The Birth of the Khalsa

SUNY series in Religious Studies
Harold Coward, editor

The Birth of the Khalsa

A Feminist Re-Memory of Sikh Identity

Nikky-Guninder Kaur Singh

STATE UNIVERSITY OF NEW YORK PRESS

Published by
State University of New York Press, Albany

Printed in the United States of America

For information, address State University of New York Press,
194 Washington Avenue, Suite 305, Albany, NY 12210-2384

Production by Diane Ganeles and Marilyn Semerad
Marketing by Susan M. Petrie

Library of Congress Cataloging-in-Publication Data

Singh, Nikky-Guninder Kaur.
The birth of the Khalsa : a feminist re-memory of Sikh Identity/Nikky-Guninder Kaur Singh.
p. cm. — (SUNY series in religious studies)
Includes bibliographical references and index.
ISBN 0–7914–6583–7 (hc : alk. paper) — ISBN 0–7914–6584–5 (pbk. : alk. paper)
1. Khalsa (Sect) 2. Women in Sikhism. I. Title. II. Series.

BL2018.7.K44S55 2005
294.6′65—dc22

2004065340

10 9 8 7 6 5 4 3 2 1

In memory of my father, who was also a mother to me

Contents

Acknowledgments

I want to thank Dr. Narinder Singh Kapany, Chairman of the Sikh Foundation of America, for getting me started with this project. Uncle Kapany has a remarkable vision for the Sikh world, and he motivates Sikh scholars, artists, filmmakers, and entrepreneurs in all parts of the world. His enthusiasm reaches me across the continent in his phone calls from California to Maine. I can still hear the excitement with which he urged me to write a book on Guru Gobind Singh for the 300th anniversary of the Khalsa. At that point I had finished my translation of a selection of Sikh sacred texts, and in fact, Kerry Brown, the editor for the Sikh Foundation, insightfully read through the draft of the first chapter of this book. I hope my maternal memory of the great Guru stirs my readers deeply and charges us vigorously to make our world a better place for all of us.

And I want to thank Ms. Marilyn Semerad at SUNY Press who saw through the finale of this project. She embodies the efficiency, cheer, and support that I received from everybody at SUNY. There are many, many in between who have helped me with this book and my heartfelt thanks to all of them. I am indebted to Mom Walker and Mrs. Fitzy for keeping Sarah happy while I'd be absorbed in my work. My special thanks to Colby College (which is much more than an institution for me!), to my students in the seminars on Sikhism for their valuable criticisms on earlier drafts, and to Jim and Linda Crawford for the wonderful gift of their endowed Chair in Religious Studies. My thanks too to my two constant muses—Harry and Sarah.

Introduction

> For there is no identity without memory—be it of a person, couple, family, neighborhood, community, tribe, people, nation, globe.
>
> —Catharine Stimpson, "The Future of Memory"

The birth of the Khalsa (from the Arabic *khalis*, meaning "pure")[1] by Guru Gobind Singh is a pivotal event in the psyche and imagination of the Sikhs. During the Baisakhi festivities of 1699 the guru and his wife prepared *amrit*, and five men from different castes sipped it from the same bowl. Their drink purified them of all mental defilements. Ending centuries of hereditary oppressions of caste, class and profession, the five were born into the egalitarian family of the Khalsa. Over time "Khalsa" and "Sikh" have become synonymous terms, and even though only a minority of Sikhs are formally initiated into the Khalsa order, all Sikh men and women trace their personality, name, religious rites, and prayers—what they do, what they wear, how they identify themselves—to this liberating Baisakhi of 1699.

But the event has been recorded only by men, with the result that its total value is far from recovered, and in fact, the imbalanced memory has imposed a heavy burden on the life of half of the Sikh community. How can its mnemonic effects forge Sikh men into hypermasculine subjects and Sikh women into passive and silent objects of centuries-old cultural burdens? Something is terribly out of joint. This study is my "re-memory" of that moment from a female perspective, which recognizes and reproduces an alternative vision to the conventional androcentric understanding and application. To be sure, Guru Gobind Singh was a man of his times. Living in a patriarchal society, he might not even have been aware of all the liberating implications of his dramatic Baisakhi event. But he set them in motion, and his followers must keep this momentum going. I hope my re-memory will inspire Sikhs to live out the emancipatory praxis birthed by their guru, and open our global society to becoming more receptive of others.

I formally began this project in the living room of our home at the Punjabi University in Patiala, India, in the summer of 1998. In the nineties I traveled from America to India to visit my ailing father as often as I could. I had lost my mother; Dad was the only link with my past, my culture, and my heritage, and I clung to him tightly. Through a paralytic stroke, he had lost the use of his right hand, and he deeply felt the loss of my mother. In his sad, sad state he was delighted to see me and showered upon me the love, warmth, and care that my mother had always shown. During the last years of his life, he was both a father and a mother to me.

Actually, even as a child I remember him being very sensitive and full of love. I'd often see Dad with tears in his eyes—which is very unusual in the patriarchal culture of the Punjab. On weekends, especially in the spring and autumn months, there would be quite a few weddings in our neighborhood. When the time came for the daughter to leave her parents' home, the air would be sonorous with doleful songs. Whatever corner of the house I'd be playing in, Dad would pick me up in his arms and cry out: "I am not going to marry off my daughter." And Granny would reprimand him: "Not marry off your daughter! What inauspicious words!"

In May 1998, I was going to be back with Dad and start my research on Guru Gobind Singh's institution of the Khalsa. The three-hundredth anniversary of the Khalsa's birth was fast approaching, and I wanted to celebrate it by exploring this historic Sikh event. On my way to India, I stopped in London for an envigorating conference at the School of Oriental and African Studies. It was a stimulating time, and I enjoyed being with friends and colleagues. On the plane, however, I felt incredibly empty and sad. As soon as I reached Patiala I knew the reason: friends and relatives had come to meet me in white *dupattas* and tears.

Dad was no more. For months I had been looking forward to finishing my semester in Maine and sitting at his bedside in Patiala to start my project. Now he was lying on ice in a living room filled with friends and family mourning in silence. I wanted to stay as close to him as possible for as long as I could. Major Sahib, whom Dad greatly admired and with whom I had intended to discuss Sikh historical texts, had also come to pay his last visit. With Dad's final departure from our house on the funeral bier, everything—my home, Punjab, India—would also be carried away from me. We were waiting for my brother to arrive from America for the final rites. I wanted to make the most of the last hours with my dad at home. Sleepless for hours, utterly confused, dejected, and lost, I began reading in Dad's "presence" Koer Singh's account of the Khalsa event with Major Sahib.

My father's life had been entirely dedicated to Sikh scholarship, and even during his very last weeks, he immersed himself completely in finishing his four-volume *Encyclopaedia of Sikhism*. Its first volume had been launched by the president of India during Dad's lifetime; the final was to be launched just a few months after by the prime minister of India, but by then my father had passed away. Dad had started his career as a lecturer in English at the Khalsa College in Amritsar, the premier Sikh institute, where he had received both his undergraduate and graduate degrees. In fact, the college authorities were familiar with his academic potential, and offered him his first academic position even before his exam results were out! Dad had joined the Khalsa College right after completing his secondary education at the Khalsa School in Muktsar. Granny would tell us about how much grandfather wanted Dad to become a doctor, and even had him admitted to the medical school in Jullundur. But Dad was so miserable for those first few days that Grandfather finally had to give in to his wish to attend the Khalsa College. Dad thrived in the creative ferment that permeated this Sikh center in the forties. He was involved in many of its interlinking and vibrant circles, and served as president of the Khalsa College Students Association, editor of the *Darbar*, and president of the Khalsa College Hockey Club.

Later in life he became involved in university administration. With Maharaja Yadvindra Singh of Patiala as the president, he served as the member-secretary of the commission that was instrumental in the establishment of the Punjabi University in Patiala. The remote area on the outskirts of the city of Patiala, where he and Bhai Jodh Singh (his revered teacher at the Khalsa College and the first vice-chancellor of the new university) would go for their evening walks, was chosen as the site for the Punjabi University—and it soon became the leading intellectual campus of the Punjab. Though extremely busy with the administrative demands of the growing university, Dad would stay up late at night to keep up with his scholarship, and he wrote many books, including *The Heritage of the Sikhs*, *Maharaja Ranjit Singh*, and *Guru Gobind Singh* (which was translated into fourteen Indian languages). At the invitation of the United States government, in 1964 he visited universities and research institutes across this country. He was greatly impressed by the American system of education, and published *Higher Education in America*. He spent a most stimulating 1968–69 academic year at the Center for World Religions at Harvard, where he wrote *Guru Nanak and Origins of the Sikh Faith*.

Upon his return from Harvard, Dad became the chair of the first academic department of religious studies in India. Called the Guru Gobind Singh Department of Religious Studies, it was established by the Punjabi University upon the five-hundredth anniversary of Guru Nanak's birth (1969). During his tenure, Dad started the publication of the *Journal of Religious Studies*, and kept up with his prolific scholarship in Sikh history and literature by writing books, contributing articles to leading journals and newspapers, translating Punjabi authors like Bhai Vir Singh, Amrita Pritam, and Ajeet Cour into

English, and editing collections of short stories, essays, and conference papers. He hosted many international conferences and brought distinguished scholars to the Punjabi University to foster understanding and peace among people of different religions and nationalities. He also traveled extensively, lecturing on different facets of Sikhism in Japan, Belgium, Holland, England, and the United States. The series of lectures that he delivered at Berkeley at the invitation of the University of California were published in book form under the title, *The Berkeley Lectures on Sikhism*. He was an active member of the World Conference on Religion and Peace, and he also joined the International Consultation in Search of Non-Violent Alternatives in Derry, Northern Ireland. Through his scholarship, travels, and warmth of personality, he developed many lifelong friendships.

So even when Dad was on his own in his paralytic condition, there was a constant stream of scholars and visitors from far and near who helped him keep his spirits high. There were also celebrations when cabinet ministers, important political leaders, and other dignitaries came to the house to present him with awards, including an honorary doctorate from Guru Nanak Dev University, Amritsar. Mishraji and Panditji, his two constant attendants, cheerfully greeted all the guests. Professor Harminder Singh Kohli, Sardar Tirath Singh Virji, and Dr. Harjit Singh took care of him as if he were their own father. I will always cherish the love and affection that our community and Sikh scholars have given my father.

The whole community bade him a deeply touching farewell for which, again, I will always be indebted. Father was given an official state funeral complete with a military gun salute. Sikh leaders who sometimes had been vehement political opponents of one another sat together at his funeral listening to the melodious verses from the Guru Granth, the Sikh bible. This was indeed a wonderful tribute to a life dedicated to welcoming people from different political, social, religious, and intellectual perspectives, and promoting, in his own unique way, the unifying impulse of his Sikh faith. Present were the President of the Shromani Gurdwara Prabandhak Committee (SGPC), Sardar Gurcharan Singh Tohra; the Congress Party member of Parliament Jagmeet Singh Brar; Captain Simran Singh Mann; and Sardar Tarlochan Singh, chairman of the National Commission of Minorities. And sharing my grief for many hours were Bibiji Mrs. Tohra, wife of the president of the SGPC; Biba Puneet Kaur, maharani of Patiala; and Biba Bunty, maharani of Burdwan. The Punjabi University honored him posthumously by prefixing his name, Professor Harbans Singh, to the Department of the Encyclopaedia of Sikhism to which he had totally dedicated himself during the last decades of his life, and he was invested with the Order of the Khalsa during the Khalsa Tercentenary Celebrations in 1999. Beginning my work on the birth of the Khalsa in that tragic hour of his death was my way of saying good-bye to my beloved dad, and this book is really a tribute to him.

A few days after the cremation, my brother and I visited Anandpur Sahib. We had gone to nearby Kiratpur Sahib to immerse in the river Sutlej the last remnants of my father, including the tiny *kirpan* and *kara* that withstood the crematory flames. Dad's death brought us to the spot where the tenth Sikh guru had given birth to the Khalsa almost three hundred years before. It was at Gurdwara (Sikh place of worship, from *guru*=enlightener and *dwara*=door) Keshgarh that Guru Gobind Singh enjoined his Sikhs to keep the five *Ks* (*kesha*, long hair; *kangha*, comb; *kara*, steel bracelet; *kirpan*, sword; and *kacha*, drawers) as symbols of their physical identity. Henceforth, they were not to cut their hair, and so the shrine of Keshgarh derives its name from the word *kesha*, meaning "uncut hair."

The memory of that historic event had something magical about it at that particular place and time, because I felt pain and estrangement literally sliding away from me. Instead, a new comfort and life arose. For the first time in days my numb body responded to the environment around me. Here I was at the beautiful white shrine, which I had visited many times before. My personal memories of coming here after the sudden death of my mother, after the birth of my daughter, with my husband, with friends, flashed and fused with communal memories: this was the place where something momentous had begun for us three hundred years ago. My brother and I were standing in Anandpur, the city of bliss (*anand*). This was indeed our birthplace. The white marble dome and pillars of Gurdwara Keshgarh serenely embraced the clear blue skies, while the skies in turn outlined the Shivalik ranges forming a diaphanous halo. In the midst of this panoramic scene Guru Gobind Singh on Baisakhi Day 1699 birthed his Khalsa. He performed a dramatic act in front of a large congregation: he asked for the life of five devotees and acted as if he had killed them. He killed five goats instead, and brought the five devotees back into a stunned gathering. He then recited sacred verses as he churned water in a bowl with his double-edged sword. His wife Mata Jitoji added sugarpuffs to the elixir. These first five who sipped the iron-sweet elixir formed the nucleus of the Khalsa. They discarded their caste, class, creed, and inherited occupations, and entered the new family of the Khalsa.

This study is a personal journey into that moment—a return to my own past. Anybody who tries to study this event soon discovers there is very little documentary evidence from that period. The accounts from Sainapat's *Sri Gur Sobha*, Koer Singh's *Gurbilas Patshahi 10*, and Sukha Singh's *Gurbilas Patshahi 10* that I will be using came from the eighteenth and early-nineteenth centuries. They belong to the genre of *Gurbilas* literature (*guru*+*bilas*=splendor of the guru), a type of narrative poetry exalting the heroism of the gurus in their fight for justice and equality. The authors are geared more toward expressing the sentiments and convictions of their contemporaries than providing us with historically accurate details.[2]

Yet these poetic narratives by Sainapat, Koer Singh, and Sukha Singh do provide a framework to approach the pivotal event that I learned as a child. They have enabled me to explore the event from my personal, cultural, and historical grounding so as to understand the *effect* it continues to have on the Sikh community. I was born in a Sikh household in the Punjab, and my first lessons in Sikh history were, of course, through my family and my community. Even then I could see the *effect* of the event for people—how it has continued to shape their psyches and their actions. This study is not a search for the historical facts of that day. It does not "simulate an objectivity." I do not claim to be epochal in my scope, for I do not intend to verify empirical evidence or rectify any historical details. I do not judge who is right or wrong in their documentation, nor do I wish to assess the accuracy and authority of contemporary scholars. I am concerned with the responses, beliefs, and attitudes of the people to the basic event, which is deeply etched in Sikh minds and hearts. My fundamental question is: how might we think about it so that it can be even more *effective*—in a positive way for Sikh men *and women*? As the leading Sikh historian, W. H. McLeod, perceptively says, "It matters little whether five volunteers were actually summoned or whether five goats were actually slain. The overriding fact is that in its essential outline the story is firmly believed and that this belief has unquestionably contributed to the subsequent shaping of conventional Sikh attitudes."[3]

My primary text consists of the basic event as I remember and as I reread it in the *Gurbilas* literature (analyzed in chapter 2). But there are some other texts I will also take up: the *Bicitra Natak*, which is Guru Gobind Singh's mythopoetic autobiography (chapter 1); the narrative from the *Puratan Janamsakhi* that describes the first Sikh guru's revelation (chapter 3); scriptural passages that shape the five *Ks* (chapter 4); and the set of five hymns that are recited daily by Sikhs (chapter 5). These sources are elemental to Sikh faith and personality, and each provides us with a crucial understanding of the birth of the Khalsa. For just as the *Bicitra Natak* shows the "fetal" Khalsa evolving in Guru Gobind Singh's consciousness, the *Janamsakhi* account traces the genealogy of the Khalsa to Guru Nanak, the founder of Sikhism. The scriptural passages highlight the five adornments of the Sikhs, while the five hymns (Jap, Jaap, Swaiyyai, Chaupai, and Anand) unfold their daily nutrition and initiation ritual. These materials are a vital part of the collective Sikh memory, and the currents formed in the subconscious from the genres of autobiography, myth, and sacred poetry flow into our feminist rememory of Baisakhi 1699. With the exception of the sections that we will be studying from the *Gurbilas* literature, these sources may not explicitly refer to the Khalsa event, but they intersect with that particular point and are extremely important in disclosing the full effect of Baisakhi 1699. These "texts" that we will study are originally heard while in the laps of mothers and fathers, and their sonorous and emotional impact continues to influence listeners for the rest of their lives. This project therefore literally becomes a "re-memory" of what I personally heard growing up in a typical Sikh home.

For me these texts occupy what Michel Foucault calls the "transdiscursive position." In his discussion of the relationship between author and text, Foucault goes beyond the narrow sense of the writer as a person to whom the authorship of a text can be legitimately attributed. He says, "[A] person can be the author of much more than a book... [he or she can be the author] of a tradition, of a discipline within which new books and authors can proliferate."[4] In the Sikh world, Guru Nanak (1469–1539) is the author who birthed a new tradition within which all of his nine successors—from Angad to Gobind Singh—have arisen.[5] Situated as he was between the Hindus and Muslims of northern India, Nanak experienced and articulated the Divine in a new and different way. He birthed a "Sikh" consciousness—generating new modes of poetry, philosophy, myth, art, and ritual. Guru Nanak is the author of the first Sikh text, called the *Jap*, a hymn in thirty-eight stanzas, which forms the opening of the Guru Granth, the Sikh holy book, and reverberates deeply throughout Sikh thought and action. In fact, Guru Gobind Singh's *Jaap*, a hymn in 199 verses, flows from Nanak's *Jap*. Nanak's *Jap* was recited during the preparation of *amrit* sipped by Guru Gobind Singh's Khalsa, Nanak's *Jap* was recited during his divine encounter in the River Bein as our myth recounts, Nanak's *Jap* is the basic texture of the five symbols worn by Sikh men and women, and Nanak's *Jap* is recited by Sikhs daily at daybreak. With such transdiscursive texts, as Foucault remarks, "the founding act is on an equal footing with its future transformations: it is merely one among the many modifications that it makes possible."[6] The works of the tenth Sikh guru elicit the same emotions from Sikhs, and are on equal footing with the works of Nanak, the founder of the Sikh tradition.

Furthermore, Foucault claims, "The theoretical validity of a statement ... is based on the structural and intrinsic norms" of its tradition rather than on the actual initiator.[7] This is very important for our study of these texts. We are interested in the theoretical validity of our textual sources, and not in proofs of authorship. What matters is their structural and intrinsic norms, and the fact that they are celebrated and lived by as a part of the ongoing Sikh tradition. Our materials indeed constitute the quintessence of Sikh philosophical and ethical ideals.

Nietzsche once remarked that the real value of history lies "in raising the popular melody to a universal symbol and showing what a world of depth, power, and beauty exists in it."[8] The popular melody in Sikhism is Baisakhi 1699, and the present study is a way of expanding Guru Gobind Singh's emancipatory performance in Anandpur to all parts of the globe. In fact, my aspirations go even farther than Nietzsche's dictum: instead of just "showing what a world of depth, power and beauty exists" in the historical Baisakhi, our re-memory is really for all of us to taste so that we may experience the invigorating drink that was sipped from the same bowl by people of different castes and creeds. Sikh scripture characterizes memory as a joyous phenomenon: "[D]elicious is the season when I remember You!" (GG, 97). The guru rejoices in the memory of the Divine, and a Sikh poet finds the same delight in remembering the actions of Mataji. When he describes her adding the sugarpuffs to the *amrit*, he exclaims, "[T]he mind is delighted by hearing her story" (Koer Singh, 9:26).

Unfortunately, the mnemonic resonance of Baisakhi 1699 has not brought much delight for women. The event recorded, recognized, and remembered by men has made them victims of hypermasculine attitudes and practices. Kanwaljit Kaur, a Sikh woman writer, laments that "Sikh history has been written by men only, who either chose to disregard women's contributions or did not think their contributions worthy of note."[9] The Canadian scholar Doris Jakobsh discusses the role of women in her book *Relocating Gender in Sikh History*. Her verdict is that "The guiding principle in Sikh history with regard to women is silence."[10] Historians are, of course, influenced by their biological, cultural, and religious upbringing. Philosophers of history like Nietzsche, Hegel, and Croce rejected the theory of the "innocent eye" of the objective historian and instead stressed the inventive aspect of the historian's own agency.[11] Gadamer is even harsher in his critique: "[H]istorical objectivism resembles statistics, which are such excellent means of propaganda because they let the 'facts' speak and hence simulate an objectivity that in reality depends on the legitimacy of the questions asked."[12]

Rita Gross has even detected a "quadruple androcentrism" coloring much of historical scholarship. As she points out, it is not only the historians who chose to record men's experiences, but also the commentators with their malestream interpretations, the academics with their interest in the study of male heroes, and contemporary practitioners with their hostility toward feminist scholarship about the tradition who have limited and distorted our perspectives.[13] In addition, it has suffered long neglect from feminist scholars, who are put off by the absence of female gurus and goddess images in the Sikh tradition. Baisakhi 1699 has been remembered by male elites, and their one-sided construction has had terrible repercussions for half of the Sikh community—which tragically has dwindled to 44 percent of our community in the Punjab because of sex-determination tests and the consequent abortion of female fetuses! Sisters and mothers and grandmothers may narrate the event, but the androcentric consciousness that has fed them "quadruply" has reduced their voices to mere echoes of male discourse—devoid of their female accents, devoid of their personal concerns, and devoid of their authenticity.

Parallel to Judith Plaskow's invitation to reshape Jewish memory from a feminist angle, we need to return to Anandpur and "stand again" at Gurdwara Keshgarh to retrieve the power of Guru Gobind Singh's momentous event.[14] We must reexperience it from a feminist perspective, with a woman's re-memory. We must remember not only those who were left out from the critical event, but also all those who are still being left out from its empowering memories. What did the women feel in the Baisakhi congregation when the guru made his call? How do they feel today as they wear the five symbols of the Khalsa? When they drink *amrit* prepared and offered by male hands? When they recite the daily hymns? When they are left out from conducting ceremonies in public? When they are given an entirely different set of expectations, roles, and obligations from their brothers, husbands, and male cousins? When their families and their society send them constant messages that they do not matter?[15] It surely does make a difference for the Sikh community whether the event is remembered by those who wield power, or by the disempowered for whom Guru Gobind Singh launched his action and in whose re-memory Baisakhi 1699 is a moment of human wholeness.

Female lenses become the key interpretative mechanism, and mine were crafted in feminist studies in religion. Over the years, Jewish, Christian, Hindu, Muslim, Buddhist, and Confucian feminist and womanist scholars have inspired me in my research into my own Sikh tradition. Yet, whatever objections and criticisms I may have of my culture, they are mine; they are not "symptoms of a disease" that I caught studying and teaching in America. Uma Narayan wisely cautions us that in Asian contexts there is a "tendency to cast feminism as an aping of Westernized political agendas." In reality, though, our Third World "feminist consciousness is not a hot-house bloom grown in the alien atmosphere of 'foreign' ideas, but has its roots much closer to home."[16] Feminist scholars—Western, Eastern, West Asian—have deepened my inquiry and honed my sensitivity to women's issues. From their different backgrounds and different orientations and different strategies, they have together equipped me with valuable approaches, frameworks, and expressions to remember the silence, invisibility, subordination, and abuse of women—all of which I have personally witnessed and continue to witness. My re-memory of Guru Gobind Singh's emancipatory deed floods with memories and more memories of tragic inequities. And yet if we just shift our perspective from the male norms by which it has been engraved in our minds, that very re-memory floods with hopes and dreams of an inclusive and egalitarian world.

In my own case, Dad's death led me to the theme of birth, bringing me much comfort and fulfillment. I began to picture Guru Gobind Singh as a maternal figure who—like a mother—birthed his Khalsa. I had imagined him primarily as a Herculean figure, who fought heroically, dressed resplendently, galloped ferociously, carried masculine weapons, shot gold-tipped arrows, and recited patriarchal poetry. I myself used to share the popular taste described by McLeod: "It is as Lord of the Khalsa that popular Sikh taste reveres him."[17] As a child, whenever I was scared of the dark, I was told to remember that I was Guru Gobind Singh's daughter. Even though these words came from my mother and grandmother, they merely covered up and denied my fear; they never reached inside me to instill courage of any sort. With false consciousness perpetuated by our patriarchal culture, to which my grandmother, mother, and I all belong, we were required to hide behind the metallic mask of our chivalrous guru. That external image prohibited me from probing my fears and feelings, and validating myself in any way. But as soon as I took off those androcentric spectacles, I began to feel close to the tenth Sikh guru. By approaching him as a mother figure, I could physically and emotionally connect with him and detect his real fears and real courage. By discarding the myth of invulnerability, I discovered Guru Gobind Singh's humanity, and many powerful dimensions of his creativity have started to unfold for me. It is my contention that when we recognize him as the Mother of the Khalsa—rather than as the Lord of the Khalsa—we experience the full force and joy of the Khalsa's birth.

I do not want to take away from the role of his wife, Mata Jitoji, and appropriate it to Guru Gobind Singh, nor do I want to neuter the male guru in any way. Nor do I want to imply in the least that "motherhood" is essential for women. The "germinative ocean" carried within every woman, mother or not, is what the male guru essentially shares with all of us women. As a feminist mystic beautifully says, "Whether or not a woman actually conceives, she always carries the essence of the germinative ocean within her, the flux of the energy in formless potential. It is a spiritual fertility, full from within, a woman's inheritance, not dependent on [an] external catalyst."[18] My goal is to recognize the female side of the heroic guru so that we can fully participate in his liberating action. The Khalsa, I argue, is birthed by the guru. It is not ordered or commanded out. Like every birth, the birth of the Khalsa is entrenched in mystery, pain, and exultation. As contemporary feminist philosophers have made us aware, a focus on birth ushers in hope and wonder and replaces the attention given to death and striving for the other world in traditional patriarchal discourse.[19] New possibilities for men and women open up with Guru Gobind Singh, who as the "mother" conceives the embryonic Khalsa inside her body (chapter 1), who goes through intense labor (chapter 2), who in the postpartum stage makes *amrit* for the newly born (chapter 3), who then dresses up the Khalsa in the five *Ks* (chapter 4), and gently whispers in the "mother" tongue the five hymns (chapter 5). His conception, labor, adornment, lactation, and maternal murmurs created Sikh identity, but they draw upon the amniotic waters of the River Bein in which Nanak first tasted the Divine Name and received his Sikh identity. The very name of this river is from the ancient Indian term for a woman's braid *(veni)*. Unfortunately, privileging the topknots of boys and men, the community has utterly abandoned the powerful flow in female braids. Androcentrism and machismo have led Sikhs astray from the physically and spiritually nutritious *amrit* that the tenth Sikh guru ultimately derives from Nanak's Bein.

It is, therefore, with a positive hermeneutic that I return to the historical Khalsa event. In fact, it is a "hermeneutics of unfolding" with which I try to recover the many meanings of the traditions and texts surrounding Baisakhi 1699. This strategy, suggested by Harold Coward, stimulates us to discover the richness and multivalent meanings and insights from our literary resources; it takes readers and listeners into account, as well as their geographical and chronological locations.[20] A "hermeneutic of unfolding" inspires each one of us to imaginatively reunite the male-female and creativity-procreativity binaries imposed by the reductive, patriarchal processes so that we can reconstruct our human subjectivity. Each of us is male and female, but we have divided ourselves into either masculine or feminine for far too long. And we have only been weakened as a result. It is not the jealous gods who cut us in half, as in Aristophanes' popularly cited myth from Plato's *Symposium*, but we ourselves who have split from the other half. While building and pumping up the one, we have subordinated and lost the "other" side of ourselves. Guru Gobind Singh created the Khalsa at a time when his Sikhs were weak and insecure. His goal was to rid them of psychological and political oppression, and change them into authentic subjects living a life of equality and justice. But after three hundred years we have subjected ourselves to all kinds of fears. Sikh life both at home and in diasporic communities is stifled by and shackled to sexism, casteism, classism, and racism. I especially sympathize with the abuse and oppression of women. In many cases, their victimization even leads to suicides, murders, and "honor killings." What an aberration of and deviation from Guru Gobind Singh's egalitarian vision of society embodied in his Khalsa! As we go forth into the fourth century of the Khalsa's birth we need to become whole and retrieve the repressed and oppressed other, our "m-other."

When fathers stop acting out their "male" roles and become like mothers, they are liberated from their prison of gender; in turn, they do not exert power over us, but rather they empower us with their tears, love, and nurture. Explorations cease to be exploitations of the other; they become gateways to discovering, experiencing, and sharing new resources with each other. The message of the Sikh gurus was precisely to strengthen us, men and women, Brahmin and Shudra, Hindu, Sikh, and Muslim. For too long we have remembered Guru Gobind Singh in some "tough guise"[21] image, and missed out on the maternal love and beauty and empowerment that are the matrix of his Khalsa institution. Sikhs will recover their true pride and authenticity not in tough and macho acts and words, but in the rejected and repressed female side of the body and words of the guru. Male and female, death and birth, creativity and procreativity are not contradictions of each other; to use Rabindranath Tagore's comforting image of life and death, they are the right and left breasts of the mother.[22]

Abbreviations

Akal Ustat	by Guru Gobind Singh, Sabdarath DG, pp.16–52. Cited by verse number.
Anand	The six prescribed stanzas recited during the amrit initiation are by Guru Amar Das. They begin on p. 917 of the Guru Granth. Cited by stanza number.
Bhai Gurdas	*Varan Bhai Gurdas,* edited by Bhai Vir Singh (Amritsar: Khalsa Samachar, 1977). Cited by chapter and verse numbers.
BN	*Bicitra Natak* by Guru Gobind Singh Sabdarath DG, pp. 53–91 Cited by chapter and verse numbers.
CC 1	Candi Caritr 1, by Guru Gobind Singh Sabdarath DG, pp. 92–127. Cited by verse number.
CC 2	Candi Caritr 2, by Guru Gobind Singh Sabdarath DG, pp. 128–53 Cited by verse number.
CS	W. H. McLeod, (editor and translator) *The Chaupa Singh Rahit-nama* (Dunedin: Unversity of Otago Press, *1987)* Cited by verse number.
Chaupai	by Guru Gobind Singh, Dasam Granth, pp. 1386–8. Cited by verse number.

DG — Dasam Granth
Shabdarath Dasam Granth Sahib Bhai Randhir Singh (editor),
(Patiala: Punjabi University, 1985) This three volume edited text goes till p. 1249.
Cited by page number.

GG — Guru Granth
Sabdarath Sri Guru Granth Sahib (Amritsar: Shromani Gurdwara Prabandhak Committee, 4th edition, 1964)
Cited by page number.

Jaap — by Guru Gobind Singh, Sabdarath DG, pp. 1–15.
Cited by verse number.

Jap — by Guru Nanak, Guru Granth, pp. 1–8.
Cited by stanza number.

Khalsa Mahima — short hymn by Guru Gobind Singh, *Sarabloh Granth (Sampuran Steek* Part III, annotated and published by Singh Sahib Baba Santa Singh Ji Chhianven Karori (Anandpur: Shromani Panth Akali Buddha Dal Panjvan Takhat, n.d.), pp. 531–32.

Koer Singh — *Gurbilas Patshahi 10,* (Patiala: Punjabi University, 1968) edited by Shamsher Singh Ashok.
Cited by chapter and verse numbers.

Puratan Janamsakhi — *Puratan Janamsakhi Guru Nanak Devji.* (Published in Amritsar by Khalsa Samachar, 1946.)
Our focus is on the "Vein Parvesh," pp. 16–19.

Sabdarath DG — *Shabdarath Dasam Granth Sahib*
Bhai Randhir Singh (editor),
(Patiala: Punjabi University, 1985).
Cited by page number.

Sabdarath GG — *Sabdarath Sri Guru Granth Sahib*
(Amritsar: Shromani Gurdwara Prabandhak Committee, 4th edition, 1964)
Cited by page number.

Sainapat — *Sri Gur Sobha* (Patiala: Punjabi University, 1967)
ed. by Dr. Ganda Singh.
Cited by chapter and verse numbers.

Sukha Singh	*Gurbilas Patshahi 10* (Patiala: Bhasha Vibhag, 1989) ed. by Gursharan Kaur Jaggi. Cited by chapter and verse numbers.
Swayyai	These ten short passages by Guru Gobind Singh are from his Akal Ustat, Sabdarath DG, pp. 20–21. Cited by Swayya number.
Var Durga Ki	by Guru Gobind Singh, Sabdarath DG, pp. 154–167 Cited by verse number.
Zafarnamah	by Guru Gobind Singh, Sabdarath DG, pp. 1238–1249 Cited by verse number.

Unless otherwise stated, all translations are my own.

Chapter One

Pregnant Text and the Conception of the Khalsa

Somewhere as a flower you bloom in floral glory
Somewhere as a bumblebee you hover drunkenly
Somewhere as a breeze you blow speedily
When I don't know the way, how can I express you? . . .
Somewhere like a deer you entice with your ways
Somewhere like a woman you are adorned in beauty.
(BN, 1: 12–13)

Beginning with Guru Nanak (1469–1539), the Sikh gurus have left a vast literary legacy, which was collected in the Guru Granth, the sacred text of the Sikhs. It was compiled by the fifth guru, Arjan (1563–1606), and placed by him in 1604 in the Harimandir, the Golden Temple of modern times. While compiling the sacred volume, Arjan included the poetry of Hindu and Muslim saints that resonated with the voice of the Sikh gurus. The 1,430 pages of the text express the longing for the spaceless and timeless One in passionate poetry.[1] The tenth Sikh guru was acutely aware of the sensuousness of its metaphysical poetry, and just a day before he passed away in 1708, he endowed the Book with guruship for perpetuity. To this day, the Guru Granth remains the Body of the Gurus, the quintessence of their philosophy and ethics, and the center of all Sikh rituals and ceremonies.

Like his predecessors, Guru Gobind Singh was a superb poet, but in addition he was a great patron of the arts. The town of Paunta (from *pav*, the foot of his horse implanted on the soil), which he founded on the banks of the River Jumna, became the center of a spiritual and cultural regeneration. The guru would hold poetry symposia and distribute awards. Many poets from different religious backgrounds gathered at scenic Paunta, and fifty-two of them, including Sainapat, Alam, Lakhan, and Amrit Rai, were permanently employed. Several Sanskrit and Persian classics were translated by the poets, who in turn were rewarded handsomely for their works. Later in his life, the guru made Damdama an important center of scholarly activities. Situated near Bhatinda in the Punjab, Damdama came to be known as the "guru's Kashi"—the Sikh equivalent of the ancient Hindu center of learning and literature.[2] He spent several months in Damdama pursuing his literary aspirations amid men from different social strata.

Guru Gobind Singh's own compositions, also esteemed very highly by the Sikhs, are preserved in the Dasam Granth (literally, the Book of the Tenth). With its 1,428 pages, the Dasam Granth is almost as large as the Guru Granth. However, it is very varied in its contents. The core of the work lies in the autobiographical *Bicitra Natak,* Candi poems, and devotional compositions like the Jaap, Akal Ustat, *Gyan Prabodh*, and *Sabd Hazare*. But it also includes a very large section on ancient Indian legends and myths, stories of moral instruction, and stories of immoral intrigue, many of them attributed to poets employed by him rather than attributed to the guru himself. It was compiled sometime after the death of Guru Gobind Singh in 1708, and it is not certain whether all that is there was written by him. Over the years the writings have elicited a lot of controversy and tension.[3] In 1950, the Sikh statutory body called the Shromani Gurdwara Prabandhak Committee officially accepted the Jaap, *Sabd Hazare,* Akal Ustat, *Bicitra Natak, Candi Caritra 1 and 2, Candi di Var,* and *Gyan Prabodh* as Guru Gobind Singh's compositions. Some of the compositions, like the Jaap and Swayyai (the ten Swayyai constitute a segment of the Akal Ustat), have long been part of the daily Sikh prayers, and are essential to the Khalsa initiation rite.

These works helped to create the beliefs I was brought up with myself, and whatever scholars may say about their historical accuracy, they are an essential part of the Sikh religion, and it would be pedantic and offensive to ignore them. Their tremendous influence in shaping the personal and communal identity of the Sikhs makes it all the more important for me to try to see them from my perspective, as a Sikh woman. What does the literature accepted as the tenth Sikh guru's by my tradition offer me? How does it speak to me? Rather than enter controversies about their authorship, I want to discern the feminine voice in those hymns that Sikhs across the globe recite and memorize and believe in as their guru's own.[4]

In this chapter the focus is the *Bicitra Natak.*[5] It is precious because in the large repertoire of primary Sikh literature, the *Bicitra Natak* is the only self-portrait. That we encounter Guru Gobind Singh—the way he saw himself and the way he wanted to be seen—is intriguing in itself. But with his panoply of artistic devices, the author also excites the reader's imagination and prepares us for creative ventures. Paradoxically, the exterior of the narrative, with its graphic battle scenes and clamorous sounds, softly whispers like a mother into our inner ear murmurs of love, creativity, empathy, and sublime beauty surrounding us all. The *Bicitra Natak* is not a linear historic account of Guru Gobind Singh's life and accomplishments; it is a stratagem by means of which we are inspired to recognize the Divine One and are motivated to respond ethically and aesthetically to the world in which we live. Personally, as I reach the end of the narrative, I am filled with the desire to see more, hear more, feel more, and to write and analyze. . . .

More immediately, the *Bicitra Natak* is very pertinent to our theme because the embryonic Khalsa is lodged in it, and life-giving oxygen and minerals for the birth of a healthy Khalsa circulate in its body. The text transcends all definitions, for *bicitra* (wonderful/amazing) in the title opens up the autobiographical discourse to a whole different plane of reality. It may not even fall under the genre of *natak* (drama) because it does not contain much dialogue, the hallmark of drama. The discourse is a magical mixture of biographical facts, literary imagination, and language—it is not meant to be a prosaic account of his life. Though scholars differ on the actual date of the *Bicitra Natak*,[6] they are unanimous that it was written prior to the momentous inauguration of the Khalsa believed to have taken place on Baisakhi Day 1699. The evidence from the text itself would put it sometime after 1696, the year that the Sikh guru fought against Mughal forces.[7] Pregnant with tension and excitement that have a larger meaning and purpose, the text is very significant in revealing the creative matrix to us. We learn about the spiritual and heroic character of the author, and, most of all, we get a glimpse into the genes and chromosomes of the Khalsa. The term "Khalsa" is not specifically mentioned, but we clearly recognize the guru's self-consciousness as it gestates in this fertile text. His own values and emotions become the nutrients that shape the physique and psyche of the future Khalsa. His vigorous meters and fiery descriptions produce heat and energy, vital to the growth of the fetus. This chapter functions like a sonogram: if we look through the *Bicitra Natak,* we see the embryonic Khalsa developing in Guru Gobind Singh's creative womb, and the nascent form that we recover in his pregnant text evolves into the Khalsa who will walk out of the mysterious tent at Anandpur on Baisakahi 1699.

Since Guru Gobind Singh's literary creation leads to the procreation of the Khalsa, our approach defies the patriarchal division between man's mental production of ideas and women's physical reproduction of species. In order to reclaim our past, feminist scholars propose that we look for the invisible women. In our re-memory we look not just for invisible women but also look for the invisible womb of men. We must, of course, discover the feminine voice of hidden women. But I want to go even further and find the hidden feminine voice in Guru Gobind Singh's text. In order to detect the womb of men, we have to use a radical new technology, the sonogram.

The composition is obviously male. It is written in a male hand within a doubly patriarchal culture. In Guru Gobind Singh's milieu, the indigenous patriarchal society of northern India with the rigid classification offered by the caste system had succumbed to yet another system of patriarchal control—that exercised by the Mughals from outside of India. Established by Babur during Guru Nanak's lifetime (1526), the Mughal kingdom had become a large and powerful empire with Aurangzeb ruling in his might. Aurangzeb did not want any religious pluralism. In 1679 he reimposed the *jizya*, a tax that non-Muslims had to pay to live in an Islamic state. Unlike his grandfather Akbar, who abolished the *jizya* and introduced an interreligious *din-i-ilahi* (divine faith), or his brother Dara Shikoh, who sponsored the translation of several Upanishads into Persian, Aurangzeb tried his best to make India into an exclusively Muslim country. All those who did not practice Islam, including Guru Gobind Singh and his Sikh community, became victims of Aurangzeb's orthodoxy. He issued repressive edicts against non-Muslims.[8] All "Hindus," with the exception of Rajputs, were prohibited from riding palanquins, elephants, or thoroughbred horses. They were also prohibited from carrying arms.

In this politically and religiously patriarchal regime of Aurangzeb, superimposed on the socially rigid patriarchal structure of traditional India, emerged the Sikh guru's *Bicitra Natak*—a work validating and celebrating the self. In a society in which the masses had resigned themselves to the imperial powers and were sunk in a mood of self-denial and self-effacement, the author of the *Bicitra Natak* grandly narrates his life story. In detail, he describes his rich ontological, ethnic, historical, and genealogical background. In order to counteract Aurangzeb's hegemonic rule, the Sikh text tries to show off its own muscle and strength. One of Aurangzeb's edicts explicitly forbade non-Muslims to carry arms; the guru's narrative—as though in defiance—opens with the image of the resplendent sword. In its deliberate attempt to challenge the prevailing political injustice, the narrative tries to stay away from the personal side of the guru's life. We do not get details about his close family. We hear neither about his wives nor about his sons. Even his succession to guruship after the death of his father is quickly brushed aside. Most of the narrative space is taken by furious battles both real and mythological. We see lightning flashing out of spears, swords, and arrows, and we hear thunder blasting from conches, clarions, and kettledrums. A Western scholar remarks how Guru Gobind Singh's battles have "an epic grandeur with vividness of detail which has hardly been surpassed in the literature of the world."[9] The voice is bold and energetic; the tempo, heroic and martial. The guru worships the Divine in the image of fiery steel, and he valiantly fights with his men against antagonistic political and social forces.

How do we find female themes and motifs here? The task is undoubtedly daunting. But it is critical, because generations of Sikhs have been fed on this overtly "patriarchal" discourse, producing and reproducing male dominant structures in their society. The Khalsa has remained a brotherhood, almost a militaristic fraternity, from which women have been pretty much excluded. The mentality of the crusader or mujahedin distorts the ideology of the Khalsa. The hypermasculine readings dwell on the surface of Guru Gobind Singh's text without looking into its deeper meaning and texture. Men immediately identify themselves with the guru's male sex; they mistake his zealous call for human rights as simply a fight for male rights, and they have not the least consideration for women's subordination and oppression. Furthermore, Guru Gobind Singh's battles against an oppressive regime are misunderstood as battles against an *other* religion; forgetting Guru Gobind Singh's pluralistic consciousness, Sikhs tend to misappropriate his commitment to pluralism as an exclusionist form of identity. The guru's thealogical vision is neglected, and so is his compassionate and creative interior. Sikhs remember the fierce battle scenes depicted by the guru, but they miss out on how those very scenes lead to women, kitchens, sacred spaces, celebrations—to an authentic mode of life and living in our variegated world.

Augustine's definition of autobiography, "a presencing of man in his deep,"[10] is very relevant, for what lies beneath the explicit text is even more significant. Our sonogram courses beneath the muscular exterior into the guru's true subjectivity, and into the folds of his deepest interior where the Khalsa is lodged. Once we start looking through our sonogram, a different reality becomes apparent. In the interstices of his textual body flow Guru Gobind Singh's human tenderness and compassion. In his womb we recover a powerful inclusivity and pluralism. In his metaphysics we discover a "thealogical" vision. In his imagination we find active women. In his aspiration we recognize the feminist urge to transform an oppressive society by changing the very sensibility of its people. The *Bicitra Natak* exposes us to the different and complex issues that were a part of the author's psyche, and its fourteen chapters become a matrix for the ideology, the reflection, and the historical contingencies that grew into the Khalsa. The Khalsa is not born yet; but the text rhythmically resounds with the pulse and the heartbeat of the embryonic Khalsa. As we try to see the earliest images and hear those initial beats, we can identify the following six features: (1) thealogical symbol, (2) woman warrior, (3) biophilic ethics, (4) pluralistic genes, (5) battles of life, and (6) inspired body.

Thealogical Symbol

The autobiographical *Bicitra Natak* does not begin with "I was born in" but rather with an exaltation of the sword. Most biographies divide the guru's relatively short life span into six parts, which correspond to the six important places in his life (see appendix for a brief biographical account divided into the six traditional phases of his life). But Guru Gobind Singh does not passively surrender to such a rigid chronology. Clark Blaise rightly comments that the autobiographical subject is distinct from the biographical object "by reason of its adversarial relationship to time." Blaise brings out the tension: "When autobiography fails, it surrenders to the artifice of creaky recollection, dutiful recitation, chronologically-correct-toe-dabbings into the flow of past events."[11]

Instead of recounting his own birth, the *Bicitra Natak* is prefaced by the first guru's articulation of "Ikk Oan Kar" (One Being Is), with which the Guru Granth opens. Thus, the very origins of the Sikh religion constitute the lining of Guru Gobind Singh's literary uterus. The text starts out with honoring the sword: "Honor to the holy sword; I bow with heart and mind." Guru Gobind Singh's self-consciousness and the autobiographical facts he chooses to record flow out of his ardent devotion to the Divine One. What is unusual is the repeated emphasis that the brilliant sword receives. As noted by M. L. Peace, "In the literature of the world no other poet has ever praised the sword in such a way as Guru Gobind Singh has done."[12] Now, the sword is not a new metaphor in the Sikh world, and here I will have to differ from Sikh scholars, including my own father, who contend that the guru provided "a new literary metaphor."[13] The sword, as we will explore in chapter 4, appears in the Guru Granth itself, and its symbolic and metaphoric significance is expressed by Guru Gobind Singh's precursors. But because the tenth Sikh guru is remembered as a military figure, the sword in his religio-aesthetic worldview is denied its scriptural significance and identified simply as Guru Gobind Singh's physical weapon. The fact, however, is that Guru Gobind Singh carries on the traditional polysemantic possibilities present in the Granth. Throughout the *Bicitra Natak* (and this goes for most of his writing), he envisions the timeless and transcendent reality in the brilliantly shining form of the sword. "Symbol" in Sanskrit is *pratik*, literally "a pointer," and the sword in Guru Gobind Singh's verse is a pointer toward the Infinite One.

The sword ushers in both male and female images of the Divine, and serves as a thealogical as well as a theological symbol in Guru Gobind Singh's religio-aesthetic *Weltanschauung*. He utilizes both masculine and feminine terms, which shows that he did not intend to limit it to a "father symbol" as Sikh scholars uphold.[14] There are no male restrictions in the fluidity of Guru

Gobind Singh's vocabulary: *khanda* and *kharag* happen to be masculine, but *kirpan*, *tegh*, and *bhagauti* are feminine. The sword points to the Infinite, which is neither male nor female, and when conceived in language, it is both male and female. Major thinkers of our century, including Paul Tillich, Mircea Eliade, Clifford Geertz, and Paul Ricoeur, have elucidated the paradoxical and multivalent quality of symbols, and how they elicit a host of different and even contradictory moods and motivations. It is therefore the "set of interpretations and the ways in which these are appropriated by an individual or culture—not the symbol itself—that finally shape a symbol's social and ethical implications or 'meaning'."[15]

Sadly, in the Sikh instance, interpretative categories have been appropriated only from one side, which has been the male side. The culture has reduced Guru Gobind Singh's manifold symbol of the sword to a mere "sign." (This is also true of the five *Ks*, the five symbols of the Khalsa, which we will discuss in chapter 4.) Instead of an opening into the Infinite as imaged by the Sikh guru, patriarchal society has selected and structured and shaped it, and made the sword to mean a male instrument. With its masculine denotations, the powerful female side of the sword and all her feminine associations and patterns are excluded. So this inspiring symbol for creativity with the capacity to function like a pen or a paint brush—an imaginative wand of sorts that can deliver exciting new horizons—ends up merely as an intimidating sign of male power. We need to apply women's agency as the interpretative category to remember Guru Gobind Singh's symbol. How is the sword appropriated by the guru? What is the religio-aesthetic matrix in which it was shaped? After all, why should we not celebrate *her* as a fecund womb?

The primacy of a mother, her being the first resort, surfaces in the opening verse of the *Bicitra Natak*. The guru is emotively drawn—with *hitu* (heart) *citu* (mind)—to the sword. She serves as a template for a dynamic interrelationship, an expression of maternal love and intimacy. As "sword" the unfathomable One is experienced in this life; the totally Beyond is seen by the eyes, held tightly in the hand. This is Guru Gobind Singh's "feminist" way of reaching out to the Transcendent and pulling That One into the day-to-day mode of existence.

We must see the sword in the context of Guru Gobind Singh's expansive mental horizon. It is *an* image lodged among his countless intuitions of the Divine. The very first canto (cited at the opening of this chapter) stretches our imagination. The infinite exists in myriad bodies—as a glorious flower, as an intoxicated bumblebee, as a speedy breeze, as an attractive deer, as a beautifully dressed woman. The guru recognizes the vast Infinite through concrete manifestations both male and female that exist in space and time. The sword belongs to this dynamic multiplicity and creativity, and it must not be truncated to a male instrument. Somehow Sikhs have neglected to take note of these lovely forms in which the Transcendent is envisioned by their guru. The beautiful female figure introduced in this first chapter of the *Bicitra Natak*— "Somewhere like a woman you are adorned in beauty"—has left no imprint on the communal memory. This lovely passage is by no means as popular as it deserves to be, and I have rarely heard it being recited in Sikh congregations. Why does my community not stress such poetically exquisite passages with their powerful female affirmations and validations? These natural associations between women and the guru's symbols, these very natural associations between his vision of the Divine and the female, are "artificially" turned off somewhere along malestream expressions and exegeses. The rich significance of female physicality overflowing in Guru Gobind Singh's religio-aesthetic world is depleted.

The reader is drawn into a feminist symbolic of natality and flourishing. The sword that can shred and grind the mightiest of evil is at once the female creatrix, *sristi ubharan,* giving birth to various species:

> You have produced the sweatborn, fetus-born, earth-born,
> You have created the egg-born and the continents and the cosmos,
> The directions and the earth and skies are from You,
> You have spoken the four Vedas, the Qur'an, and the Puranas.
> (*BN*, 1: 24)

The poet is constantly in awe of the inner impetus of natural energy and the overflowing vigor of the cosmos. We get a sense of his abiding joy in the wonder of life and his respect for all wombs, human and other. Birth is a wondrous process shared by diverse species—a natural happening out of sweat, fetus, earth, or egg. Creation here is not ex nihilo, it is not a command, or an artist designing and examining abstractly; rather, it is an inner dynamic of physical energy and overflowing—an embodying of life. The mother giving birth (be it a bird, an ant, or a mammal) flashes on our mental screen. Guru Gobind Singh's verse coheres with contemporary feminist reminders of the interconnectedness of the ecosystem and of the web of life in our biosphere.

The above passage also unites procreation and creation. The biological birthing is immediately juxtaposed to literary productions, for That One is regarded as the author of all the scriptures, Eastern and Western. The Sikh guru acknowledges that the four Vedas, the Qur'an, and the Puranas share the Divine Composer. Hindus and Muslims in his society were divided on the authority of their sacred literature, and as a consequence, forced conversions and religious persecutions were rampant. Guru Gobind Singh brings home the point that the creator of the physical world is also the generator of all thought, the narrator *(kathayam)* in both the Sanskrit and Arabic languages. As we hear Guru Gobind Singh's expressions of respect for the sacred texts of the Hindus and Muslims, we also hear dualistic models collapsing and breaking. The tyrannical emperor he fights against may happen to be a Muslim, but the Sikh guru recognizes the Qur'an as the voice of the Divine. The different and distinct languages and religious systems emanate from a sole source, and thought itself is of and from the physical body. A "paternal symbolic" and "maternal semiotic" (a distinction we will explore in our final chapter) come together in his religio-aesthetic *Weltanschauung*.

Even for his own literary and artistic creation, the guru solicits the support of the sword. In his words, "I'll complete this text, only if you help me please" (*BN*, 1:1), the sword carries creative energies, for she assists him in stringing ideas and images together: *granth* (book) literally means something that is "bound" or "strung together." The sword is an instrument that connects, and her sharpness performs the role of a needle that sews and gathers and knits together the rips in the fabric of life. Body and mind are not divided, for the sword is not just a weapon used in physical self-defense but equally valuable for mental acumen. Guru Gobind Singh extols her for different facets of his life: for his very subsistence, for his triumph over tyranny, and for the composition of his text. He immediately juxtaposes the creator of all art to the wielder of the sword (1:3). His literary structures pulsate with the fecundity of the sword. Rather than an instrument of death and destruction, she becomes instrumental to rhythm, imagination, dynamism, and life itself. The sword is motion, not stillness; she is life, not death; she is birth, not end.

She is a very positive metaphor, for her piercing light of intelligence gets rid of nescience and dark brute force. The *Bicitra Natak* honors the sword for "comforting the good" and "scaring evil away." The infirmities of the psyche like ego, deceit, and desire are won over by the sharp and shining sword. She is the eternal light *(joti amandam)*, she is the most powerful and luminous energy *(tej pracandam)*. So luminous is the sword that the sun can barely equal her brilliance! The powerful weapon deflates arrogance, ignorance, and false consciousness; it illuminates our true consciousness so that we can give birth to compassion, truth, and reality. The geographical battlefields of the *Bicitra Natak* could very well be our own bodies, where contrary forces are at war with each other, and the sword is used to get rid of our internal pathogens and afflictions. In our feminist re-memories she is welded to female powers: like the womb the sword can hold life; like the womb, the sword can get rid of life.

The resourcefulness of the sword ripples out from the individual into the community. As the individual psyche becomes communal, the sword serves as the medium to disrupt the infirmities of society, and a womb for a new life of justice and freedom. Guru Gobind Singh's thealogical symbol fits in with his creative impulse. The sword would instill courage in the masses resigned to political and social oppression; she would uphold righteousness and resist tyranny. His glorification of the sword was to secure the fulfillment of divine justice. Both at the symbolic and functional levels, the sword draws together word and action, text and battlefield, creation and destruction, male and female, personal and public.

Guru Gobind Singh's *Bicitra Natak* brings about a disclosure of the power of imagination, for the image, that was imprinted on the guru's mind soon became the instrument to shape Sikh moods and motivations. It became the center of Sikh rituals and ceremonies. On Baisakhi Day 1699, Guru Gobind Singh's artistic symbol entered the practical sphere. It cut the umbilical cord that constrained people within patriarchal restrictions. The newly born Khalsa was fed the *amrit* churned with the double-edged sword: this first drink, the "mother's milk," was made through and with the sword. Just as the mother transforms her own nutrients into nurturing milk, so the sword transforms water into *amrit*. Sikhs of both genders continue to be initiated into the Khalsa with water churned by a double-edged sword. Since the day of the Khalsa's birth, it is also worn by both Sikh men and women. It is one of the five gifts that the Khalsa received: some wear it as a tiny symbol studded in a comb tucked in the hair, others as a charm worn on a chain around the neck, and many carry a real sword varying in length. By having it touch their body, men and women should feel its *multivalent* vibrations. Faced with external hostilities and inner turbulence, her touch should bring them comfort and clarity. The sword extolled by Guru Gobind Singh in his *Bicitra Natak* has become an essential element of Sikh personality and religious ceremony. The artistic symbol gestated in his fecund religio-aesthetic matrix, and in the course of a few more than nine months, evolved into a maternal reality that was to feed, clothe, and sustain generations of Sikhs for perpetuity.

Woman Warrior

The woman who figures quite explicitly in the *Bicitra Natak* is the mythological heroine Kali. In Guru Gobind Singh's milieu, the image of the goddess Kali was extremely popular and she was worshipped in the surrounding hills as Camunda, Bhadrakali, Durga, and Mata. The female figure belongs to an ancient tradition flowing far back to the banks of the Indus River. The Sikh guru was fascinated with her warrior aspect, and she was a heroine in many of his compositions. But her strong female presence has been very threatening for many of Guru Gobind Singh's readers and exegetes, who one way or the other have obliterated her from public memory.[16] The courageous mythological warrior is made utterly irrelevant in the Sikh world. Although she is not a central character in the *Bicitra Natak*, she is a strong force throughout the drama, and I find her unexpected presence here even more telling than in compositions directly about her like *Candi Caritra* and *Var Durga Ki*. The female figure and her feminine energy, including both creation and destruction, passion and compassion, are deeply imbedded in Guru Gobind Singh's subconsciousness—so much so that Kali and her strength show up even when he is writing about quite different subjects and events.

There are several reasons why Kali would surface in his *Bicitra Natak*. Firstly, Kali devours Time. With scissors in her hand she cuts off the life span of all creatures. The personification of time would hold a special interest for the guru who constantly addressed the Ultimate as Akal (Timeless One). Since the entire first chapter of his *Bicitra Natak* is a praise of the Timeless One, how could the most spectacular goddess of time (Kali) not figure into Guru Gobind Singh's artistic horizon?

Secondly, she was worshipped by women and people of the servile and untouchable classes.[17] Her association with those excluded from orthodox Vedic rites must have touched a chord in the Sikh guru, for whom human equality was of paramount importance. As he aspired to rid his society of priestly hegemony, the goddess espoused by those on the margins would have appeared very attractive to him.

Thirdly, she is what Kant would describe as the "sublime." Not pleasantly beautiful, Kali is very conducive to evoking the *raudra rasa* (heroic mood), and so the ancient Indian goddess functions as an important aesthetic device for the Sikh guru. He writes the *Bicitra Natak* to incite courage in his readers and devotees, and Kali with her heroic character is utilized by the poet to accomplish his aesthetic goals.

Fourthly, he probably felt that the very process of importing from another tradition would act as "an anti-inertial" device and help his society to escape from the trap of its patriarchal structures. As Wendy Doniger insightfully reveals, other peoples' myths can contribute to the new life that we want to live ourselves. "But we may break out from all of these various prisons with the help of other peoples' myths, which, coming from outside our own closed system, may provide an external influence, an anti-inertial force, to move us off our own treadmill, our own track, onto an entirely new path."[18] The tenth Sikh guru wanted to move his stagnant society into a new world of freedom, and this popular mythic model from the Hindu world would have been a good device for animating his Sikh readership.

Fifthly, the image of the Hindu goddess would challenge the pervasive fanaticism of his milieu. In the oppressive regime of the fundamentalist Muslim emperor Aurangzeb, the Sikh guru freely retells the courage of a Hindu goddess! This is a daring gesture of rebellion on his part. I see him acting in ways quite like his father, the ninth Sikh guru, who gave up his life for the sake of religious freedom—precisely, for the right of the Hindus to wear their sacred thread and practice their rites.

And most of all, how could his comprehensive aesthetic horizon exclude anybody or anything—he even sees the drunken bumblebee as the Infinite One! Guru Gobind Singh's expansive imagination follows the exciting goddess rather than excising her.

Actually, at the end of his *Bicitra Natak* Guru Gobind Singh informs the reader that he wrote it between his two *Candi Caritra* poems (*BN*, 14:11). Durga-Kali, the revered subject of *Devi Mahatmaya*, is the heroine of Guru Gobind Singh's *Candi Caritra* compositions. She is the central figure in *Devi Mahatmaya*, a Sanskrit work written in the sixth century (which forms chapters 81–93 of the *Markandeya Purana*). It is the most famous of all Hindu texts celebrating Durga-Kali's mythological exploits. This Puranic story of her titanic battle against the demons is retold by Guru Gobind Singh in his ornate Braj compositions, the *Candi Caritra* poems, and in his Punjabi work, *Var Durga Ki*, commonly known as *Candi di Var*. Even his Akal Usat, a hymn written in praise of the Timeless One, contains a panegyric to the prowess of the invincible goddess. The Sikh guru was very attracted to *her*, the kinetic energy of the Divine. Without her, there would be no creation, and without her, the male gods would have lost to the demons. The goddess legitimizes the war against injustice. In his poems on Candi, the Sikh guru recalls the classical Indian myth recorded in the *Devi Mahatmaya*, and amplifies the warrior role of the female protagonist with all his artistic zest and fire. The fact that he situates the *Bicitra Natak* between the two goddess poems affirms and substantiates her configuration in his artistic landscape, and in turn provokes and stimulates our senses to recognize other female associations and appropriations in his narrative.

Now, the goddess is not an incarnation who actually fights in Guru Gobind Singh's battles. Surely she is no Lord Krishna helping out the Pandu brothers in their battle in Kurukshetra. She is by no means literally present by his side. Nowhere in the text does Guru Gobind Singh worship or invoke her, and the goddess never descends (*avatara*) to help him out. The guru remains ever devoted to the singular, transcendent One—envisioned in a plurality of ways, including the form of a beautifully dressed woman. The reverential tone in which the goddess is extolled in Hinduism as the object of worship and ritual is absent in Guru Gobind Singh's discourse. The Hindu goddess is not idolized by the Sikh guru in any way. Without succumbing to any theory of incarnation, Guru Gobind Singh artistically and very playfully brings the ancient goddess into his poetry. Kali remains a classical paradigm of those who valiantly fight against injustice and ignorance. By vigorously retelling a female story from the past, the Sikh guru participates in the process of "remythologizing" put at the heart of the contemporary feminist movement by spokeswomen like Ellen Umansky and Bella Debrida.[19]

The *Bicitra Natak* carries direct references to the goddess's invincibility when attacked by the evil forces of Sumbha, Nisumbha, and Raktbija, an invincibility recorded in the *Markandeya Purana*. We get gory scenes of how the demons are "shredded into tiny, tiny bits by Time" (1:64) and how "they are killed by the sword of Time" (1:95). In the magical world of the *Bicitra Natak* we vividly see the goddess in action, and we also hear her. The tinkling *ghungaram* (bells) that ring through the drama lead us to imagine *her* body. Her laughter is loud and free. With "a skull-bowl in hand, Kali thunderously laughs in the skies" (3:23). She is heard again; "Devi thunders in the skies" (3:31). In later chapters of the *Bicitra Natak*, "the shrieks of Camunda and her attendants are heard in the battlegrounds" (8:18), and as the horses begin to dance, "Kali roars ferociously" (10:5). Her ankle bells, her laughter, her roar, and her clanging weapons demonstrate her power in different ways.

The sounds of Kali are an impressive contrast to silence, the prized virtue of women in Guru Gobind Singh's culture. In the guru's moral imagination the female breaks out of her "booby-trapped silence" and vigorously charges to deliver a just society. Whereas the Sikh guru could easily hear a female voice, his followers seem to have a tough time recognizing her, for Sikh patriarchs cannot bear to hear either the mythological goddess in their guru's compositions, or the voices of their daughters, sisters, wives, or nieces.[20] Kali's sounds announce liberty and freedom for a stifled people. Out of the millions of gods and goddesses of ancient India, it is Kali who roars against injustice, and she is the heroine who is bred in Guru Gobind Singh's literary production. It is often said that a child responds to sounds in the mother's womb: I read the aural depiction of the goddess in the *Bicitra Natak* as a prenatal technique for instilling fearlessness in the embryonic Khalsa.

Because the sound of his Kali goes unheard in Sikh circles, some scholars banish the goddess entirely from Guru Gobind Singh's imagination, claiming Hindu poets to be the author of his goddess poems.[21] Some, like D. P. Ashta and Trilochan Singh, concede the goddess's presence in his secular works but find her presence inappropriate in the devotional poems.[22] And some even convert her into a male figure! In translations of the *Bicitra Natak*, Time is invariably addressed as a male and presented in masculine terms and images, and only the male side of the formless Time is brought out and underscored. What is surprising is that even when the poet clearly has the goddess in mind, the translators give her a masculine identity.[23] This trend continues to dominate, and even an important contemporary work on the Dasam Granth distorts her female figure. This recent translation reads, "Fragmenter of the pride of Madhu (the demon), the decimator of Sumbh and keeper of white canopy over your head, O Lord, the weapons adorn your hands."[24] Now, in the original text there is no gender specification, no vocative such as "O Lord." The preceding acts of the goddess who destroys the demons imply that the hands that hold weapons are female: *lasam hath atram* means "the weapons *(atram)* shine (*lasam*) in hand (*hath*)." Obviously, the poet means *her* weapons and *her* hands, but the English version accidentally interprets his words as referring to a supreme male lord. Such scholarly "accidents" recur with alarming consistency, because his poetic images are feared as worship of a goddess. Guru Gobind Singh's poetic utilization of the mythological figure is misconstrued, and therefore erased.

Androcentric interpretations leave us impoverished artistically, spiritually, and morally. We distort the guru's artistic landscape in which the female sword wielder is a fascinating literary protagonist; she is *not* the Ultimate who is the sole subject of Guru Gobind Singh's belief and worship. At the same time, we sever ourselves from the maternal contact and protection extended by the female hand. Through his fabulous literary techniques, the guru incites us to imagine a woman's body, drawing us to her strong female hand. We can see *her* flesh, *her* fingers as the source of his sword: "The sword in hand, crores of sins crossed over" (*BN*, 1:47). As long as we refuse to recognize the mythic heroine in Guru Gobind Singh's poetry, we devalue the legitimacy and beneficence of female power in his religio-aesthetic worldview. I want to emphasize that the Sikh guru does not worship Kali.[25] Sikhs are rightly upset about the slightest hint of incarnation, but there is none here. Yet, at the same time, he artistically projects her female figure and energy. Now, there would be no problem if the guru were referring to a Hindu male god and his legendary activities. A Shiva or Indra or Rama would simply be understood as a literary device with metaphoric associations. As soon as the female is introduced, theologians and exegetes get all ruffled, and suspicions and fear of "Hinduism," "polytheism," or "pantheism" immediately begin to surface. The goddess Kali affects Sikhs at a visceral level, which her male counterparts do not.

Guru Gobind Singh's remythologizing of the goddess discloses traits and unleashes energies that the poet and his readers, both men and women, could identify with and incorporate into their own lives. Male paradigms needed to be balanced by female paradigms. The rejuvenation of society depended on the actions of both men and women. The fact that Guru Gobind Singh was able to imagine a female hand holding the sword is a vital signifier that he could confidently see the instrument held in the hands of women in his own society. In fact, Sikh history records the case of Mai Bhago, who fought valiantly with the guru. She was from the Amritsar district of the Punjab. When she saw how some Sikhs of her area had fled rather than help the guru in Anandpur, she chided them for their pusillanimity. Mai Bhago led them back to fight for the guru, and she herself fought in the battle that took place in Muktsar on December 19, 1705.[26] During the period of Sikh persecutions that followed the guru's death, women not only took care of their families but also fought courageously. The period is replete with the heroic deeds and sacrifices of Sikh men and women like Mai Bhago. The guru who remembered the mythic woman warrior could have a valorous Mai Bhago by his side.

By refusing to acknowledge the artistic image of the goddess in their guru's literary horizon, the Sikh community only loses out. Staying blind to her image and deaf to her sounds, we weaken ourselves: we fracture the Sikh guru's universality that experiences the Infinite One, we fracture our community in which both men and women are equal, we fracture our self which contains both the male and the female, anima and animus. By obliterating Kali from Guru Gobind Singh's memory we give up a valuable paradigm to counter patriarchal theologies and patriarchal social systems that keep reinforcing each other. Sexism festers in the Sikh community. The prospect of translating Guru Gobind Singh's ancient Indian story into the contemporary social and political affairs of the Sikhs has not been realized, and unfortunately, "mythos" has not led to "ethos."

Biophilic Ethics

In *Metaphors of Self,* the literary critic James Olney comments that the act of autobiography constitutes "a bringing to consciousness of the nature of one's own existence, transforming the mere fact of existence into a realized quality and a possible meaning."[27] The *Bicitra Natak* gives us a firsthand account of the author. The way he identifies himself and understands the meaning of his life can best be characterized as "biophilial." In contrast to necrophilia with its preoccupation on death and the other world, biophilia is literally a love for life. Feminist thinkers have appropriated it as a psychological and philosophical category to reshift the necrophilic imaginary rooted in misogyny. The feminist philosopher Grace Jantzen argues that in their love for the immortal, the spiritual, and the father, philosophers, mystics, and psychologists have hated the mortal, the physical, and the mother. Her comprehensive study *Becoming Divine: Towards a Feminist Philosophy* incorporates the views of important Western feminists who condemn Freud's equation of the child's desire to control the mother's absence with Thanatos, the death drive. Jantzen cites Diane Jonte-Pace, who describes death as "the unrepresentable, the ultimate absence, is symbolized as woman; woman becomes through metonomy, death. . . . "[28] Jantzen, Jonte-Pace and their peers make us face the harsh reality that the obsession with death is linked to the obsession with female bodies.

The September 11 tragedy painfully brings home the point that the lovers of a God, conceived as male, were haters of women. The Al Qaeda hijackers were indeed obsessed with death. The eighteen-point "Last Will and Testament" of their leader, Mohammed Atta, reveals his joy at the prospect of death. Preparing to meet death, Atta and his companions had their hair cut about an hour's distance from where I live in Maine. They were neatly shaved and eagerly awaited death. It is hard to fathom that these daring fighters had such disgust for—or fear of? —women! Point number 5 of Atta's will reads, "I don't want a pregnant woman or a person who is not clean to come and say good-bye to me"; number 11: "I don't want any women to go to my grave at all during my funeral or on any occasion thereafter."[29] In their love for death and a paradise somewhere out there, the earth and women are horribly despised.

The warnings of feminist scholars are extremely important in the context of our text, because what we have is a text full of battles and bloodshed. Death and the dead are everywhere. Could the *Bicitra Natak* be read as necrophilic? I am afraid such erroneous interpretations of the guru's text have found their way into Sikh society. The patriarchal psyche has remembered the guru's depictions of death as though life did not matter, as though body was not important, as though the guru's orientation was toward a heaven somewhere out there, as though women were irrelevant and inhuman. But to the contrary, the whole purpose of the birth of the Khalsa was to celebrate an authentic mode of existence here on earth with fellow men and women. We desperately need to see through the male surface of the *Bicitra Natak* in order to rectify our misinterpretations, and redirect ourselves.

In fact, our sonogram shows a person who deeply values a fruitful and abundant life on earth. We may recall his opening chapter celebrating the Infinite in the myriad forms of earthly existence—"Somewhere as a flower. . . . Somewhere like a woman." That One is the source of the flourishing world, and the resource of every embodied, gendered, situated self. We are drawn in by Guru Gobind Singh's respect for wombs from all species. His sense of wonder and joy resonant at the outset of his narrative—"You have produced the sweat-born, fetus-born, earth-born, You have created the egg-born"—lingers with his readers till the very end.

Even when he identifies himself, Guru Gobind Singh's love for life and living comes out strikingly. He is proud of his embodied self, the self that was born of his mother and father:

> My father and mother worshipped the ineffable One,
> they meditated and contemplated in many ways
> They served the ineffable One,
> and the supreme Guru was pleased with them.
> (*BN*, 6:3–4)

There is a hint here that the parents had some difficulties in having a child (actually, Gobind was the only child of Mata Gujari and Guru Tegh Bahadur). But both parents were devoted to the Divine, and their efforts bore a wonderful result. Guru Gobind Singh does not point toward any immaculate conception. His was a birth in blood and placenta. In his re-creation of himself, the guru validates the physical and sexual mode of procreation.

He is adamant that he not be confused as an incarnation of the Supreme One.[30] He categorically identifies himself as personal slave *(dasa)* of the Supreme One and rejects all other appropriations: "If anyone calls me the supreme being, they shall fall into the pit of hell. Know me as the slave of That One, for there is nothing hidden in it. I am the slave of the highest Being..." (6:32–33). The guru enfolds his readers into his poetic enterprise and invites them to accept the dignity of human life and experience—finite though they may be.

Grounded in human history, he hears his divine call to launch a community that would steer people away from ignorance:

> "I cherish you as my son, to propagate the Panth [Community]
> I have created you.
> Go there and launch Dharam [moral system], restrain humanity
> from ignorance."
> I got up, my hands folded together,
> and with my head bowed, I responded:
> "The Panth will begin in the world when you help."
> (*BN*, 6:29–30)

The earliest inklings of the Khalsa are visible here. The guru is endowed with a divine mission that can be consummated only through a community that will radically change the affairs of his contemporary society. Justice does not belong to another time and space, and the guru reminds us of the responsibilities we owe one another. His future organization is to bring out the best of humanity by erasing "ignorance" *(kubudhi)*. We hear his commitment to a fulfilling life on earth. The guru accepts his mission in and through his body: his hands are folded together and his head is bowed.

Guru Gobind Singh's mission is accomplished through love and emotions. Body is good. Senses are validated. Morality comes in life, through our bodies. The guru adamantly says: "I will not keep matted hair nor wear glass-rings in the ears" (*BN*, 6:51), "I will not blindfold eyes" (6:62) nor "shut my nostrils "(6:57), "I will not keep false faiths nor display acts of piety... " (6:52). These cultural codes for annihilating the body, shutting off the senses, and breaking all natural links with our bodies, with our families, and with our community are loudly rejected in the *Bicitra Natak*. Morality is not fostered in some distant cave or a faraway forest; rather it is practiced in the immediate world of here and now. The sensuous experience—with eyes, with ears, with nose—of the Transcendent One, constitutes Guru Gobind Singh's sole method.

And the story of his life takes shape in a nexus of relationships that helped him in the "cultivation of the self": "They nurtured my body in various ways; they gave me instructions of many different types" (*BN*, 7:3). The care of the body *(tan racha)* is instilled in him in his early years. In fact, the five *Ks* that he gave his Khalsa (long hair, comb, drawers, bracelet, and sword) are a means of taking care of the body, and must have their genesis somewhere in this early phase of Guru Gobind Singh's life.

The guru also reminisces about the affection he received: "I was caressed by many different nurses" (*BN*, 7:2). Different arms must have cuddled him; different voices must have sung him lullabies. When he was born in Patna, he must have been raised by women from Bihar, and after his move with his family to Anandpur, he would have been brought up by women from the Punjab and the hill areas of Garhwal and Bilaspur. A variety of languages and accents and myths and legends would have echoed in the little person. Being nurtured by a variety of people in his childhood is likely to have contributed to Guru Gobind Singh's open and embracing personality. The more love he received as a child, the more love the guru was able to give to others during his adult life. Having a healthy relationship with women in his impressionable years solidified his positive attitude toward the opposite sex for the rest of his life. Sikhs popularly recite his childhood friendship with Queen Mania, who had no children of her own. When the four-year-old Gobind promised that he would be like a son to her, Mania gave him grain. In recognition of the friendship between Gobind and Queen Mania, grain continues to be served in the community meal at Patna Sahib Gurdwara. Queen Mania may have introduced him to the mystery and power of procreation. Guru Gobind Singh's subterranean self was constructed through his intimacy with women.

Guru Gobind Singh entered the variegated world with love and joy. The world blossomed with the Infinite, and he entered the blossoming world through the body of his mother. As he grew up he became actively engaged in upholding the morality and freedom of his society. The battles he fought were short-lived, and they were intended for the goodness and liberation of everybody, so that the intrinsic blossoming could be felt by his society. Our rememory of his autobiographical narrative fills us with respect for our mothers, a celebration of our entry into the world, a love for our own bodies, and a responsibility to make life fulfilling for ourselves and for our fellow beings. The clues that we find in the narrative are not inconsequential ones that can be ignored in the development of Guru Gobind Singh's ethical philosophy; rather, they constitute his self-consciousness and the consciousness that he passed down to his future Khalsa. Above all else, it was by his obsession with life and living that he became pregnant with the Khalsa.

Pluralistic Genes

The *Bicitra Natak* gives us a firsthand account of the author in which he looks at himself from diverse angles—spiritual, cultural, historical, and biological. The guru identifies himself as the servant of the One, as the descendant of legendary Indian kings, as the successor of Guru Nanak, and as the son of Guru Tegh Bahadur and Mata Gujari. The manifold past is very much alive in the author's consciousness, and those diverse and plural patterns of his own integrated personality are passed on to the Khalsa.

Spiritual

The Divine, of course, is the ground of Guru Gobind Singh's life and imagination, and is naturally regarded as his progenitor. This One is the common denominator of the universe, the voice of both Eastern and Western scriptures. The guru introduces himself as the "servant" of That One, commissioned to bring about justice in society. His notion of selfhood constantly retains its physical and metaphysical dimensions. Perhaps it was Guru Gobind Singh's feeling of transcendence that made him search deep inside of himself and express his birth into this world with the imagination of a poet and the insight of a philosopher. In chapter 6 of his work, the guru writes that on the lofty Hemkunt mountain, he became totally saturated in the One: "[F]rom two it became one form" (*BN*, 6:3). Absorbed in the Sole Reality, all his doubts and dualisms disappeared. In the intensity of his experience, the subject of the devotions and the object became One, and he experienced total unity. On their side, his parents were also devoted to That One. The Transcendent was the focal point on which his parents' and his own ardent devotions converged. As he was absorbed in that timeless moment (not in some previous birth), the parents lovingly conceived and received him. The infinite source was carried by Mata Gujari in her womb for nine months and entered this world.

That his divine source was both male and female was critical to Guru Gobind Singh's self-understanding. In his final canto, he experiences transcendent time in terms of a parental bond: "All human time is our transcendent father; all divine time is our biological mother" (*BN*, 14:5). The guru comes into this world not as a detached individual who is "thrown" but as the progeny of a couple who share a rich organic intimacy. He draws our attention to both dimensions of time—male (*kal*) and female (*kalika*)—for they are the father and mother who together constitute our world and reality. Every birth restores transcendent time into the seconds, minutes, and hours of our days, weeks, months, and years. Birth and being alive are therefore natural phenomena completely contingent on time, which in nature and function is *both* father and mother. Thus Guru Gobind Singh recovers his physical identity lodged in the Divine.

The male and female dimensions are also equally vital to his intellectual, emotional, spiritual, and moral self-construction. In the very next verse he says, "Male mind is our guru, female mind is our mother who taught me all right action." The word *man* (mind) defies either-or categories and means mind, heart, consciousness, spirit. All good action toward the human family is learned from this mental, spiritual, and emotional hub, which is personified by the figures of a male guru (*manua gur*) and a female mother (*mansa mai*).[31] This acknowledgment in the final canto of his autobiography discloses that all that the guru thought, all that he imagined, all that he sensed, and all the good deeds that he performed came from this reservoir flowing with male and female currents. His is a holistic notion of the self in which the female is not denigrated, denied, or repressed. Guru Gobind Singh's integrated self-awareness vigorously contests the mind-body dualism, and in turn offers new livable possibilities for spirituality and action for men and women alike.

Cultural

The Guru shows us his link with the soil and soul of India by connecting himself with the protagonists of both the *Mahabharata* and the *Ramayana*. Guru Gobind Singh was born in India, he studied the classical Indian languages, and he was familiar with the ancient Indian literary and intellectual tradition. The *Bicitra Natak* amply illustrates that the guru was proud to inherit his extensive pan-Indian cultural legacy. There is an inner confidence in him that allows him to celebrate his selfhood *with* and not *against* his ancient past.

With all his narrative details, Guru Gobind Singh introduces us to his cultural ancestry, which goes back for more than two millennia. The guru claims, "[T]hrough self-discipline I landed at Hemkunt, the site bedecked by seven mountain peaks" (*BN*, 6:1). While we are introduced to his spiritual activities amid the beauty, sturdiness, and loftiness of the Himalayan locale, we are also introduced to his association with the ancestor of the Pandavas, since Hemkunt "was the spot where the Pandu king practiced austerities" (6:2). The guru must have cherished the Pandava clan because of their display of courage in the *Mahabharata*, in which they fought against the immoral forces of the Kauravas. When the Pandava brother Arjuna showed some reservation, Lord Krishna urged him to fight for the upkeep of Dharma, and his divine advice is enshrined in the Bhagavad Gita. For the Sikh guru, the Pandava undertaking was crucial. Immorality and injustice had to be quelled. But even more important was the sequence: intense contemplation by their greatest warrior preceded the mighty war fought by the

Pandava brothers in Kurukshetra. The Sikh guru's engagements follow a parallel path: only deep reflection and meditation prepare one to fight for justice; only after intense concentration did he create the Khalsa in the Shivalik Valley to fight oppression.

Simultaneously, he contextualizes himself within the framework of the other great Indian epic, Valmiki's *Ramayana*. In cantos 2–6 of the *Bicitra Natak*, the author traces the lineage of the Sikh gurus to King Aju, who is known to have descended from Raghav, a brilliant star of the Solar dynasty. Guru Gobind Singh describes the forefather as "a fabulous warrior and a fabulous archer" (*BN*, 2:20). But the guru admires King Aju for leaving behind all his wealth and power to King Dashrath and retreating to the forest to meditate. The combination of secular and spiritual aspirations is the striking characteristic of all the ancestors he mentions in the *Bicitra Natak*, be they Sodhis, Bedis, or the forefather King Aju himself. C. P. Loehlin tersely comments that there was a kaleidoscopic succession in which Guru Gobind Singh's warrior ancestors turned into scholars, ascetics into rulers, and rulers into ascetics.[32]

Interestingly, he traces the origins of the cultural centers of the Punjab—Lahore and Kasur—to Lav and Kush, the "sons of Sita" (*BN*, 2:23). Sita surfaces in the Sikh guru's memoir as the progenitor of civilization in northern India. He praises those cities of *madra desh,* the region between the Rivers Beas and Jhelum: "[S]uch is the grandeur of Lahore and Kasur that Lanka and Amravati were put to shame" (2:24). Sita's offspring gave birth to new cultural centers that would draw people from different geographical, linguistic, religious, and social backgrounds. In an earlier section of his narrative as well, the male Guru remembers the foremothers—the incredibly beautiful daughters Banita, Kadru, Diti, and Aditi. They were married to sages and gave birth to serpents, gods, and demons (2:17–18). He reminds us that "It was [Dashrath's] first wife who gave birth to Prince Rama " (2:22). In a culture where genealogy is traced solely through males, the *Bicitra Natak* takes note of mothers, wives, and daughters. In fact, the Solar clan decends from the womb of Aditi, the female principle of creation or infinity.[33]

Clearly, Guru Gobind Singh's India is not divided into Hinduism, Buddhism, or Jainism; for the Sikh guru India represents universal morality, oneness, and justice. The Sikh guru burrows deep into India's heart and experiences her pluralism, which takes him out of provincialism and narrowness into a vaster and profounder reality. In his Akal Ustat he strikingly denounces the difference between Hindu and Muslim forms of worship and their sacred places, the temple and the mosque, proclaiming "all humans are one" (Akal Ustat, verse 86). When India was bleeding from the wounds of partition in the twentieth century, political leaders like Mahatma Gandhi tried to bring peace and harmony by reviving Guru Gobind Singh's vision.

According to Dr. S. Radhakrishnan, Gandhi got the idea for his popular public prayer "Ishvara and Allah are your names..." from Guru Gobind Singh.[34] Gandhi often claimed to be a follower of the Sikh guru, and because of his aspirations for a united India, he felt to be closer to the ideals of Guru Gobind Singh than to contemporary Sikh political leaders who wanted a separate Sikh homeland: "I had said to no one else than Master Tara Singh that I was the true heir of Guru Govind Singh and not he...."[35] We hear Gandhi lavishly praising Guru Gobind Singh: "He was a man given to charity, he was unattached, he was an incarnation of God,"[36] though Guru Gobind Singh would not have wanted anybody to go that far.[37] Just a few days before his death, Gandhi broke his fast for Guru Gobind Singh's birthday (January 18, 1948). Clearly the Sikh guru's pluralism and humanism had great appeal for Mahatma Gandhi in twentieth-century India.

Guru Gobind Singh's own sense of the past continued into his future occupations and became embodied in the Khalsa members, who would remain in touch with their ancient roots. The first five initiates into the Khalsa family not only came from different sectors of society but also from different parts of India: North, South, East and West. The nucleus thus represents a wide and diverse spectrum of Indian culture. The universal morality and justice and the power of poetry embodied in India's rich past had to be reproduced in the future. Indomitable warriors are made up of delicate poetry. Guru Gobind Singh's ideal of the Khalsa was generated by the ancient figures that he remembered in his drama.

Historical

The origins of the Khalsa are directly traced to the Sikh gurus. While maintaining his pan-Indian links, we find that Guru Gobind Singh is very specific about his Sikh genealogy. The detailed exposition of the Bedi and Sodhi families in chapters 2–4 of the *Bicitra Natak* is a logical progression to his Sikh origins, to the appearance of Nanak (*BN*, 5:4). Guru Gobind Singh devotes three and a half verses to Guru Nanak. But in those few words he underscores Guru Nanak's pluralistic mandate, which must have made a deep impression on him.

First of all he celebrates Nanak as the founder of a new ethical order. In his own words, "[H]e launched *dharam* in this age" (*BN*, 5:5). By *dharam* Guru Gobind Singh means the Sikh way of life. He retains the traditional Sanskrit term *dharma* (that which holds together) to indicate that Nanak initiated something new and that "he popularized *dharam* [Punjabi version of *dharma*] in this world" (5:7). We have here an important testimony from Guru Gobind Singh that the first Sikh guru transformed his society and created a new energy, which became consolidated into a new religion. The tenth

Sikh guru maintained his ancient links and remained ever in close touch with the eternal wisdom of India, but the origins of his Khalsa are specifically rooted in Guru Nanak. In the new path launched by the founder of Sikhism, the *varnasharamdharma* upheld by traditional scriptures is overturned, and so the warrior is no longer limited to the Kshatriya caste; the fight for justice is not only Arjuna's dharma but action shared equally by all men and women, at all stages of life. Though Guru Gobind Singh's Khalsa would carry on the ideals of heroism and poetry from ancient epics, it would also be something radically different from any historical paradigm.

Guru Gobind Singh further compliments his predecessor for showing the way "to all good people" (*BN*, 5:5). Nanak made no religious, cultural, or social distinctions. The tenth Sikh guru emulated his inclusive approach and made it the very ground for his philosophy and ethics. People from different castes, different professional backgrounds, and different cultural parts of India could join the new family of the Khalsa. Their rebirth into the single caste of humanity was marked by their sipping *amrit* from the same bowl. This practical gesture started by the tenth Sikh guru on Baisakhi Day 1699 was modeled on his memory that Guru Nanak had received a bowl full of *amrit* from the Transcendent One (a metahistoric account that we will explore in more detail in chapter 3). Guru Gobind Singh had to ensure that nobody belonging to the human family was ever to be weaned away from that divine *amrit* first tasted by Nanak.

The final point that Guru Gobind Singh makes about Nanak's ministry is that he instilled Lahina as his successor.

> Nanak gave his form to Angad
> He spread his religion in this world.
> Then he was called by the name of Amar Das
> Like one lamp lighting another.
>
> (*BN*, 5:7)

Guru Nanak's disciple Lahina is made Angad, literally, a limb (from Sanskrit *anga*) of his own body. Guru Gobind Singh's lamp analogy has a precedent in the Guru Granth itself (GG, 966), and has also been used by Bhai Gurdas in his Punjabi ballads.[38] One flame kindles another. In spite of the fact that the gurus were born in different families (Bedis or Sodhis), Guru Gobind Singh categorically claims that the same light, the same message, and the same physicality was carried on from Nanak to Angad and to his successor gurus. The historical succession from Nanak to Angad etched in the tenth Sikh guru's memory was eventually reproduced by him: he made the Khalsa a limb of himself on Baisakhi 1699, and a day before he passed away, he invested the Granth with guruship. The corporeality of *angad* continued to sustain his vision and praxis.

Biological

The author continues with his historical account, depicting how each guru was embodied in the next till he comes to the ninth, Guru Tegh Bahadur (*BN*, 5:12). Here the narrative speaks of his biological father. With the mention of Tegh Bahadur, the poet's attention is instantly drawn to the ninth guru's martyrdom, and this tragic event reveals yet another layer of the Khalsa's fertilization.[39] The final four verses of chapter 5 of the *Bicitra Natak* form an intersection between the author's past and his present. The memory they recount and the sentiments that they express reveal how deeply affected he was by his father's phenomenal sacrifice for the sake of religious diversity.

Guru Gobind Singh's very first comment about his father is that "he protected the frontal mark and sacred thread" (*BN*, 5:13). Compassion and sympathy for others are the characteristics that stand out foremost in the mind of the son. Guru Tegh Bahadur was not a votary of either *tilak* (the mark on the forehead) or *janeu* (the sacred thread worn by upper-caste male Hindus). Yet, the ninth Sikh guru staked his life for the right of those who believed in them. The defense of these two religious symbols signified the right of each individual to practice his or her religion freely. The son is struck by the fact that his father overcame narrow religious barriers, and performed his "momentous deed" for the sake of people of another faith (5:14).

Guru Gobind Singh's admiration for his father's tremendous courage flows out in verses of haunting beauty. We hear in rhythmic assonance: "[H]e gave up his head, but did not utter a sigh" (*BN*, 5:13). In the next verse, "[H]e gave up his head but not his faith" (5:14). Again, "[A] deed like Tegh Bahadur's none has dared to do" (5:15). The *Bicitra Natak* does not go into any of the details of how Guru Tegh Bahadur was cruelly beheaded in public in Chandni Chowk, near the Red Fort in Delhi on November 11, 1675. Young Gobind, who was nine years old at that time, was far away in Anandpur with his mother.

Historians report that for fear of Mughal reprisals, the mutilated body of Guru Tegh Bahadur was left unattended in Chandni Chowk. At night there was a storm that helped Sikhs to escape with the bodily remains. Lakhi Shah, with the help of his son, lifted the headless trunk and carried it off to his home in a cart. Since open cremation would not have been allowed, Lakhi Shah set fire to his house, burning with it the body of the martyred guru. The spot is now the site of the popular Sikh shrine Gurdwara Rikabganj in Delhi. Bhai Jaita took the severed head and made a hazardous journey with his revered possession to Anandpur. Harbans Singh tenderly captures the tragic scene: "The rocks of the hills around Anandpur must have melted to see the dust-laden, severed head of its founder."[40] It was the nine-year-old Gobind who received the head from Bhai Jaita, and with due ceremony he cremated it. No wonder the "head" is mentioned so often in those few verses in chapter 5 of the *Bicitra Natak*. And years later, on Baisakhi Day of 1699, when Guru Gobind Singh began the Khalsa institution with the call for a "head," he must have been unconsciously remembering his father's gift to humanity. The demand that stunned the Baisakhi congregation of 1699 was but what Guru Tegh Bahadur had already met in his lifetime. The pluralistic motivations of his father must have resonated deep within the son and eventually led to his ideal of the Khalsa, which would valorously defy all sorts of religious and social exclusions.

Guru Gobind Singh's personal loss, pain, and anger were sublimated into a dynamic and creative mode of living. His father's death did not make him vindictive, as is commonly assumed.[41] The *Bicitra Natak* throughout shows how Guru Gobind Singh remains full of love for the Transcendent One and for the beauty of the world around him. The notion that revenge of his father's death became the dominant force behind his actions would be a gross misreading of his autobiography, a gross misinterpretation of the devotion he had for humanity at large, and a gross misunderstanding of the conception of the Khalsa. In fact, what his father was for him, Guru Gobind Singh became for the Khalsa. His procreation of the Khalsa was prompted by his feelings of compassion and love, and on Baisakhi 1699, he and Mataji become parents of their newly born Khalsa.

Guru Gobind Singh's multifaceted identity was transferred to the Khalsa. The pluralistic genes from the Infinite Reality, from epic figures of ancient India, from the first Sikh guru, and from his own parents, Tegh Bahadur and Mata Gujari, would naturally flow into Guru Gobind Singh's Khalsa. As the *Bicitra Natak* unfolds for us, the multiple sources of his own birth become the resources of the Khalsa. He erases all boundary markings, a strategy that is implicitly feminine, since such boundaries are a "part of patriarchy's exercise of power, a power connected to ownership and deploying of identity politics that must know itself *as against* the other and fails to embrace what 'could happen with others.'"[42] Guru Gobind Singh identifies himself by accepting himself as a part of human history, and our failure to recognize his total personality is our loss.

Like him, his Khalsa is fertilized by the Divine One and gestates in Guru Gobind Singh's expansive religio-aesthetic *Weltanschauung*; while its cultural and ethnic cradle is ancient India with its manifold models of warriors and poets, the Khalsa is specifically rooted in the pluralistic vision of the Sikh gurus from Nanak to his own father. Guru Gobind Singh bred the Khalsa precisely to fight against monolithic structures and conceptual rigidities. When the orthodoxy and fundamentalism of the Mughal empire stifled diversity, the guru vigorously challenged the Mughals. The conception of Guru Gobind Singh's Khalsa therefore needs to be remembered not in terms of exclusivism, but in terms of pluralism. According to Diana Eck, a popular contemporary voice on the subject, "[T]he pluralist . . . stands in a particular community and is willing to be committed to the struggles of that community. . . . The challenge for the pluralist is commitment without dogmatism and community without communalism."[43] The Khalsa he conceived would not simply tolerate people of other faiths; the Khalsa would try its best to create a space where different communities could live together freely and harmoniously. The Infinite would not be slighted or insulted in any *body* from any caste, class, religion, or gender.

Battles of Life

Chapters 8 through 13 of the *Bicitra Natak* chronologically outline the battles of Bhangani and Nadaun, and the many skirmishes against the neighborhood hill chiefs and Mughal forces that Guru Gobind Singh took part in. The six chapters come toward the close of the *Bicitra Natak*, and each of them focuses on a particular battle and names and describes the warriors and their actions. This section of the *Bicitra Natak* has received considerable attention from scholars, who study it with the objective of gaining historical information about the specific battles and collecting biographical facts about Guru Gobind Singh. Our reading expectations are somewhat different, for what we want is to discern the poet's sentiments and concerns, and to recognize the allusions to life and living that underlie his graphic battle scenes. It may very well be that we are following Virginia Woolf's dictum "to make serious what appears insignificant to a man, and trivial what is to him important."[44]

In spite of all the vivid battle scenes and heightened dramatic scenarios, what we notice is the lack of divine rewards for the warriors. The guru who is so talented in depicting the scenes of this world has no descriptions of the "world of the gods" that he hastily mentions in connection with his father's sacrifice (*BN*, 5:16) or with the heroic death of his men who bear the shots from their enemy (*BN*, 8:26). Guru Gobind Singh does not lead his readers away from our earthly setting to a paradise beyond with eternal delights awaiting his heroes. He makes no such promises to whisk us away from this world of ours. Nor does he offer any rationalization or legitimization for expansion and conquest. The guru is not fighting for any political aggrandizement or economic gains. There are no enticements of booty or territories of any size or kind. As a result, the various battles and skirmishes with their ferocious actions and blaring sounds do not possess either the intensity or the fervor of crusades or jihads.

The battles he takes part in are fought in self-defense. At the beginning of chapter 8 he writes, "Fateh Shah, the king then, was angry; without any reason he made the attack on us" (*BN*, 8:3). The guru is not the aggressor, and is actually quite perplexed about his adversary's motives. So according to the *Bicitra Natak*, the fierce Battle of Bhangani (which took place in September 1688) was actually forced on the guru by Fateh Shah—without any purpose *(binu kaja)*.

Similarly, the guru happened to go along with his neighbors in the battle that took place in Nadaun (March 1691). When his neighbor, the ruler Bhim Chand, saw his opponent Mian Khan coming down to strike him, "the king called upon me" (*BN*, 9:2). The guru casually repeats that he was asked to take part in the battle: "[A]ll the warriors were called; I was called too" (9:6). Evidently, there is no religious calling, only a plea from a neighbor. Guru Gobind Singh does not fight out of acrimony, and he does not fight for the sake of territorial conquest.

And once involved, he seems to enjoy his fights tremendously. Although he was the leader and commander of his forces, he was always in close proximity, fighting with and beside his people. Through his artistic sensibility the battlefields become playgrounds, and fright and terror are replaced in him by adventure and excitement. Death is made light of. It is not the ultimate concern, nor is it looked upon as an entry into another world. The guru's absolute mission is to make *this* world a better place with the help of the Transcendent One. His literary technique triumphs in heightening the reader's imagination and talents for creative action, and it induces an appreciation for this world with its domestic, seasonal, and sacred scenes and rituals. We sense in him a deep desire to connect the public and private worlds. The *Bicitra Natak* is not a simple autobiographical account. As Guru Gobind Singh works through the historical events, he plays upon the reader in many fascinating ways.

It is a mark of the guru's poetic genius that in his narrative of the brutal battles, he can evoke the colossal war fought in Kurukshetra, on the one hand, and the delightful pranks that Lord Krishna played in kitchens, on the other. His allusions to and evocations of ancient Indian figures and events has an altogether unique and powerful effect. While reading Guru Gobind Singh's narrative of the Battle of Bhangani, the reader is swept into the ancient and gigantic world of the *Mahabharata*: "Daya Ram, honored like the gods, fought furiously as though perfected by Drona in the great war" (*BN*, 8:6). Dronacarya was the great teacher who taught the skills of war to both Kauravas and Pandavas, the cousins who fought against each other in Kurukshetra. In his subtle way, Guru Gobind Singh not only praises his Brahmin ally Daya Ram for fighting valorously as though he were taught by Drona himself, but he also makes the point that a revered Brahmin can and does fight heroically. The instruction originally given to the Kshatriya princes is opened up to the other castes.

The compliment to Daya Ram is followed by one to Kripal (the maternal uncle of the guru), who finishes off a sturdy enemy as though it were child's play. The gruesome scene of Hayat Khan's death is framed with the lovely antics of baby Krishna (*BN*, 8:7). The enemy's shattered skull and the spilling out of the horrible gray matter is compared with the fragile pitchers of the cowherdesses from Brindaban and their scattered butter. The reader quickly moves back and forth between the bloody Battle of Bhangani and the warm, nourishing kitchens in Brindaban where baby Krishna would be stealing butter from the cowherdesses. The male space is linked with the female space; battlefields of crimson blood with kitchens flowing with white milk; the hurling of weapons with the churning of butter; the historical event with fanciful legends. Guru Gobind Singh's similes are not prosaic or hackneyed; his comparisons are couched in drastic contrasts that are then beautifully synthesized, as though the poet were using Mother Yashodra's wooden blender himself and bringing out rich new experiences for his readers.

In spite of its evocation of battle after battle, the *Bicitra Natak* probably does not shock its readers very much. The readers of his day were familiar with depictions of wars in Sanskrit and Persian literature and may have even witnessed the many battles fought between and among Mughals, Indians, and Europeans on their soil. His modern readers are also only too familiar with equally gory images. With guns and weapons chemical, biological, and technological all around us, and a constant bombardment of brutal images in movies, novels, news, documentaries, and video games, we are as a matter of fact quite anesthetized to violence. The horrendous attack on the World Trade Center was initially registered as but a scene from a movie! Obviously, the power of the guru's narrative is not in his gruesome depictions of battles—there have been far too many registered in our human history. Rather, it lies in the unique way he negates those usual scenes of blood and weaponry and opens the reader to nurturing vistas and life-sustaining utensils. The real shock to the reader comes when we are led from bloody battles to warm and comfortable spaces. It is upon entering our homes that we are challenged to rethink each experience in our own lives in new and different ways. Guru Gobind Singh's artistic strategy "reorients" us, and we begin to gather butterlike nutrients that come from the churning of Mother Yashodra. Instead of the deathly stillness that follows the hurling of weapons by warriors mythic and real, the guru awakens us to dynamic activities in our kitchens and offices. As we read on, the *Bicitra Natak* leads us to a reorientation of our familiar preconceptions, in a subtle way that has been nicely articulated by Wolfgang Iser, the famous exponent of the German school of reception theory:

> The efficacy of a literary text is brought about by the apparent evocation and subsequent negation of the familiar. What at first seemed to be an affirmation of our assumptions leads to our own rejection of them, thus tending to prepare

> us for a re-orientation. And it is only when we have outstripped our preconceptions and left the shelter of the familiar that we are in a position to gather new experiences.[45]

The sweeping and speedy patterns of evoking and negating familiar scenarios continue on, and the equally fierce battle of Nadaun culminates in Holi, the traditional spring festival of northern India. During this celebration, people throw brightly colored paint and dye on one another. They dance and they play practical jokes on one another. Friends and strangers, high and low alike, are sprayed, splashed, and smeared with reds, yellows, greens, and blues. With scenes of burlesque and merrymaking as the backdrop, Guru Gobind Singh describes the defeat of Alif Khan and his men. The enemies are repelled and thrown into a stream flowing from the River Beas. Those warriors left on the bank "sit as if [they] had just finished playing Holi" (*BN*, 9:19). He extends the analogy of Holi: "Their clothes are colored as if they had been having fun at the Phalgun festival" (9:20).

Holi is celebrated on the full-moon day of the month of Phalgun on the Indian calendar, just as winter mellows into spring. That mood of joy, that exhilaration, that anticipation of vitality that comes with spring, is re-created in Guru Gobind Singh's description. The guru does not lead us to death or another world beyond death; his battles are not endowed with any heavenly promises of eternal life. His graphic descriptions open us to springtime with its change and finitude, and they stimulate us to create new possibilities in our world here and now.

The *Bicitra Natak* reveals the many facets of the author. While we hear him proudly and playfully relay the defeat of his enemies, we also hear his tender sympathy for the destruction caused by the battles, and the loss and suffering of the innocent. In chapter 10, he describes enemy troops stealthily preparing an attack in the middle of night. But the guru's guard, Alam, came to the rescue: "Alam came and woke us up" (*BN*, 10:3). The word got around, and everyone got up, inebriated with the spirit to fight. Taken aback by the alacrity of the response, the enemy made a hasty retreat from Anandpur but avenged themselves on the neighborhood village of Barwa, wrecking it completely.

The guru felt compassion for the people of Barwa. The finale of his chapter is a unique simile in which we hear him sympathize with the innocent victims of Barwa, and we hear him poke fun at their enemy: "By Your strength they could not get us here, but they looted Barwa. Like the vegetarian who tries to make a rich curry out of a paltry leek" (*BN*, 10:10). We enter a kitchen again. Failing to acquire the hearty treasures of Anandpur, the khan and his men loot and pillage Barwa. They vent their fury at the poor and pathetic village, and like a cook with his vegetables, do their best to suck out all they can from the destitute villagers. We get a feel for Gobind

Singh's war ethics, which, scholars say, "allowed no looting, no raping, no killing of innocent civilians, no pursuit of he fugitive enemy, and no ill-treatment of war-prisoners."[46]

We enter spring festivals, we enter kitchens, and we enter temples. Guru Gobind Singh's artistic repertoire evokes a vast range of beautiful images. While recounting another fierce battle, he leads us into a religious space where "The arrows poured out sacred waters, the bows recited Vedic chants" (*BN*, 11:38). As warfare gets identified with religious activity, ceremonial rituals and worship are imported poetically into the din and clamor of the battle. The arrows in the *Bicitra Natak* perform the ceremonial adoration in which rose water is lovingly sprinkled over deities. The sensation of touch is accompanied by melodious sounds—the strongly strung bows recite Vedic chants! The guru poignantly fuses the battlefield with the temple, and all the fury of warfare with the serenity of sacred rituals and recitations. His multidimensional architecture refuses to erect any demarcations.

Ancient Indian religious motifs are very much a part of the mosaic of the *Bicitra Natak*, for Guru Gobind Singh does not see himself separate from the continuum of human history. His mental matrix is inclusive of all cultures. With his imagination soaring far above any religious or ideological boundaries, the Sikh guru explores new areas of human experience through new diction and meter. He weaves together the daring deeds of the goddess Kali and the colorful Holi, the baby Krishna's antics in Brindaban, and a lovely Hindu mode of worship to enhance the aesthetic effect of his narrative. Lord Shiva and other Hindu deities also figure prominently in scenes of gruesome battles. Guru Gobind Singh utilizes popular images and themes from Hindu mythology and culture in novel and unique ways. They illustrate his extraordinary breadth of vision, and in turn they enrich and expand his narrative, opening it up to wider and wider audiences. Charged with cultural significance, Guru Gobind Singh's literary devices vividly bring out his feelings of fury and tenderness. By mixing the events of his life with events involving popular mythic heroes and heroines, Guru Gobind Singh provides his narrative with a surrealist quality. We are turned away from the facticity of his narrative and become imaginatively involved in the actions of its mythical protagonists, and thus the reading of the *Bicitra Natak*, in Iser's words, "reflects the process by which we gain experience."[47]

Guru Gobind Singh's belief and devotion remain focused on the One that is ever formless and transcendent. His categorical statement

> I will contemplate the name of the Infinite One
> And acquire the supreme light;
> I will not meditate on any other
>   Nor recite the name of another.
>
> (*BN*, 6:38)

resonates throughout the text. That One remains the guru's ultimate concern and his constant support. In the last chapter of the *Bicitra Natak*, he writes, "Deeming me your slave, you helped me, / By your hand, I was saved from all enemies" (*BN*, 14:2). Here again, he palpably feels the presence of the Transcendent One. The protection from his mighty enemies comes from the "hand" extended over him through all his trials and tribulations. The hand (*hathu*) is not specified as either male or female, and if it is sensuously felt by Guru Gobind Singh, it has to be *both* male and female. The primal touch he experienced was that of his mother's midwife, of his mother, and of his grandmother, and his first conscious memories were of his nurses who affectionately carried him around: "I was caressed by many different nurses" (7:2). How can we obliterate the female from Guru Gobind Singh's experience and imagination?

Inspired Body

The *Bicitra Natak* rejuvenates the psyche so that reform in the real sense of the word can come about. As we all know, rules and regulations simply fail if there is not also a change in the consciousness of the people. The dedicated activist and founding editor of *Manushi* (a leading Indian journal of women and society), Madhu Kishwar, aptly comments that laws and regulations are useless gestures and concessions by governments.[48] Guru Gobind Singh probably understood this political reality, and so his literary discourse was aimed at radically changing his oppressed and subjugated society from within. The guru wanted to reach into the very marrow and psyche of his people, and through his passionate urge and his artistic devices, he achieves his effect.

The *Bicitra Natak* may not provide us with much biographical information. But the readers are stirred by his absorption in the Divine and by the titanic energy of his narrative. The work is more a disclosure of his self *(autos)* than of his life *(bios)*. Through his splendid literary talents, the ferocious fights come together—at once gently and strikingly—with the playful, the festive, the very domestic, and the most sacred activities. The details of war do not leave the reader in fear or dread; they do not orient us to a world *out there*. His love for life dominates all his writings, and his descriptions excite the intellect, the spirit, the imagination, and the senses, inspiring his readers and directing them toward immediate moral action in their home, or their nation, and in the international community. The *Bicitra Natak* is not a call to fighting but to writing, speaking, painting, communicating, loving.

Guru Gobind Singh heightens his fresh images, his poignant similes, and his fantastic analogies by using a rhythmical tempo. Out of the nine *rasa* or moods elaborated in Indian art, Guru Gobind Singh uses the *raudra rasa*, the martial mood, both as the content and as the form of his magical memoir. Actually, the *raudra rasa* pervades all of Guru Gobind Singh's compositions. His repetition of sounds like *bha, gha,* and *jha* reproduces the heavy sound of feats, and their alliteration, assonance, and consonance lend a stimulating rhythm and music to his narrative. He also uses quick and short meters to reproduce the speed of action. Through the dynamic rhythms readers are led into exciting landscapes. We become saturated with the frenzy of action, and feel creative currents flow in our blood and nerves.

The literary enterprise is vital to the guru. His engagement in battles does not deter him from his poetic productivity, and as the *Bicitra Natak* comes to a close, the guru is ready to begin his next project: "First I composed the *Candi Carit* describing deeds from toe to head; / In detail I told the story and now leaving these stories behind, / I wish to give praise again" (*BN*, 14:11). An ending expresses what is ultimately important to authors and what they want to leave with their readers, so this final verse reveals how vital the writing process was for Guru Gobind Singh. Perhaps as his autobiographical narrative comes to a close he feels a sense of loss and longs to start anew. The male guru who is fighting with and against men has an inner compulsion to tap into the recesses of his self and think about the actions of a female protagonist again. His adventurous spirit aspires to produce poetic expressions that have no utilitarian value; there is just the artistic abundance in him that he labors to give birth to. But he wants to conceive a topic that he has already dealt with extensively. And so the lasting impression he leaves on our minds is that of a poet who values mnemonic reverberations. His life story with its battles and war drums sketched surrealistically in the *Bicitra Natak* essentially ends up being the life story of a creative artist who wants to give birth to new patterns and tones by returning and remembering and re-creating the past. Indeed, we find here a justification for our own methodology: we re-member the past to make sense of it for ourselves. With him as our model, we enter his world from the depths of our own being. Guru Gobind Singh grants us the freedom to think about the past differently from the ways in which we have been taught to think.

It is a crucial insight into his personality that he has the need to reflect upon a female subject, and that he shares his thoughts with his readers. In this way he makes the point that women cannot and must not be forgotten. Her activities he described in an earlier composition, and now he looks forward to beginning another work in praise of Candi. In fact, written in 1684, *Candi di Var* is his very first composition, and his only major work in the Punjabi language.[49] Clearly, the image of the courageous woman is deeply imprinted on his psyche, and he returns to her again and again. Now, Candi does not come close to any romantic ideal. She is not the typical submissive female consort. The black goddess is not the stereotypically classic beauty, who is white, smooth, and perfectly unblemished—as we see flashed endlessly in our glossy magazines—but her rage against exploitation and injustice and her powerful peals of laughter as she fights for freedom carry great significance for the Sikh guru. He values and welcomes her again and again.

Resisting the androcentric processes that have curtailed or suppressed the powerful role of ancient women, the Sikh guru tells the story of the mythic heroine in full detail—literally, from "toe to head" (*nakh sikh*), as he says! Merlin Stone and Bella Debrida have warned us about patriarchal influences curtailing and degrading the prestige of womanhood in many cultures. Guru Gobind Singh's artistic canvas depicts his heroine in all her glory, and as Durga-Kali fights valiantly against injustice, she opens doors for other women to action and victory. She serves as a model for all of us—Hindu, Sikh, Muslim, Jew, or Christian. But male fears and phobias twist and transform the perception of Guru Gobind Singh's poetic genius, constructing barriers along the vast range of his social and poetic imagination. Yet again, male scholars transform his female subject into a male deity. The final words of the *Bicitra Natak* read "I wish to give praise again," but when these scholars translate it, they add the words "The Lord," and force it to mean that the Guru will praise the Lord.[50] Alas, even Guru Gobind Singh's forthcoming project, which he clearly specifies as another *Candi Caritra* poem on the legendary female figure (and this poem is actually the next one in the Dasam Granth!) is misconstrued as a project on a male god!

The guru seems to take up the role of his guard, Alam. As mentioned, when the Mughal troops tried to launch their attack in the middle of the night, "Alam came and woke us up" (*BN*, 10:3). Soon everyone was up and about, animated with a new kind of motivation. Similarly, through his literary compositions, the guru tries to awaken and quicken the spirit of his readers and hearers. The biographical event becomes a metaphor: in the dark night of rigid systems and hierarchical systems, we have to wake up and courageously face our oppressors. Guru Gobind Singh's text is not a preparation for conquest or territorial expansion, but for vigorous defiance of oppression and tyranny. There are no economic benefits to be gained—neither the spices and rubber plantations of yesterday, nor the mines and oil fields of today. The aim is not power over others; the aim is self-empowerment. One has to stop being afraid of oneself and become heroic. Patriarchal structures with their "isms" of casteism, classism, racism, and sexism have to be faced squarely and confidently, and like the residents of Anandpur, we have to react immediately. Otherwise, the enemy advances even further, inflicting more and more casualties. Guru Gobind Singh's resistance to exploitation and injustice is motivated by his love for this world. How could political, religious, and social oppressions destroy the abundance of life palpitating with the Divine?

It is also important to encounter the enemy face to face. The guru would never have proposed a nuclear holocaust, and the sword carries such importance precisely because she confronts the enemy closely and directly. During the Battle of Nadaun, the guru "gave up the gun and took the arrow in hand" (*BN*, 9:18). While meeting the "enemy"—be "he" psychological, social, or political—the guru's experience shows we must reject mechanized techniques and instead foster our physical, mental, and spiritual faculties. The sharp sword embodies a rarefied sensibility. And just as all the residents of Anandpur got intoxicated, so must all the readers and hearers. No one, no male or female, is barred from hearing and being touched or provoked by his compositions. The fiery diction of Guru Gobind Singh has, of course, engendered outgoing and autonomous roles for Sikh men. But it was directed at women, too, so it is appalling that, in the popular memory, his narrative has been distorted to reduce Sikh women to passive and utterly dependent roles! The mnemonic effects should be the same for both male and female readers. They must hear the same rhythms, murmurs, and meanings in Guru Gobind Singh's literature, and they must together follow the guru's example and combat the deplorable sexism and inequities plaguing their society.

A magical mixture of history and imagination, the *Bicitra Natak* is a precursor to the institution of the Khalsa. While it discloses the values cherished by the author, it is also the way to the establishment of the Khalsa. The text is the fertile womb in which his readers are nourished and nurtured. The reorganizing and restructuring of his community envisioned in the Khalsa could take place only through a previous reorientation and revitalization. Without real commitment, institutions do not work. Guru Gobind Singh's *Bicitra Natak* was the gestation process for transforming his contemporaries from within; his fervid literature was to enlighten and inspire his people.[51] Otherwise, how could there be the birth of a healthy Khalsa? Like modern feminists, Guru Gobind Singh appeals to the moral consciousness of his society. Reading or hearing his narrative quickens the heartbeat. It releases endorphins. It pumps out adrenaline. The text produces heat and food, the very things necessary for the conceptual and perceptual growth of his readers, making them physically and spiritually strong. Surely, art is not simply for art's sake; rather as Leo Tolstoy said, the infected artist through his work creates a community. And so, through his magical poetry, Guru Gobind Singh wished to awaken the slumbering and passive masses and re-create a community of bold and creative subjects. Only when the people were internally strong would they be ready to hold the sword in hand—or the pen. He himself was ready and led the way; he took up the pen and went back to his poetry once more: "[A]nd now I wish to praise her again." And his readers can follow him. As we scan the Khalsa lodged in the many folds of his autobiographical uterus, we too are fed by his life-giving muse, and are empowered to make exciting excursions into our own oceanic wombs.

Chapter Two

The Guru in Labor and the Birth of the Khalsa

> Mother's light permeates land and water,
> the mind is delighted by hearing her story
> (Koer Singh, 9:26)

The imagination and creative sensibilities of the author of the *Bicitra Natak* emerge splendidly in the drama par excellence of the Sikh religion, the Baisakhi of 1699. The poet and the artist whom we described in the preceding chapter emerges as the director and chief protagonist of this drama. Soon after writing the *Bicitra Natak*, Guru Gobind Singh staged a wondrous performance in the town of Anandpur. Years of deep reflection and commitment to his moral vision culminated in a creative choreography. But scholars and historians generally neglect its orchestration and theatricality. Carried away by purely theological and ethical concerns, they find no meaning in the dramatic elements by which the Khalsa was engendered. The event is brushed aside as too familiar, or too untenable a story to deserve full attention. Some even consider it in "conflict with the basic Teaching of the Guru."[1] But as we discern from both the content and form of his compositions, Guru Gobind Singh was fascinated by dramatic discourse. Even the title of his autobiographical *Bicitra Natak*—the "Wonderful Drama"—reveals his fascination with theater. It is in keeping with his artistic sensibilities that he would give birth to the Khalsa in front of a huge Baisakhi audience in a scene fraught with suspense. What had been gestating in Guru Gobind Singh was fabulously delivered on the "due date."

The Khalsa was born as a healthy democratic body on the maternity ward of Baisakhi 1699. Five men from different castes, professions, and regions of India offered their lives to Guru Gobind Singh's sword. But instead of dying, they were invigorated. The guru gave them *amrit* fused with the alchemy of his sword, he gave them sacred poetry, and he gave them sugarpuffs from Mata Jitoji. The five sipped it together! Guru Gobind Singh's dramatic praxis was intended to emancipate his society from the shackles of religious and social oppression. The performance took place not in some secret chamber but in the open, in front of the entire gathering, so that spectators, male and female alike, could participate. Ancient norms and laws enforcing the segregation and hierarchies of caste and creed were dramatically eliminated in front of their very eyes. In Gadamer's phenomenological reflections, "artistic presentation by its nature exists for someone," and at the Baisakhi gathering, the birth of the Khalsa did indeed "exist for" everyone.[2] Guru Gobind Singh generated the exciting new mode of selfhood and freedom for all the men and women, but sadly, as we have said, the emancipatory birth of the Khalsa is submerged in an androcentric historical memory, and this event "exists for" men but does not "exist for" women.

Gadamer discloses the impact of sociohistorical conditioning on our mental faculties. As he says, these are not mere psychological equipment: "Keeping in mind, forgetting, and recalling belong to the historical constitution of man and are themselves part of his history and his Bildung.... Memory must be formed; for memory is not memory for anything and everything. One has a memory of some things, and not for others; one wants to preserve one thing in memory and banish another."[3] The memory of the paradigmatic birth of Sikh democracy has been formed by male historians, theologians, and exegetes, and it has preserved male privilege and legitimized patriarchal control. Sikhs fervently remember the guru as a heroic "king" and a most benevolent father who on that day created a virile fraternity to fight fearlessly, and prescribed rules of army discipline to be followed faithfully. Their memories have focused on a militaristic brotherhood—without any liberating implications for women. What happened to the equality and dignity birthed by Guru Gobind Singh for all people? The democratic principles he engendered? The low and the weak that he included in his egalitarian family? The equality between men and men generated in the historical event is zealously preserved by Sikhs, but the equality between men and women, or the mutuality between women and women, is banished from Sikh memory. The cultural stereotypes and inscriptions of female otherness and subjugation that should have been severed by the Khalsa's birth have only been reinforced and internalized over the centuries.

The memory of Guru Gobind Singh's delivery has been distorted to reproduce structures of domination and authority.

Come to think of it, when does Sikh society ever remember the birth of a girl? While families jubilantly celebrate the birth of their sons, the birth of daughters is quite another matter. As far as I see, the alarming growth in the abortion of female fetuses in Sikh families is hooked up with the way in which female memories are aborted from Sikh consciousness. Mnemonic feticides cannot reproduce healthy bodies in society. By banishing women from our mental worlds, we banish them from our daily lives. The patriarchal culture of Punjabi society continues to breed sexism, and as a natural consequence, male voices constantly remind us about the "maleness" of the Khalsa. Repeatedly reciting the fact that the first five who fearlessly responded to the "male" guru's call were "men," malestream narratives discount and dismiss the meaning of the historical occasion for women. With the exception of two of Guru Gobind Singh's wives, the contributions, voices, thoughts, feelings, and support of mothers, wives, sisters, and daughters in the Khalsa family are scarcely acknowledged. But even these two women have a single walk-on part in the drama, without any spoken lines. Mata Jitoji, the first wife of Guru Gobind Singh, is remembered for adding sweetness to the *amrit* as it was being prepared by the guru. She glides across the stage briefly, and apart from this glimpse, scholars have shown no interest in her. They have not asked where she was before or afterward. The other female figure with a walk-on part, Sahib Devan, was Guru Gobind Singh's third wife, and she did not become a biological mother. Sikhs declare her as the spiritual mother of the Khalsa. But they have yet to experience the joy that comes from truly remembering Sahib Devan as the maternal matrix for the Khalsa. They have not asked about the rest of the women from the guru's family, either. Where were they during the historical Baisakhi festivities of 1699? Even the sweetness poured by Mata Jitoji into the historical *amrit* has not quite reached the Sikh community's bloodstream. Women remain forgotten both in the symbolic and practical dimensions of Guru Gobind Singh's radical delivery.

Actually, one of the earlier Sikh ethical manuals, entitled The *Chaupa Singh Rahit-Nama*, explicitly forbids women from joining the Khalsa family. It is attributed to a tutor and aide of the tenth guru. It dates between 1740 and 1765, and it is said that "no existing rahit-nama carries us nearer to the time of Guru Gobind Singh than this work. . . ."[4] But this Sikh text contains several misogynistic injunctions that ignore the guru's radical Baisakhi and revert to the norms of *stridharma* [moral system for women], spelled out in the traditional *Dharmashastras*. It is not the Guru's Baisakhi but Manu's prescriptions and proscriptions that loudly echo in Chaupa Singh's manual. He dictates a Sikh woman's primary mode of religiosity as her worship of her husband; she is to "know her husband as god," and give other men the status of fathers, brothers, and sons (Chaupa Singh, 556). She is to "keep fasts for the sake of her husband" (567). The ideals and practices of the first Sikh community established by Guru Nanak in Kartarpur, where men and women together recited sacred verse, together cooked, and together ate, are totally overturned by Chaupa Singh! Instead, he stipulates segregation and discrimination: women may listen to but are prohibited from reading the Guru Granth in public (538). "A woman must read in the midst of women; a Sikh sitting amongst other Sikhs" (539). He even misconstrues a scriptural passage to bolster and disseminate his own misogynistic commands that "the Guru-oriented Sikh never trust a woman—neither his own nor another's. Never share secrets with her. Know her as the body of guile" (100).[5] And among many other dos and don'ts, Chaupa Singh categorically prohibits men from administering *amrit* to women: "[H]e is an offender who gives Sikhni *amrit* prepared by the sword" (506)![6] The waves of wonder, joy, and equality generated in the Baisakhi of 1699, had, in just a few decades, found their way back to a stagnant pond of discriminations and misogynistic constructions that were definitely outside of the Sikh practices instituted by Guru Nanak and his successor gurus. The voices and views of patriarchs like Chaupa Singh have been very harmful for the community as a whole.

Later Sikh renaissance movements tried to rectify some of this sexism. In the middle of the twentieth century, several Sikh reformers developed an ethical code, The Sikh Rahitmaryada, in which some rules combat female oppression. According to this standard Sikh code of personal and communal conduct, any Sikh, male or female, can receive the *amrit* initiation. But though their ethical code admits them, Sikh consciousness denies women their true equality and freedom. Memories of male moralists like Chaupa Singh are kept alive by Sikhs, and McLeod is unfortunately correct when he says that the "printed word of Sikh Rahit Maryada makes little or no impression on them."[7]

We find that even in America, in the land of liberty and equality, diasporic Sikhs bring their sexist attitudes with them. If anything, the threat of Westernization makes patriarchal control and superiority even more vehement. A second-generation American Sikh recently shared her predicament with me: her male peers categorically told her she could never be their equal because none of the Five Beloved during the Baisakhi of 1699 was female! The young woman, who was enthusiastically organizing a workshop at George Washington University for her peers to learn about their religious and cultural heritage, was reduced to silence and tears. What a detrimental effect androcentric memories have! They rob women of their selfhood and authenticity—abandoning them to alienation, injustice, inferiority, and exploitation. For me the recollections of these young men—or that of Chaupa Singh—are a complete reversal and distortion of the actual Baisakhi event. And it is critical that such distorted "recollections" be disrupted.

In this chapter, then, I want to return to Guru Gobind Singh's dramatic performance in Anandpur with the wish to change the way things are. Past and present are closely linked for me, and Baisakhi 1699 serves as a site of justice and moral goodness. On the surface it is a masculine event. A male guru asks for the life of five disciples. Five men rise up. The guru takes them into a tent where he kills five male goats. The audience outside hears loud thuds and sees the flow of blood. The five men are brought back into the congregation. Sure enough, male protagonists perform macho activities, and when the story is told and retold in male language and consciousness, it has nightmarish consequences for Sikh women.

But Baiskahi 1699 is an open-ended drama that sets in motion the experience of transformation and liberation. It is not a static event. There is something very powerful about it that touches my female sensibility and inspires me as a woman. I feel it has tremendous potential for transforming our nightmares into dreams. The guru's radical enactment of the principle of equality in front of all the people gathered in Anandpur was intended for both genders, and it is imperative that it be remembered and utilized for both. If we return to Anandpur and resee Baisakhi with our own eyes and hear what went on that day with our own ears, Guru Gobind Singh's paradigm of transformation could be actualized. If we changed our angle just a bit, we could experience the emancipation wrought through his spectacular drama.

All we have to do is make one simple change in our perspective: we must shift our image of the guru from a patriarchal view to a maternal one. Once we have made this adjustment in our attitude, we will quickly perceive his birthing of the Khalsa as a manifestation of the reproductive energy that belongs only to women. But as long as our minds remain engraved with the guru as our "kingly lord," "our father," we will keep ourselves from ever welcoming the mother's unbound love and delight that he brought to us on that day. Western thealogians have argued about the problems and dangers of the male model for the Divine. As Sallie McFague concisely puts it, the "king as dominating sovereign encourages attitudes of militarism and destruction; the king as benevolent patriarch encourages attitudes of passivity and escape from responsibility."[8] In a rather similar vein, Guru Gobind Singh is fixed in Sikh memory as a powerful and magnificent monarch. Instead of this "untouchable" royal image, I propose that we remember him in the figure of a mother intensively delivering her children. My purpose here is not to idealize motherhood, nor would I ever want to equate womanhood with motherhood. Motherhood is one aspect of womanhood, and surely all women are not mothers, and many may choose not to be mothers. Women who do not give birth—or in Sikh society, who do not give birth to *sons*—are *not* failures in any way! But conception, gestation, birth, and lactation are powers held by the female alone, and Guru Gobind Singh's Khalsa is generated in and through them.

And so the male guru in his regal bearing and militaristic attire is not riding off into the distance to hunt or do battle, but like a mother, he draws near, touching our deepest selves. The maternal model has the potential of engendering a different historical consciousness in which the humanist values and vision of the Sikh guru can be illumined for all of us, both male and female. Guru Gobind Singh's aspirations for his newly born Khalsa are not limited to men or a band of elite warriors. They have great significance for all Sikhs, and for all times.

The maternal framework enables us to see that the agency and activity of Guru Gobind Singh on Baisakhi Day 1699 was fundamentally feminist, but this framework is also the most fitting device for capturing the phenomenal birth of the Khalsa. The natality of the Khalsa is not modeled on a commander or king who calls into being a new regiment or institution. Nor is it based on an organic model like that of the Vedic Purusha. The hymn (Rig Veda 1:10), which describes the creation of the universe from the sacrifice of Purusha's *body*, is in fact quite hierarchical. For despite its organic structure, the society is four-tiered: the Brahmins created from the mouth of the Purusha enjoy the highest status in society. The Kshatriyas coming from the arms are next,[9] the Vaishyas from the thighs are lower still, and born from the feet of the cosmic Purusha, the Shudras are the lowest of the low. This model of male creation is diametrically opposed to Guru Gobind Singh's feminist procreation, which eliminated all castes and divisions. Nor is the guru's birthing of the Khalsa modeled on a father, who despite his benevolence remains perfectly uninvolved. Rather, it is modeled on the mother, who carries new life in her womb and gives birth in intense labor. So the mother's biological process is the only appropriate way for understanding the birth of his Khalsa. Like a mother, the Sikh guru births his Khalsa. Like her he goes through agony and exhilaration. Like all births, the birth of the Khalsa is most natural. Like all births, it is most wondrous, complex, and intense, and with its flow of blood, placenta, and milk, it is profoundly dramatic.

By imagining the guru as our mother, our consciousness is transformed. Our attitudes become less rigid. We become more open, more excited, more confident, and less willing to accept disparities. Once we realize that the whole "operation" of the Khalsa is based on her body and on her biological process, how could we possibly exclude women as vital reproducers of the Khalsa family? If we remember that the guru charged the entire Baisakhi audience with responsibility to create an egalitarian community, how could we be satisfied by merely reciting the narrative of our lordly guru and not do anything about the horrible sexism festering in our society? In our feminist mnemonics, the Khalsa was procreated from the maternal body, and birthed a new life of liberty and equality not only for Brahmins and Shudras, Hindus and Muslims, but also for men *and women.* Our re-memories should provide us with the capacity to change our patriarchal reality. By reappropriating the past and showing that the purpose of Baisakhi 1699 was to liberate women, we accomplish Joan Kelly's objective of restoring women to history and history to women.[10]

The historical documents are not sufficient to provide us with an objective testimony of what exactly happened on that particular day and hour. But as I have been stating all along, rather than being drawn to empirical evidence I am drawn to the imprint that Baisakhi 1699 has left on the popular Sikh imagination, and to the attitudes and emotions that it continues to elicit. We do have a few poetic sources written sometime after the event that relay its effect and psychological impact rather well. Poets like Sainapat, Koer Singh, and Sukha Singh evoke it from their personal, cultural, and religious perspectives. They are not writing as remote observers, but as ardent enthusiasts, and their individual experience enters into their historical narrative. Through their metaphors, similes, rhythms, and mythological allusions they try to bring out the mystery and power of Guru Gobind Singh's drama. Birth is not something sweet and passive; it is fierce and bloody. The poets offer us textual traces to make meaning of that past experience—they take us into a present in which both the past and the future of the Khalsa can be understood. So with Sainapat, Koer Singh, and Sukha Singh, we journey back in time to the procreative moment of Sikh history and recreate it with our imagination.

The Delivery

We arrive at Anandpur, a maternity theater. It is Baisakhi, and all of nature is ready to welcome new life. Guru Gobind Singh is very much the mother in childbirth. As he delivers a healthy Khalsa, he goes through intense emotions of pain, fear, and ecstasy. But as with most childbirths, we do not know much about what really happened.

The earliest account that mentions the birth of the Khalsa is *Sri Gur Sobha* (Splendor of the Guru), completed three years after the passing of Guru Gobind Singh. Eminent scholars including Pandit Tara Singh Narotam, Baba Sumer Singh, Bhai Khan Singh Nabha, and Dr. Ganda Singh have confirmed that Sainapat, the court poet of Guru Gobind Singh, was the author of *Sri Gur Sobha.* Sainapat's first chapter, entitled "Description of the Panth's Manifestation," highlights the importance of his own work: "[L]iberation is attained by reciting, hearing, and reflecting upon the splendor of the Guru"

(5). Serving as the intermediary between the guru and the community, Sainapat writes his narrative to bring joy and liberation from the cycle of birth and death (Sainapat, 1: 11). He does not allege that his is a day-to-day eyewitness record of the guru's life, and even admits that "whatever I describe is partly from what I heard and what was told before"(8:7). In chapters 2–4 he describes pre-Khalsa battles, and in the fifth chapter ("Manifestation of the Word"), we hear about the birth of the Khalsa.

Sainapat begins with beautiful descriptions of the spatial and temporal setting that are later reproduced by Koer Singh and Sukha. Anandpur is identified, Baisakhi is identified; so are the large gathering and the grandeur of this important spring festival. "Messages are sent from town to town" says Sainapat, (5:3), indicating that something momentous is in the offing. Anticipation and expectancy fill the air, but as to the actual event, Sainapat is brief:

> Gobind Singh ushered joy in, made the community happy,
> He then created the Khalsa, and so removed all traps.
> The entire community gathered on the banks of the auspicious Sutlej
> Hearing him, many became his Khalsa, and many discontent.
> (Sainapat, 5: 4-5)

This is about all we have. The versions of Koer Singh and Sukha Singh, which were to follow, are much more detailed. Brief though Sainapat may be, his narrative unequivocally points to a specific historical event: "*kio pragat tab khalsa*"—(he then *[tab]* manifested the Khalsa). Obviously, Guru Gobind Singh did something "tremendous" (to use Rudolph Otto's term), which inspired many to adopt Khalsahood and left many others discontent. Sainapat does not give any sequence to the guru's performance; he only alludes to its intensity and suspense. Instead of recording Guru Gobind Singh's speech and action, Sainapat registers the different responses that emerged from the congregation. Perhaps he did not feel the need to recount the guru's actions, since he and his contemporaries would have been familiar with them. It is also possible that a full description was a part of Sainapat's text, but a scribe found the text with its flow of blood unsettling, and deleted it. Come to think of it, the absence of details in this instance is no different from any other childbirth: after the delivery nobody pays much attention to the actual process. The mother herself forgets about the most painful labor instantly! Sainapat takes the guru's epic action for granted and instead writes about the repercussions, which impinged on his own psyche and those of his contemporaries. He focuses on the new mode of life that came into being.

To learn about the delivery, we turn to Koer Singh's *Gurbilas Patshahi 10* (Splendour of the Tenth Emperor). It is striking that Sainapat regarded Gobind Singh as his guru alone and entitled his biography *Splendour of the*

Guru, but Koer Singh quickly transformed this image and turned the guru into an emperor. Guru Gobind Singh was already being altered from a feminist guru to a macho ruler! I have reservations, therefore, in using his work, and Sikh scholars have been troubled by his work on other grounds. They have argued over his dating, and questioned certain parts of his work where he makes the guru seem too Hindu.[11] In spite of these reservations, Koer Singh poetically unfolds the episode in a form that I have known ever since I was a child. Our focus is specifically on "The Creation of the Khalsa Panth" (Koer Singh's chapter 9), which concurs with and elaborates upon Guru Gobind Singh's human drama etched in the popular Sikh imagination.[12]

His narrative begins with the appearance of light: "Night ended, dawn was illuminated. Sun, the revered jewel of the day, bedecked its ever-turning throne. Supreme light, the comfort-giving lord, seated himself in revered Keshgarh" (Koer Singh, 9:2). The "supreme radiance" *(param joti)* and "comfort-giving lord" *(sahib sukh+dai)* emerges as a homologue to the cosmic sun: as the jewel of the day enthrones itself in the infinite skies, Guru Gobind Singh seats himself in Keshgarh. Keshgarh, the "fort" (*garh*) of "long hair" (*kesh*), retains the human body's natural power of growth, and leads us into a female space, for long hair, especially in that milieu, would be typical of women.[13] While the guru is linked with the brilliance of the sun, we also find that he has the glow of a pregnant woman carrying new life in her. His body radiates with the hormones produced in the natal process.

The guru is called the giver *(dai)* of comfort (*sukh*). But the word *dai* also means midwife. So he is not just a male lord (*sahib*) giving comfort (*sukhdai*); he is actually a midwife bringing comfort (*sukh*) into the world. Thus we find Guru Gobind Singh endowed both with the creative power of motherhood and the professional talents of a midwife who works hard to bring new life into the world. His "spiritual" energy is something internal; it is something that he shares with the cosmos, and it also belongs to the body and expertise of women.

Soon however, the poet conjures up images of darkness and secrecy. His depiction serves as a prelude to what the poet calls "the wonderful trick" that the guru has set up for the "refinement of his community": "He sent for more than four tents, and had them pitched separately./Secretly, he sent for five young male goats and had them tied up during the night" (Koer Singh, 9:7). The fact that the guru "secretly" sends for five male goats and has them tied up in the dark of the night creates an air of suspense. The mystery is intensified by the lack of explanation for the preparations. Night passed. The day broke. All men and women woke up on the day of the Baisakhi, continues the account. The presence of women *(nari)* is specifically acknowledged. They are an integral part of the gathering, which the guru "miraculously" brought together. When they had all assembled, the guru spoke. Everybody saw the guru in his regal attire, burning with spiritual fire, and heard him, like a roaring lion, announce, "Is there anyone (*koi*) here a full Sikh / Who would offer their head to the guru?" (9:9).

What to make of this stunning address? The congregation was utterly baffled then. Engrossed with the dynamics of the rest of the narrative, scholars have missed out on the complexity of this dialogue. For us these words are the birth pangs, inducing labor, which would soon push the Khalsa out.

The crown on the head of the earth, standing on a spot that itself is the head of the region, demands the gift of a head. Indeed, it is a most painful demand, especially since it is made on such a joyous occasion. What did the guru have in mind? How did the huge audience read his words? The guru provides no rationale whatsoever. Although the poet recording the event decades later keeps repeating that the motivation behind the guru's word (*vak*) was the refinement (*sudhara*) of his community, the congregation at that point could find no discursive meaning behind the guru's tortuous request. The ultimate faith and love of his devotees, male and female, are put on trial.

The Baisakhi event comes across as an analogue of the founding event in the Hebrew Bible—God's testing of Abraham by asking him to sacrifice his beloved son Isaac. In fact, we can read Guru Gobind Singh's trial as a Sikh *aqedah*, "a trial in which an ambiguity, a negativity, and an uncertain potentiality are to be worked out." As David Shulman explains, *aqedah*, from the root *qd*, to bind, is a specific pattern of sacrifice with two defining features: "(1) The sacrifice proceeds out of a divine command *or* from a demand made on the father, implicitly or otherwise, by the metaphysical ultimate; (2) this sacrifice must have no easily recognizable or comprehensible logic, above all, no utilitarian explanation or rationale. . . ."[14] Both these characteristics are present in the Sikh context. Guru Gobind Singh is the spiritual leader of his people, who must fulfill his divine mission. The second feature of the *aqedah* also applies, because there is no motive or rationale provided by Guru Gobind Singh in his call that morning. The Sikh *aqedah*, however, betrays an emphasis on the "gift" (*bhet*) that the conscious and faithful Sikh had to offer rather than on the "sacrifice" that Abraham had to make in the land of Moriah. And unlike Abraham, who was chosen to make the sacrifice, anybody in the huge Baisakhi gathering could volunteer his or her life.[15] For what purpose, though? Sikh men and women had come only to celebrate the spring festival in the presence of their guru. There was no battle to be fought, no agriculture god or goddess to be appeased, no offering to be made, no stranded Greek fleet to be restored, or ship to set sail as in the case of Iphigenia's sacrifice by her father; indeed, there was no utilitarian purpose at all—just as in the case of the biblical *aqedah*.

Yet, if they are lacking in explicit purpose, the Jewish and the Sikh narratives are fraught with immense meaning. Koer Singh reports: "On hearing this greatly weighty command, the entire world went into shock" (9:10). Guru Gobind Singh's words leave the entire audience speechless. His discourse is direct and literal, but his refusal to express any motive creates an overwhelming tension. His speech in the biblical style "indicates thoughts which remain unexpressed."[16] What Auerbach finds effected in the biblical episode is also true of Baisakhi 1699: Guru Gobind Singh accomplishes Schiller's goal of the tragic poet—"to rob us of our emotional freedom, to turn our intellectual and spiritual activity in one direction."[17] Shocked, they concentrate exclusively on their present crisis.

We read the situation in the context of a mother in labor. All her emotions and all her faculties are concentrated on bringing out the life she has generated and nurtured in her own body for such a long period. It is the moment of supreme power, suspense, pain, and some deeply hidden joy. That ultimate creative moment joins every mother with Schiller's poet, Guru Gobind Singh with Abraham, East with West.

Silence remains. In a way, the power of the guru reverts to his audience. They hold a positive advantage. He asks for a head; they have the power to deny him. It is the severe hour of labor. The guru makes his call three times.

> When the revered lips spoke three times
> A devotee came with folded hands.
> The guru seized his arm and drew his sword,
> Assuming thus a very fiery form.
> (Koer Singh, 9:11).

The devotee who emerges from the gathering says nothing. As he "comes" to offer his head, we wonder what is going on in his mind. His hands are folded in utter humility. His absolute faith is on trial. Is he afraid? Is he overjoyed? Is he simply overflowing with love for the guru? Does he remember Guru Nanak's verse:

> If you want to play the game of love,
> Enter my road with your head placed in your palm;
> If you want to tread this path,
> Don't hesitate to offer your head.
> (GG: 1412)

In the absolute silence of the stunned Baisakhi gathering, the ideal of love rings out in the wordless response of the Sikh devotee. Offering of one's head in the palm of the hand was enunciated as the prime symbol of love by the first Sikh guru. This Sikh ideal was actually put into praxis by Guru Tegh

Bahadur when he offered his head for the sake of humanity. What did he feel as he walked over to his executioners in the Delhi jail in 1675? What did Guru Gobind Singh's devotee feel as he walked up to the guru's thirsty sword in 1699? On the other side of the Baisakhi stage, what does Guru Gobind Singh feel when he makes his call for a head? Does he think of his own father? The head for centuries has served in the Indic world as an ideological apparatus—a locus for the superiority of the intellectuals. In Plato it is referred to as the lofty citadel (*akropolis*) best suited to rule over all bodily parts.[18] What did the nine-year-old undergo when the head of his martyred father was delivered to him? He has already confronted a human head; what impact would another have? The only gesture we have is of the folded hands of the volunteer, a sign of obeisance, a vivid expression of his total gift of himself.

And what about the women who had come to celebrate the spring festivities in Anandpur and see their revered guru? They are seated in Keshgarh too, and we must not lose sight of them. The guru's call was openly heard by both men and women, sitting together side by side. Mothers, wives, daughters, sisters, and aunts were not asked to leave when he came fired up into the congregation, demanding a head. Guru Gobind Singh does not exclude women from a full and active participation in the birth of the Khalsa. Unlike Sarah, who is left behind by Abraham when he fulfills his obligation, women are not absent from the Sikh *aqedah*. But no woman dared to stand up. Why not? Have we ever considered their feelings? The inner conflict they must have gone through? Women were equally devoted to their guru, and they too must have had the urge to offer themselves. But would their cultural conditioning have allowed it? Where silence is imposed as the jewel of woman, how could a woman speak up? If she had actually stood up in public, how would her husband, father, brother, uncle, or son have reacted? *Would it have been an act of honor or of shame?*

The devotee who offered himself is in a fetal position. Folded in upon himself, he has no voice of his own. He cannot feed and he cannot breathe on his own. Like the child in the body of the mother, he is totally dependent on the guru. He is, in fact, a part of the guru. He is "carried" by him in every sense of the word. The devotee's gentle gesture of folded hands forms a contrast to the violent gesture of the guru, who with one hand grips the supplicant's soft flesh and with the other reveals his weapon. The kind and compassionate guru acquires a consuming persona, and he even becomes the embodiment of fire. The importance of the devouring fire in sacrificial rituals across cultures is provocatively brought out by J. C. Hesterman. The lapping flames of fire central to Vedic Indian, Iranian, and Greek rituals are physically missing on the guru's stage, but they are psychologically present, because "his body acquires tremendous heat."[19] The absolute love of the devotee is juxtaposed to the absolute fury of the guru. The two men go off together, one to be killed, the other to kill—both bonded together at some very deep level. We see Guru Gobind Singh as a fired-up and sweating mother who is struggling to push out the life from inside her.

We are not told where the guru goes with his volunteer. Or for how long. But he comes back outside again. However, this time he is alone. The volunteer remains in the womblike dark and mysterious world, utterly unknown to the audience outside. The guru holds the devotee's life inside of him. Recipient of the ultimate gift of life, he carries the power of his devotee's love. "He slaughtered a male baby goat, and a current of blood flowed. / With sword soaked in blood in his hand, the refuge of the universe came out again" (Koer Singh, 9:12). The poet informs us that a male baby goat was killed. But if we are the audience sitting outside, all we hear is a thud. All we see is the free-flowing, fresh blood. The guru, we infer, must have performed an immensely creative and nurturing task for the poet to call him "the refuge of the universe" as he reemerged with his sword soaked in blood.

Sword and blood. Both, holding vital powers of life and death, come together powerfully. The sword is a crucial metaphor in the poetic intuition of Guru Gobind Singh. In his autobiographical narrative, he had used it profusely as a synonym for the Transcendent itself, and for the powers of generation and sustenance. The sword was his prime symbol for intelligence, justice, and freedom. During the delivery of the Khalsa, the symbolic sword is concretely present, and becomes the recipient of the devotee's ultimate gift.

The role of Guru Gobind Singh's sword is similar to that of the knife that Abraham carries to the land of Moriah to kill his beloved Isaac. Abraham's knife is called *ma'achelet*, from the root *achol*, to eat, and according to the Midrash Rabbah, "everything that Israel eats in this world is by virtue of that knife."[20] But whereas the biblical narrative does not reveal any blood on Abraham's knife, the sword held in Guru Gobind Singh's hand triumphantly carries the essential substance of the "volunteer," and the sight of the crimson fluid running around its sharp and strong and sparkling body can be deeply unsettling.

For us the blood on Guru Gobind Singh's sword is a powerful prelude to the new family he is birthing. Whatever one's skin color, the color of blood is the same for white, brown, black, or yellow; the same for Brahmin and Shudra; the same for man and woman; the same for goat and man. By displaying it so unabashedly in public, the guru emphasizes the essential unity that permeates our cosmos. The graphic scenes filled with blood reveal Guru Gobind Singh's staunch belief that in spite of all our superficial differences, we have the same biological makeup. We can see what he means in his Akal Ustat: "We have but the same eyes, the same ears, the same body, the same voice" (verse 86). The expert dramatist sends his message of oneness into the bloodstream of his Baisakhi audience.

As we look more closely, our eyes recognize that the fluid on his sword is saturated with the creative powers of mother's blood. The guru's thealogical symbol of the divine vividly upholds the female flow—dramatically affirming *her* physiology. Our society is horrified at the sight of her blood—whether it is the monthly period or the blood that accompanies every birth. Considered a private, shameful process, it is equated with being ill or weak. As feminist scholars and artists have been reminding us in the West, the disdain for this natural feminine phenomenon has contributed to the low status of women. Indian society has been even worse. Through laws codified by the mythic Manu, Indians have feared the gaze, touch, and speech of menstruating women. The house in which a woman gives birth is deemed polluted for forty days. Wendy Doniger has shown that the *Manu Dharmshastras* still affect Indian society as a whole.[21] For example, "A man who has sex with a woman awash in menstrual blood loses his wisdom, brilliant energy, strength, eyesight, and long life... food should not be touched by a menstruating woman."[22] Sikhs have not yet fully expelled such rules from their daily life.

The image of Guru Gobind Singh's sword seeped in blood does not make us cringe. For us seated in the Baisakhi gathering, it comes across as a piercing statement that the age-old hegemonies need to be discarded. In fact, on the metal sword held in Guru Gobind Singh's hand, the fluid crimson patterns create a female calligraphy. In these powerful designs, written in the mother's language, we can read Sikh scriptural affirmations of women's life-generating power. Images of conception, gestation, giving birth, and lactation are unambiguously and powerfully present in the Guru Granth. The Sikh text is unique among world scriptures in its celebration of the centrality of menstrual blood. It affirms menstrual bleeding as an essential, natural process. Life itself begins with it: "[F]rom mother's blood and father's semen is created the human form" (GG, 1022). Here priority is given to *ma ki raktu* (mother's blood). Other scriptural passages confirm the natural process of birth beginning with mother's blood (GG, 706). Guru Nanak even condemns pollution associated with childbirth (GG, 472), and reprimands those who stigmatize the garment stained with menstrual blood as polluted (140). These scriptural verses, which are rare in the religious history of humanity, are, of course, glossed over by malestream exegesis, and very sadly, Sikh women themselves have had no access to them.[24]

As he replays the Sikh message of equality and unity, the tenth Sikh guru is dramatically reminding us of the ideals we have forgotten. The crimson sword in his hand is an integral part of his mnemonic performance. The Khalsa could not be born without the maternal flow. The blood that is dripping on his sword is not dark or congealed or dead in any sense; its life force is palpable, which creates an awesome tension that is, heightened even further by Guru Gobind Singh's demand for yet another head.

The audience is shocked even more. The words and actions recorded by Koer Singh in verse 12 are repeated in verse 14. The guru makes his call three times. The dramatic effect is deeply enhanced by the fact that the audience does not know the mimetic act of the guru. Who could see through Guru Gobind Singh's performance? Surely, the men and women sitting side by side in the Baisakhi congregation were not at a play; they were full participants of the event, and, in fact, they were the tragic victims of their revered guru's outrageous deed. Guru Gobind Singh is a most successful director and actor, because he has the audience utterly and intensely involved in his drama. How could a theatrical performance be so real? In *The Magic of Ritual*, Tom Driver explains the complexity of such a performance: "A performance, being never purely mental nor entirely imaginary, is a material as well as a rational event. It takes place in an environment both physical and mental, both actual and imaginary, both immanent and transcendent."[24] Involved solely in the physical and actual event, the audience does not recognize its imaginary and transcendent dimension. They become very critical. Koer Singh again mentions both men and women voicing their disparagement. "From where did he catch this insanity that he has slaughtered Sikhs like goats and dogs?" (9:16). They repeat their complaints using the same simile: "[H]e is killing Sikhs like goats!" (9:18). Ironically, they do not realize that their verbal similes stumble upon the reality of the situation!

On their part, they try to make sense out of the apparently nonsensical deed of the guru. Their first thoughts go to the powerful goddess: "The coming of the ferociously strong Kali he could not bear. The goddess has had a contrary effect[,] that is why his intelligence has gone awry" (Koer Singh, 9:18). The goddess Kali was very popular in the region. The Kangra hills were a stronghold of Hinduism, and "the people were fanatically steeped in the Devi cult."[25] The Baisakhi gathering would of course have known about her mythology and iconography, in which she is almost always associated with blood and death. The Sikhs must also have recognized her from the compositions of their own guru. So when they encountered the frightening and dangerous dimension of their guru, it was natural and logical to associate him with the goddess Kali. She emerges in the mind of the Baisakhi congregation as a negative force who has infected their guru. She is criticized—not exalted. She is accused—not worshipped. The violent performance of the Sikh guru was her doing. After all, they knew how powerful she was, for all the gods together were no match for her: "Poor Brahma, Vishnu, all the gods and all the celestial beings! Who are they in front of Kali?" (9:21). Their general consensus: "What happened is that Bhavani revealed herself and put an embellished sword in his hand. That is why he could not endure its blaze." (9:21–22) So all the men and women identified Bhavani (Kali) as the source of Guru Gobind Singh's imbalance.

Psychologically it was difficult for the Sikh congregation to accept their guru's violence, and so they tried to shift the blame to the powerful and popular Hindu goddess. With their total faith in their benevolent father, they could not imagine him taking the life of his own sons. So it had to be the goddess putting her sword in his hand—and the luminosity of her mighty gift must have overwhelmed the guru's senses! Mentally, the Sikhs substituted her sword for his, the dazzle of Kali's sword for their guru's will and actions.

The guru, in turn, displayed another kind of substitution. He came out of the tent along with his glorious Sikhs. His was in fact a mimetic violence where the goats were killed instead of the Sikhs. Just as the ram served for Isaac, the five goats ordered the night before by the guru served as the surrogate for the five Sikhs. The Baisakhi congregation was amazed to see the five, whom they had thought to have been sacrificed to the guru's whim, enter in flesh and blood. Still in shock, people were further puzzled to see the five come out in such splendor. The joy of the tormented congregation knew no bounds. The guru had performed the supreme drama of birth. The Baisakhi audience hailed him for his wonderful delivery: "Hand in hand he came out with them, and sat again on the miraculous throne. 'Blessed!' 'Blessed!' exclaimed all men and women./He then gave those five many ornaments. Graciously he made them like himself, he made the disciples most beautiful" (Koer Singh, 9:24).

No longer were the five Sikhs in that subdued fetal position with folded hands. Together, most tenderly, they walked out "hand in hand" with the guru. They had given themselves to death and were born anew. The blood that flowed and soaked the guru's sword was in fact procreative—it proved to be an essential part of the birthing process. It is the symbol par excellence of life and equality, and therefore Guru Gobind Singh must have felt it important to display it so openly. Blood, as we know, carries basic nutrients to our cells. Caroline Bynum's study of medieval physiological theory posits blood as food "because it feeds flesh and when processed into milk, blood feeds the young."[26] The sword and the blood together produce and sustain the Khalsa.

In this postpartum scene, Guru Gobind Singh comes across as a proud mother, bringing her offspring forward, affectionately showing them off. He is also busy dressing up his Sikhs, adorning them with jewels. The description *bhukan anik* (lots of jewels) opens up the realm of female accoutrements, and closes off the either-or gender roles that Western culture dictates. (This openness was completely reversed under the colonial rule when British officers in the Punjab forbade men to pierce their ears and wear earrings.)[27] If these tender scenes of the guru dressing up his beloved were etched in our minds, we would experience the new sensibility that came with the birth of the Khalsa. The five symbols (known as the five *Ks)* that Sikhs believe he gave at that point to mark the new identity of his people are not militaristic weapons, as ingrained in our psyche; they are adornments that ensue from his postpartum feelings of tenderness, beauty, and love. But because the communal memory neglects such lovely maternal moments, the guru's Khalsa is basically remembered as an organization that does admittedly abolish caste but remains male, macho, and militaristic. The love and tenderness with which he greets and dresses the Five Beloved puts his behavior in the previous act of this drama in perspective. We fully comprehend that Guru Gobind Singh had to go through the maternal trauma to experience this ineffable delight. What is so "untenable" about such a natural female process? It only seems "untenable" or "confusing" if we view him as an unapproachable, benevolent, all-powerful "father" or "master."

Through his *aqedah* Guru Gobind Singh gave birth to emotionally and spiritually strong Sikhs. He was not driven by male ego to show off his authority. He was filled with a mother's affection that yearns to instill confidence, endurance, love, and courage in her offspring. This was not drama for drama's sake, nor a selfish test on his part; rather, it was an intense and painful delivery that helped the Sikhs discover themselves. Guru Gobind Singh's procreative act was to strengthen his devotees with their own inner power. Though only five from the congregation went through the process, the entire Baisakhi 1699 gathering was intensely involved in it. As Koer Singh noted, "'Blessed!' 'Blessed!' exclaimed men and women." The guru's *aqedah* had psychological significance for both the individual Sikh and the community at large. Upon their birth, they are holding hands; the five are joined intimately with the guru and with one another, and through the five, the entire Baisakhi gathering is united in a profound way. Something new came into the world of Sikhism. By putting them through the death crisis, Guru Gobind Singh gave his Sikhs a new attitude toward life and living. It was the moment when he made them aware of their self-determination and love. The *aqedah* was his way of bringing them into consciousness—instilling inner confidence, and providing them with psychic energy to grow and develop even more. A male guru performs a creative act with five volunteers who happen to be men. But it is essentially through a mother's love and her female process that the Sikh *aqedah* took place, and it involved both men and women who were a part of the Baisakhi of 1699. In every respect, Guru Gobind Singh is the mother in childbirth, delivering a new world of love and courage to both men and women.

The Nutritious Drink

As the work of labor ends, Guru Gobind Singh takes on the role of the new mother. The blood had given form to the five, and now the semiotic fluid was necessary. They needed nutrition. They needed to build up their immune system. Together with Mataji, he prepares and pours out the most invigorating drink for his Five Beloved. The guru must have been deeply touched by their response. It had to be known and experienced by future generations. Through *amrit* initiation, he assured the reality and durability of the Khalsa's birth, and with it, the specific moment of Baisakhi 1699 was projected onto an eternal plane.

While the guru is in contemplation on the lofty stage, Kirpa Ram from the audience "runs over to Mata and reports the event":

> Having heard about the Khalsa Panth from beginning to end,
> The mother came, and at that time she put sugarpuffs in.
> Seeing the guru's spouse the people said:
> It has become the progeny of both father and mother,
> by doing this act of love the mother expressed herself.
> (Koer Singh, 9: 25)

Koer Singh does not name the mother (*mata*). Sikhs popularly remember Mata Jitoji, the guru's first wife, as one involved in Baisakhi 1699. It would be curious if on such a festive occasion, she were not a part of the Baisakhi gathering, especially when the poet repeatedly mentions the presence of both men and women. Where was she that Kirpa Ram had to run over? Where was Mata Gujari, the guru's mother? How about Mata Sundari, the guru's second wife? Did they know about the guru's venture? Where were the rest of the women from the guru's family? Male chroniclers seldom pay attention to women. But obviously Mataji is an important figure, for Kirpa Ram sensed the urgency of informing her about the events in minute detail. Jitoji must have recognized the significance of the guru's *aqedah* and was eager to take part in it herself. So Jitoji joined Guru Gobind Singh, and put the sugarpuffs into the iron bowl. As Koer Singh narrates, she did this out of her own will and out of her love for the Khalsa community. In Max Arthur Macauliffe's account, Mata Jitoji was denied any initiative of her own and simply followed the directions of the guru who "asked her to throw the sweets into the holy water."[28]

However historians may describe the event, a woman participates vitally in Sikhism's most profound rite of passage. No stigma is attached to *her* body, and no cultural taboos are associated with her performance. In contrast with many religious traditions in which women are barred, the woman is essential to the sacred moment in Sikhism. It is with her input that the historical drink reaches its perfection. Iron is mingled with sweetness, and Baisakhi 1699 enters another level. The inner fruition is tasted, blending physical sugar with the metaphysical experience of joy and unity. Sikhs were delighted to have Mataji as an active agent in the phenomenon of birth and to become recipients of her love. She validates their birth, and they declare themselves as "the progeny of both father and mother." Their new identity is contingent on her. They all honor her as the historical mother of the Khalsa, but at the same time women are barred from entering that very same Khalsa!

The next verse again resounds with their delight and gratitude:

> Now the mother put sugarpuffs in, and the congregation became ecstatic
> "Blessed, blessed is she!" they all said,
> "blessed is the mother who did this benevolent deed."
> Mother's light permeates land and water,
> the mind is delighted by hearing her story.
>
> (Koer Singh, 9:26)

Her role in the birth of the Khalsa is greatly cherished. In spite of the fact that the guru is male, that the five disciples who offered themselves were male, and that the poet who is reporting is also male, Mataji is praised as an active copartner in the process. Women were not absent from the audience; they were not absent from the emergence of the Khalsa. The *aqedah* is fulfilled by *her* expression of love. The entire gathering extols Jitoji for her benevolent act. They taste the sweetness she added to the mixture, making it as nourishing as the im+mortal fluid, the *amrit* (*a* = not + *mrt* = death) of mother's milk. They are sustained by her "light" *(joti)* pervading the land and waters. The Baisakhi audience connects Guru Gobind Singh's wife with the cosmic mother, the matrix out of which everything that is originates and evolves. She is the life-giving *jal* (water), all the rivers and oceans that flow through and support the earth. She is the life-giving *thal* (soil or land), all the countries and continents that hold and sustain diverse creatures and cultures. She is crucial in the event, and as the author claims, "[T]he mind is delighted by hearing her story."[29]

Koer Singh is telling us that we must remember the role of women. Her mnemonic presence is deemed essential by the author both as an intrinsic part of Sikh identity and as an innately joyous phenomenon. Clearly, female reality must not be erased from consciousness; otherwise we only deprive ourselves of our authenticity, and of the happiness that her remembrance brings.

At this point there occurs a curious break in Koer Singh's text. The praise and respect for the mother is followed by the poet's assessment of his own narrative: "I have narrated fully, without any omission; thus the guru had staged this play" (9:26). The statement seems to be a concluding remark, and yet, immediately thereafter, the poet resumes his description of the *amrit* initiation. Perhaps this was his way of unfolding the two aspects of Baisakhi 1699: the delivery of the Five Beloved once and for all, and the initiation ceremony, which was to recur again and again for his Sikhs. In the poet's discourse, Mata Jitoji forms the center of the birth of the Khalsa and its postnatal rite.

His narrative then zooms in on the initiation. The guru asks for an iron bowl that contains water from the river flowing by, and "after preparing the *amrit*, the guru performed the ceremonial Ardas" (Koer Singh, 9:27). The ambrosial drink and the ambrosial word go together. Koer Singh does not specify the way in which Guru Gobind Singh prepares the *amrit*. His emphasis has been entirely on Mata Jitoji's action. Since the liturgical Ardas (recited while standing up) begins with the remembrance of the sword, we assume he acknowledges its symbolic presence. Later accounts, however, are very explicit about Guru Gobind Singh stirring the water in the iron bowl with his *khanda*, the double-edged sword, and that is why the *amrit* ceremony is popularly known as *khande ki pahul* (initiation through the double-edged sword).

The guru then pours out the drink, and a very physical relationship emerges between the five who drink the *amrit* from their cupped hands and the guru and his wife who had prepared it: "He has them drink the *amrit* with cupped hands. He has them recite "waheguru" with their lips" (Koer Singh, 9:28). The *amrit* reinforces their new relationship and energy. Five men from different castes drink together! This would be a revolutionary sight in a culture where even the shadow of a lower caste person polluted all food or drink. With each sip, notions of social hierarchies are rinsed out. Their drinking together defines their new birth and equal membership into the family of the Khalsa. Just as drinking milk from the same maternal breasts unites children to a family, so taking *amrit* from the guru's iron bowl welds the Five Beloved into the Khalsa family forever.

Earlier we saw them hold hands with one another; now their hands receive the nectar of immortality, which then flows into the very blood and marrow of each of them. Their joy and devotion is expressed as they utter "waheguru!" Since Guru Nanak, "waheguru" has been a popular Sikh expression for the *mysterium tremendum* and *fascinum* of the Transcendent One. The tongue that tastes verbalizes the Infinite. The energy from the steel, the sweetness from the sugarpuffs, the elemental power of the water, and the force of the divine word are all swallowed simultaneously and absorbed totally. Their imagination is startled to a new awareness and a sense of wonder. Flesh and spirit are equally stimulated by the *amrit* prepared by their guru and Mataji.

Though Koer Singh does not give details, Sikhs firmly believe that the guru at that time gave each of the Five Beloved five palmfuls of the *amrit* to drink, just as he asked them to keep the five *Ks* and recited five hymns while preparing the *amrit*.

Twentieth-century scholars also spell out the heroic posture in which the five received *amrit*. In *The Baisakhi of Guru Gobind Singh* Kapur Singh writes that this hero posture *(bir asan)* consists of putting the left knee up and the right knee on the ground. *Bir* is related to the word *vir* (virile), and means a hero; and Kapur Singh in a lengthy note explains that this "heroic posture is the one considered most appropriate for shooting arrows from a bow."[30] But such one-sided hermeneutic of militaristic bodily postures have deflected us from recognizing a supplicant's posture in Sikh initiation. A knee down on the ground is a universal gesture of humility and respect, and we must not confuse it with arrogance and aggression. Such distortions tell us everything about the minds of interpreters and nothing about Guru Gobind Singh's event itself. By seeing this gesture simply as a matter of being ready to shoot arrows, we miss out on the spiritual serenity and stillness of the Five Beloved as they await the *amrit* drink. Bending the knee brings us close to Mother Earth who feeds and sustains us, and makes us feel at home in this world. Guru Gobind Singh and his Five Beloved were showing humility before the Divine, and respect toward one another. They were not getting ready to shoot arrows. Our memories have to be cleared of such macho distortions.

After giving them the *amrit*, Guru Gobind Singh asks the five their names and their places of origin. As Koer Singh reports,

> Having initiated the five in this way, he asked them their name and town.
> First they told their name and residence,
> then the invincible guru repeated with them.
> "I am from Lahore, your kindness,
> my name is Daya Singh, the Compassionate One's slave.
> In a previous birth I was Lau from the Sobti Khatri clan."
> Then the second one said, "I am Nihchal Singh resident of Dwarka.
> I was formerly Namdev from calico-printer's class."
> The third was called Sahib Singh from the town of Bidar.
> He was formerly Sain, the barber, from the caste known as barbers.
> The fourth was the immortal Dharam Singh, who was from Hastinapur.
> Saint Dhanna in a former birth, he was even now Jat by caste and color.
> Then the tenacious Himmat Singh sang that he was from Jagannath: in a previous birth he was a bird-catcher from the comfort-loving jhivar caste.
> These five who had been companions in the ancient golden age
> Now came together as the guru's companions.
>
> (Koer Singh, 9:28–34)

Guru Gobind Singh obviously knew all five of them, since they were his disciples and lived in Anandpur.[31] So in his dramatic overture he is not merely introducing his Five Beloved to the congregation at large: he is exhorting all the men and women to follow their example of identity construction.

The guru asks his Five Beloved for particular information, but all of them discard their different family names and respond with the same last name: "Singh." (Sikhs also mention that on that day Guru Gobind Singh gave the name "Kaur" to Sikh women.)[32] Distinctions of caste, class, and family profession are therewith abolished; a new egalitarian and kindred identity is announced in the new family name of Singh. Koer Singh's narrative fluctuates between the direct voices of the Five Beloved and the indirect voice of the author. Three of the five trace their lineage back as far as the medieval Indian saints. Although they were all Hindu saints, the figures of Namdev, Sain, and Dhanna were very familiar in the Sikh world, because their poetry had been included in the Guru Granth, compiled by the fifth Sikh guru in 1604. Each of these saints had ardently loved the Divine, rejected social divisions, and stressed the human core. The pattern of inclusivity of the Sikh sacred text is reproduced in the newly born Khalsa members, who regard themselves as heirs to the diverse saints of medieval India. The Five Beloved do not show off any physical talents or accomplishments. They are proud of the spiritual delicacy and emotional sensitivity of their ancestors. Historians, however, have only reinforced their muscular strength, as if the guru expected only the "physically" strong as his offspring. They have buttressed their "maleness," as if the guru would not have welcomed women into his new family. From childhood we are fed on the battles that the Five Beloved virulently fought against imperial troops and how they killed hill chiefs. What is banished from our communal memory is the pride with which the five trace their lineage to the sensuous lovers of the Divine. In Koer Singh's narrative, the way the five introduce themselves connotes the timeless link that they seem to have enjoyed with Sikhism, and in turn, their joyous acceptance by Guru Gobind Singh shows his admiration for their emotional and spiritual sensitivity.

When commentators overlook the fascinating details in Guru Gobind Singh's *aqedah,* they deny these five their individuality, and make them into abstract virtues. Indeed Daya, Dharam, Mohkam (who is called Nihcal in Koer Singh's work), Himmat, and Sahib—compassion, duty, tenacity, effort, and honor, respectively—are important Sikh values, which constitute the very personality of the Khalsa. But an overemphasis on their representational value only hides the power of Guru Gobind Singh's *aqedah.* The five introduce themselves by their first names, which certainly imply moral values but also specify their geographical locale and former profession. They are not some distant, disembodied ethical principles; the Five Beloved are made of flesh and blood, and they come together from different social backgrounds and from different cultural centers of India. They congregate in Anandpur and reproduce a glorious and diverse spectrum. Each one of them brings his unique heritage into the Khalsa family. By overlooking their individual identities, we overlook the intrinsic diversity and pluralism of the Khalsa. With them Anandpur becomes the center of the large Indian peninsula.

The presentation of the Five Beloved is followed by a list of rules and regulations. The Khalsa is born, and it must develop its own personality, so there is a need for definition and discipline (we shall return to this theme in chapters 4 and 5). Verses 35–52 of Koer Singh's text carry both negative and positive stipulations, and though his report is very long and not arranged in any particular order, the welfare of women is a top priority. What catches our attention is that at the very outset, the Khalsa is forbidden to consort with those who oppress women (Koer Singh, 9:35), and the subject is taken up shortly again:

> He who kills or sells a girl
> His flesh will be thrown into the lowest pit.
> (Koer Singh, 9:37)

From the time of Guru Nanak, the Sikh gurus were extremely sensitive to the subjugation and victimization of women. The marginalized objects of medieval Indian society became significant subjects for the Sikh gurus, who loudly condemned the grisly practices of sati, purdah, and female infanticide. In the newly created family of the Khalsa, the prevalent custom of killing or selling off daughters is utterly forbidden. Young girls were the most vulnerable members of society, and the Khalsa was given a collective responsibility to ensure their protection. They were not to associate with *kanyapapi*—literally, "sinners against girls." Anyone participating in any of the customs harmful for girls was to meet with the severest punishment: "His flesh will be thrown into the lowest pit." Gambling and prostitution are also prohibited (Koer Singh, 9:43). The guru's sensitivity to the objectification of women comes across strikingly, for any kind of game playing with "her" is severely forbidden: "[H]e doesn't frolick around with women" (9:41).

But who remembers such injunctions? Sikh society is not concerned about the subjectivity of women, or the guru's prohibitions against women's mistreatment and objectification. In the horrid dowry customs they follow these days, Sikhs are literally selling off their daughters; in order to preserve their so-called honor they are even killing their daughters; and in their desire for sons, they are aborting female fetuses. Utilizing modern technology to determine the sex of the embryo, couples are regularly getting rid of female fetuses. Though sex-determination tests have been illegal since 1994, this law has not been enforced. As the *New York Times* reports, these couples may be denounced as *kudi-maar* (daughter-killers), but this name calling does not have any effect on people's behavior. The word *kudi-maar* is a modern equivalent of Guru Gobind Singh's term, *kanyapapi* (sinners against girls) with whom Sikhs were not even allowed to associate. Now, in spite of his condemnation, Sikhs themselves are sinning against women: there are now only 793 girls for every 1,000 boys in the Punjab, where most Sikhs live![33] Any minor detail that would foster male agendas and male superiority is sure to be kept alive in the Sikh communal consciousness, but emphatic stipulations against female exploitation get buried away.

Sikhs fervently remember that by drinking the *amrit* prepared by the double-edged sword of the guru (*khande ki pahul*), they changed from "jackals into lions, from sparrows into hawks."[34] I must say I admire the natural confidence and strength of the lion more than the conniving powers of the jackal. But I have problems accepting the change from sparrows to hawks. Not only is the hawk an emblem of the Mughal emperors, but I doubt Guru Gobind Singh would have ever wanted his Khalsa to imbibe its predatory mentality. Somehow, however, the hawk has really become stuck in the Sikh imagination. Paintings of the guru show him with a hawk perched on his shoulder. I even received an award from the Sikh community in Windsor, Canada, that was a sculpted hawk clawing a dead rabbit. Such violent sentiments and actions could not be the effect of the nutritious, life-giving elixir prepared by Guru Gobind Singh and Mata Jitoji! Even the five goats that were killed were not displayed before the Baisakhi audience. The guru did not rejoice in their death. There was no feast that followed, and the act of killing any animal was never made a part of *khande ki pahul*. Actually, Sikhs are forbidden to eat the meat of an animal that is slowly bled to death (Koer Singh, 9:37). Considered pure (*halal*) in other traditions, the method is denounced because of the extended pain that it brings to the animal. The intimidating and aggressive images that monopolize Sikh memory need to be seen anew in light of Guru Gobind Singh's maternal empathy and tenderness.

I don't want the female sparrow erased from Sikh memory, either. She holds a special place in the Guru Granth. The first Sikh guru exalts her. Unlike the male elephant that devours mounds of butter and molasses and then puffs and belches and raises dust, the delicate female sparrow eats but half a grain and flies longingly to the Divine, singing "khudai khudai!" (GG, 1,286) The symbol of royalty and physical power is no match for the psychologically refined sparrow that warbles its longing in an Islamic expression. The Khalsa's new rite was not meant to discard the emotions treasured in the Sikh past; it was designated to build on them, as we shall explore more fully in the next chapters. We have to hold on to the sparrow in all of us.

The Five Beloved are also rooted in the Guru Granth, and the script for their performance can be found in its opening hymn. There is a typological relationship between the Five Beloved birthed by Guru Gobind Singh and the five (*panch*) envisioned by Guru Nanak in his Jap. The word *panch* is frequently mistranslated as "the chosen" or "the elect," but this mistranslation is not only incorrect from a linguistic point of view, it also completely distorts the significance of the five in Sikhism. In Guru Nanak's words:

> The *panch* are accepted, and the *panch* lead on
> The *panch* receive honors in the court,

> The *panch* shine splendidly in the royal gate,
> The *panch* meditate on the one and only guru.
> (Jap, 16)

Nanak's *panch*, like Guru Gobind Singh's *panj pyare*, are not an elite. because the gurus were opposed to such a thing; they were not the elect, or specially chosen ones, because the gurus were opposed to all such choice specimens. They were ordinary, nonelitist, nonelect, nonchosen people who in their complete devotion opened the way for others in their community. In the passages preceding this one, Guru Nanak explains that freedom is experienced by hearing (stanzas 8–11 of his Jap) and remembering the Divine Name (stanzas 12–15). His *panch*, then, are the five who fathomed the Infinite and lead others to that joyous experience. Stanza 15 had specifically mentioned that liberation is open to everybody, and those who hear and remember the Transcendent rejoice in the wondrous name themselves, and lead their family and community toward that experience as well.

As Nanak describes, the *panch* become role models for divine love, and they are fully acknowledged for this. They receive honors, they shine resplendently, and they meditate on the One. In fact, this Nanakian passage serves as a script for the dramatic emergence of the Five Beloved in Anandpur. Drenched in their love for their guru, the five give themselves to his sword. In turn they become the guru's beloved, and leaders for their community. They show the Sikh path of liberation to their families, and their friends, and everybody else gathered in Anandpur—the path launched by Nanak himself for all people, from all different castes and classes. Like Nanak's *panch*, the five are shown utmost respect and dignity. They are not chosen as such; they volunteer themselves. They prove themselves in their infinite love. Like Nanak's five, they are honored—in fact, in front of the vast Baisakhi gathering. The guru adorns them lovingly in such radiant garments and jewels that they physically resemble the splendor of Nanak's five. And just like them, the Five Beloved learn to relate with the Enlightener. By feeding them the *amrit* churned with the poetic praises of the Infinite coming down from his predecessors, Guru Gobind Singh provides his *panj pyare* with an immediate taste and recognition of That One. In effect, the drama that was enacted out on the Baisakhi stage was penned by the first Sikh guru in his Jap.

And the *khanda* used by Guru Gobind Singh during his fabulous performance must be duly remembered for cutting the umbilical cord and all its connotations of dependency and submission. In the Keshgarh shrine itself, several weapons of Guru Gobind Singh are preserved. Each of them is connected with an important event in Sikh history, and among them, his double-edged sword elicits the deepest reverence. We revere Guru Gobind Singh's *khanda* because it has freed us from the constricting gender roles of patriarchy.

In order to enter a postpatriarchal world, we need to move beyond gender equality to getting rid of gender roles altogether. As Rita Gross says, "Any concept of gender equality presupposes the continued existence of gender roles and all the imprisoning implied in such conditions."[35] Her feminist insights help us see that in the maternity ward of Anandpur, Guru Gobind Singh not only delivered all the castes as equal; he also ripped down the divisive rules that their society had enforced on them for centuries—simply on the basis of their biological sex. The birth of boys automatically puts them higher on the social ladder. Through *khande ki pahul*, the guru birthed a new morality: he vehemently rejected the notion of biological castes and the specific roles assigned to people at birth. Guru Gobind Singh thereby rejected discrimination based on physiological sex and the disparate gender roles imposed at birth. If all the castes were encouraged to take up one another's roles in the new family of the Khalsa, why would men or women be kept from taking up each other's roles, functions, and professions? Why would there have to be a double standard for sons and daughters? It is in the Sikh guru's radical elimination of birth rights and birth obligations that we recognize the elimination of gender roles. *Khande ki pahul* was the transforming ritual that cut off cultural constructions and breathed new life and freedom into all recipients. The delicious maternal drink with all its nutrients began to nurture generations of Sikhs. The mother's milk flows equally for her sons and daughters. Its supply never changes because of the sex of the child! It should give men and women the strength and sustenance to be whatever they want to be.

Bonding Together

The full force of the Khalsa's birth emerges when the progenitor and the offspring are reversed: Guru Gobind Singh, who had given birth to the Khalsa, is now born from the Khalsa. After serving the nutritious drink to the Five Beloved, the guru receives it from them. It is a sequence of natural growth and progression. In their intimate bonding, the Khalsa member leaves childhood behind, and acquires the maturity and responsibility of the guru. In psychoanalytic terms, it corresponds to Lacan's mirror stage in which there is a complete harmony between the *Innenwelt* and the *Umwelt*: "We have only to understand the mirror stage *as an identification*, in the full sense that analysis gives to the term: namely the transformation that takes place in the subject when he assumes an image—whose predestination to this phase-effect is sufficiently indicated by the use, in analytic theory, of the ancient term *imago*."[36] In this new phase, the Five Beloved acquire a heightened sense of selfhood and authenticity, and the old patriarchal structures of authority and subordination crumble before our very eyes.

Our poets graphically describe the scene of the "kingly" guru humbly beseeching his offspring to initiate him into their democratic new world, just as he had initiated them: "Coming down from the throne with folded hands, / The comfort-giver himself took the ambrosial nectar" (Koer Singh, 9:53). Whatever lordly image he may have had, the guru at this point sheds it entirely. All sorts of hierarchies dissolve as the movement anticipates the merger between the sovereign and citizen, the guru and disciple, the parent and child. With hands humbly folded, the guru approaches the Five Beloved and receives *amrit*. A perfectly inclusive circle is produced on the Sikh horizon. That a guru gives up his high status and joins in with his own disciples is a rare event in the history of humanity, and Sikhs in all corners of the world continue to recite their miraculous union: "[W]onderful, wonderful Gobind Singh who himself is guru as well as disciple."[37] But I feel we do not really remember or enjoy the implications of this unique bond.

The poet Sukha portrays Guru Gobind Singh's memorable actions and dialogue with equal verve. He even tries to describe the indescribable brilliance of the guru's ornaments, garments, and weapons as he descends from his throne (*Sukha Singh*, 12:72). The figure is so regal and grand in these verbal portraits drawn by our Sikh poets that painters and artists of the "kingly" guru do not have to rely on any secular models like the "glorious body of Maharaja Duleep Singh" suggested by Brian Axel.[38] But this imperial figure humbly folds "his hands together" (*hath milai*) and "respectfully" *(adar su)* addresses the Five Beloved. In the communal memory of the Sikhs the majestic and elevated image of their tenth guru is so massively engraved that his sensitive and intimate love for others is forgotten. The majesty of the Sikh guru lies in his value for and maternal closeness with his Sikhs; his greatness lies in his humility, in his desire to be one with his disciples, in his tender tone, in his harmoniously joined hands. The memory of the guru galloping strident horses, with hawks perched on his shoulders and carrying weapons, is a partial one. Displayed in homes, businesses, sacred spaces, and embedded in our minds, it carries the "untouchable monarch" far, far away from us. We need to recollect and celebrate the mother's rhythms with which the guru drew close to his Sikhs for all time.

Guru Gobind Singh's own initiation is the point at which we hear his side of the story. Why did he perform the *aqedah*? What did he feel as he put his Sikhs through the torturous test? His introspection unfolds the intense love he has for his Sikhs, and his apologetic tone resonates with a mother's tenderness. To return to Koer Singh's rendition: "From his revered lips he uttered the words, 'Listen Khalsaji! Attentively! / You are most dear to me. / When I asked you for your head in my previous words with you / I chose that deed after much searching..." (9:53–54) The birth of the Khalsa is ontologically rooted in love. Guru Gobind Singh addresses the five respectfully, and tells them that they are his "most beloved" *(param piare)*. He is fully aware of the trauma he put them through, and even though it was couched in his love for them, the guru is rueful. As he explains, his act was not impromptu or frivolous. It was the result of much contemplation and deliberation. There was a transcendent goal he envisioned, and he explored different ways to realize it. He does not hide himself behind the mask of a supreme commander or a distant director. Clearly, he shares his trials and emotional conflicts with his beloved ones, and like them, the reader encounters the human side of the guru. Putting his beloved Sikhs through the test was not easy for him. The power of the guru lies in his empathy and tenderness.

His own birth into the Khalsa family is a concrete rejection of monarchical distance and hegemonic relations. The magnificent scene of the guru-Khalsa bonding articulates feminist interests and aspirations. It obliterates patriarchal systems of domination and mediations, and establishes a direct and spontaneous relationship between them. Sainapat, who does not give many details about the events of Baisakhi 1699, repeatedly juxtaposes Guru Gobind Singh's creation of the Khalsa with the death of the *masands*.[39] *Masands* were local community leaders who took care of the Sikh congregations in various parts of India. Guru Arjan had started the *masand* structure, which initially helped in the expansion of the Sikh faith. Over time, however, they became neglectful of their religious office and started taking advantage of their intermediary position by exploiting innocent Sikhs. An early Sikh feminist, the sagacious Punjab Kaur, brought the hypocrisy and tyranny of the *masands* to Guru Gobind Singh's attention. She fed Guru Gobind Singh's determination to abolish the oppressive *masand* system.[40] The Khalsa born from his own body would help the guru embrace his people; it would bring the groups splintered by the *masands* into a family united by blood; it would supply the wholesome mother's milk to all the members. In a poetically charged passage, Sainapat compares the renewed intimacy between the guru and his Sikhs to that of fish and water (5:6). Koer Singh, too, reports that with the birth of his Khalsa, Guru Gobind Singh brought his Sikhs close to himself.[41] Through the life-giving maternal bond, he abolished authoritarian structures.

Similarly, the hegemony of the male Brahmins is disposed of. They wielded great spiritual and religious authority in his milieu. Spokesmen for Hindu society, Brahmins were the only ones who had access to the scriptures and philosophy, and the only ones with the potential to attain *moksha*, the freedom from the cycle of birth and death. They were the only ones to officiate at religious ceremonies and all rites of passage. The Sikh *aqedah* broke such ideological and ritual fetters to produce a new mode of natality and life.

That is why the Khalsa is not created from individual parts of the body, as in the Vedic hymn of creation, but through the natural, maternal process, with all its emotions, complexities, and hormonal effects. Unlike the Brahmins, who were born from the mouth of the cosmic Purusha and were demarcated from the rest of the castes, the Five Beloved were born from the *whole* maternal body. They came from the same womb. They were fed from the same breast. By asking the Khalsa to initiate him into their fold in the same way, Guru Gobind Singh concretizes the bonds of equality and unity. This new relationship would free Sikhs from oppressive male religious officers, and enable them to form an egalitarian and loving bond, among themselves.

The guru three-dimensionally shows men and women how to shift their loyalties from those in power to themselves. On the maternity theater of Anandpur, Guru Gobind Singh visually and aurally replays the message of his predecessors enshrined in the Guru Granth. Their critique of the pandit in Hinduism and of the ulema in Islam is emotionally communicated in the scene of Guru Gobind Singh beseeching his followers. The Five Beloved had been no different from the rest of the men and women seated in the Baisakhi congregation! They had been sitting beside them, and they heard the guru's call along with the rest of them. As they now see their revered guru with folded hands, down on one knee before those very five, the congregation sees the age-old superiority of the *masands* and the pandits and the ulema crumble away. With their very eyes, the entire Baisakhi audience witnesses the patriarchal operations of control and manipulation fall apart.

The guru's initiation is a bold enactment of the feminist protest against the patriarchial priests that reign inside our heads and on our altars. It is an explicit confirmation of the charge and responsibility of the Sikhs to be active citizens and officiate at their own rites of passage. J. D. Cunningham's observation that "Guru Gobind Sigh abolished caste rather by implication than by a direct enactment" is therefore a drastic understatement.[42] It is, of course, implied everywhere in Guru Gobind Singh's writings, but it was directly and dramatically enacted on the maternity theater of Anandpur. No matter what caste anybody was born in, the Khalsa was equated with the high-born Brahmin: *bipr su khalsa* (the Khalsa itself is the Brahmin). Beginning with the most profound rite, the initiation of their own guru, the Sikh community was henceforth to conduct all their birth, death, and marriage ceremonies by themselves: "Perform all rites of birth, death, marriage without worship of Brahmins./The Khalsa itself is the Brahmin, so entertain it and look at it./This is the guru's word" (Koer Singh, 9:99). By removing hegemonic structures that stood between himself and his Sikhs, he shook off their passivity and dreary acceptance of age-old customs. He instilled a new sense of responsibility and power in all his Sikhs. The Baisakhi gathering was not an audience of spectators; they were "seers" who were to subjectively register the guru's deed and put it in practice for generations to come. The guru performed his spectacular drama so that everyone would be motivated to react. The direct and intimate maternal bond created in front of all put an end to the continuing spiral of patriarchy "perpetuating its perpetuation."

In fact, the Baisakhi audience instantly witnessed its emotional effect. In the beginning there was trepidation on the part of the Five Beloved, who did not deem themselves worthy of conducting the rite for their revered Guru (Sukha Singh, 12:78). But the praise, love, and intimacy with which Guru Gobind Singh related to the five transformed them. They began to stir water and sugarpuffs. The disciples followed the same sequence as their guru, and even asked him his name and his place of origin, and gave him the code of conduct as they themselves had received it. The guru's act is repeated and replayed vigorously by the disciples. Their bodily motions of "standing up erect" and "coming forward" betray their newfound emotional strength. They respond actively and dynamically to their new role as people in charge. Impelled to initiate their most revered figure, they immediately acquire self-esteem. There is no undue hesitation on their part, and even their speech illustrates their self-assurance: "Sir, tell us your name and residence," says the Khalsa, "do not delay" (Sukha Singh, 12:104). In turn, the guru responds to his empowered and reconstructed disciples with respect and equanimity. Unlike a benevolent patriarch who would rather promote passivity and escape from responsibility, as Sally McFague points out,[43] the guru performs the role of the mother who fosters growth, autonomy, and responsibility in her offspring.

By joining with his beloved, the male Guru celebrates values of relationship and community. By accepting *amrit*, the guru himself becomes a member of the Khalsa institution, and like the Five Beloved he adopts the last name Singh. So instead of patriarchal hierarchies and individualism, he establishes a relationship of mutuality and reciprocity. We find here a feminist transformation that rejects the patriarchal preference for power, control, and alienation. The male infatuation with violence, aggression, and warfare that prevails both in the Punjab and in our Western culture stems from the lack of the primacy of relationship. Males are afraid of losing their individuality and autonomy, and as Katherine Keller warns us, "in such a fear of self-loss lurks a profound fear of women."[44] We sense the real strength of the guru not in his muscle or horsemanship or imperial grandeur, but in his notion of selfhood that could extend to others and embrace them. Assured and confident, he relinquished his individuality and guruship and merged totally with the collective body of the Khalsa. And as the Khalsa becomes his alter ego, his own self is enlarged, too. Guru Gobind Singh is physically, emotionally, and spiritually empowered by them. Indeed, his *aqedah* is not a one-way progression that strengthens the other Sikhs alone; the guru is likewise strengthened. The mother's energy is not sapped by her children. Love expands the giver and the receiver into infinite realms of exhilaration and awareness.

As they invest their guru with Khalsahood, the Five Beloved in turn are invested with guruship. The consciousness and conscience of Guru Gobind Singh, which we tried to grasp through his autobiographical *Bicitra Natak,* is now physically reproduced in the Khalsa. Their list of instructions to the guru elucidates their moral vision. The ethical blueprint of the Five Beloved combines an internal change of consciousness with responsible action against external exploitation and manipulation:

> Immerse yourself in selfless service, love, and devotion,
> Get rid of the corrupt, abide by the good;
> Have faith in none but the absolute sword,
> Let the mantra of true Name your lips absorb.
> (Sukha Singh, 12:106)

While Sikh communal memory fervently recollects the valiant battles fought externally by the Khalsa members, it sadly forgets their stress on inward spirituality. Their stand against political, social, and political oppression is grounded in the passionate experience of love and devotion. Self-examination is necessary. Guru Gobind Singh's heroic Khalsa posits a psychic interiority and sensitivity that contemporary feminists urge we tap into.[45] Political and social mobilization have to come from within each person, and the sword of the Khalsa reaches into those inner depths. Stirring the Transcendent at the core of our bodies, it motivates us to just and liberating praxis. Action is not for action's sake, it is not following the masses, it is not acting like a predatory hawk; it is a reaction to our deepest reflections, a response to our inner voice.

The gesture of the guru receiving the *amrit* from his Khalsa is a profound statement that henceforth the Khalsa lead, not be led; that the Khalsa rule, not be ruled. "I have given the rule of the world to you, / In turn I have made you my guru" (Koer Singh, 9:56). Clearly, the rule or *raj* that Guru Gobind Singh projects for his Khalsa is not a patriarchal dominance over a territory or a people. It is their investment with guruship. The master-disciple relationship is ended, and an egalitarian and enlightened mode of being in this world is given birth. In his autobiographical *Bicitra Natak* we never find him battling to conquer any place or title. His notion of *raj* does not imply a conquest or a founding of a kingdom. Rather, his is a feminist vision, which integrates the entire life of the individual, a life lived freely and authentically, a life lived in consonance with all modes of knowledge—emotional, intuitive, sensual, and spiritual. Of course oppressive forces that stand in the way of liberty and self-empowerment have to be squarely faced. But the life engendered by the Khalsa is not lust for power or control over others; it is an enjoyment of true power and confidence *with others*. The Khalsa rule tries to create the golden age of divine rule, when, according to the Guru Granth, the creditor and debtors will live in the same neighborhood, and there will be no religious taxes to be paid by anyone (GG, 430). The Khalsa was a collective and democratic institution, one in which all the members were royalty—all, including the guru, and *equally* both Singhs and Kaurs. Each is no more and no less than the other. It is really the first Sikh guru's injunction "By conquering the self, we conquer the world" (Jap) that constitutes the essence of Khalsa Raj.[46]

Bonded with his beloved, the guru is elated. The element of delight is important to modern feminists who find monotheistic religions ubiquitously promoting self-denial and suffering. "A blanket of pessimism, of dolor, hangs over the practice of religion in patriarchy…and pleasure is the ultimate enemy," laments Sheila Ruth.[47] The guru rejoices and praises his beloved, admitting that no tongue—be it that of Sheshnag, or Wisdom—be it that of the goddess Sarasvati, can fathom the greatness of the Khalsa. He avails himself of ancient Indian mythological figures to exalt his newborn Khalsa. The praise of the Khalsa attributed to Guru Gobind Singh has been one of the favorite hymns for Sikhs across generations. This short poem called the Khalsa Mahima is full of endearments. In the language of the mother, the guru repeatedly rejoices in the Khalsa as his physical embodiment: "[T]he Khalsa is my special form / the Khalsa is my chief limb / the Khalsa is my body and breath / the Khalsa is my life of life" (Khalsa Mahima). The mother's own body with its senses and emotions, its rhythms and motions, is reproduced and celebrated in the body of her offspring. In his maternal surge, the guru rejoices in all aspects of their union. There is no body-mind, immanence-transcendence, male-female split in his experience and imagination. The Khalsa is his body, the Khalsa is his "social and political success," and the Khalsa is his "subtle consciousness and wisdom." In a brief but arresting statement, the guru speaks of their intimate bond: "I belong to the Khalsa, the Khalsa to me" (Khalsa Mahima). The fluidity of their relationship comes out best in Adrienne Rich's words: "The flow of energies between two biologically alike bodies, one which has lain in amniotic bliss inside the other, one that has labored to give birth to the other.…[48]

Through their mutual flow of energies, they were able to encompass the entire Sikh community. The Five Beloved created a new relationship between the guru and all his Sikhs, for on that day Guru Gobind Singh pronounced the Khalsa and the Sikh identical: "[T]he entire congregation, from the beginning to the end, is my Khalsa" (cited in Sainapat, 5:30). Triumphant in their love, they fulfilled the Sikh scriptural dictum: "[T]hose people become *khalsa* who know the devotion of love" (GG, 655). Love cleanses by dissolving constricting prejudices and expanding the self. This is the identity of the Khalsa birthed by Guru Gobind Singh. In his flood of mother's love, the Baisakhi gathering nestles comfortably on his maternal breast and hears him murmur a mother's boundless praise.

Centuries later, re-memories of these scenes and sounds of the Sikh *aqedah* fill us with feelings of confidence and self-worth. Obviously, Chaupa Singh and his peers must have remembered something drastically different and listened to somebody other than Guru Gobind Singh to have codified the sexist and hegemonic rules that have regulated Sikh society. The Baisakhi congregation included men and women, so how could we limit the Khalsa to a mere brotherhood? How could we prevent women from receiving or giving *amrit*? How could we treat our daughters any different from our sons? In all honesty, have we ever considered this question: if a woman had offered herself to the guru, would the guru have ever ever, excluded her from being one of the Five Beloved? It is necessary for all of us to return to Anandpur and, without heavy male blinders and mufflers, reexperience his profoundly liberating performance. On the Baisakhi stage, the guru did without *masands* and Brahmins, and it is imperative that we emulate his momentous action. Without intermediaries, we too must relate with our guru directly, intimately, profusely, "like fish with water."

Guru Gobind Singh may have begun his dramatic *aqedah* with the splitting of a head, but it reaches its climax in the union of head and body. This quintessential phenomenon is expressed in his own words: "Sikhs are the guru's body to which the head is joined. This complete mixing of Guru and Sikhs, I so cherish" (Koer Singh, 9:58). The guru is delighted that the "body" (*tan*) and "head" (*sees*) are henceforth joined together. In this organic metaphor fuse together many factual events of Sikh history. It is, of course, a recollection of the vital moment when Guru Nanak joined himself with his disciple Lehna, making him Angad (a limb of himself). The metaphor vividly brings to mind Guru Tegh Bahadur's execution by the imperial rule in Delhi, his severed head carried in fear and trembling all the way to Anandpur to be handed over to his young son, Gobind. The metaphor replays Guru Gobind Singh's demand for a head at the festive Baisakhi celebrations of 1699, pulling us into the maternity theater as the Khalsa pushes out amid the flow of blood, placenta, and milk. The metaphor stages the disappearance of the patriarchy of priests and *masands* into the intimate bond between the mother and her offspring, and as the guru lowers his head to the Five Beloved, the "heads within us" and on altars dissolve. It is, of course, the metaphor for our human wholeness. Patriarchal thought has dualized our totality into mutually opposed body and head, with women being identified with the "body," matter, and bondage, and men with the "head," spirit, and liberation. Indeed, with the birth of the Khalsa in Anandpur on that momentous Baisakhi day when winter and summer come together, the severed body and head come together in Sikh consciousness forever.

Chapter Three

Mythic Inheritance and the Historic Drink of the Khalsa

The multitreasured drink of the divine Name
Rests within the body itself.
(GG, 293)

Since that Baisakhi Day, Sikhs are being fed on the nurturing drink made by Guru Gobind Singh and Mata Jitoji. Sikhs who go through the initiation ceremony by drinking *amrit* which is prepared by the churning of water with steel, are called the *amritdharis*. There may be variations in the actual practice among Sikhs, but as Pashaura Singh has cogently said, "Each group claims to follow the 'correct' procedure laid down by Guru Gobind Singh at the Baisakhi of 1699 and transmitted orally through successive generations."[1] The vast majority of Sikhs do not go through the formal ritual, yet they continue to be fed on the *amrit*, prepared by the guru. Called *kesdhari* Sikhs ("those who keep the long hair"), they fully identify with the rite of initiation conducted during Baisakhi of 1699. They too maintain the "heroic" spirit of the Five Beloved, keep the five Ks given to the Khalsa, recite the same verses that the guru and the Five Beloved did during the preparation of the *amrit* rite, and follow many of the injunctions remembered to have been given to the Khalsa on that day, especially abstinence from tobacco and from meat that is not *jhatka*.[2] There is no division between *kesdharis* and *amritdharis*, because all *amritdharis* must be *kesdharis*. Whether they sip *amrit* literally (as in the case of *amritdharis*) or symbolically (as in the case of *kesdharis*), the *amrit* rite of Baisakhi 1699 continues to have a profound impact on the individual and collective identity of the Sikhs, and all who partake of that Baisakhi *amrit* are united as Sikhs.

In my re-memory, Guru Gobind Singh's rite evokes the primal moment of Sikhism—Guru Nanak's sipping of *amrit* recorded in the *Puratan Janamsakhi*. The myth narrates how Nanak, a simple worker at a grocery store, was initiated by the Divine in the River Bein, and became the founding guru of the Sikh religion. The river that is called Bein in modern Punjabi is written as Vein in the *Puratan Janamsakhi*, and it is the exact same word as *veni* in Sanskrit, which means braid.[3] The word *veni* has for thousand of years been a very important term for "river" on the Indian subcontinent. This deep-rooted image validates typical female hairstyles. In fact, one of the most important sacred places in India is called the "triple braid"—Triveni. Triveni is the sacred spot where the holiest rivers of India—the Ganga, Jumna, and Sarasvati—come together. It is significant that these three rivers are visualized as goddesses. The *triveni* is a common style for plaiting women's hair. But this everyday women's practice has always had a cosmic significance, so the connection between the River Bein and the woman's braid is a very ancient and powerful one. The primal waters of the Bein clearly resemble the braids that are worn by women, especially Sikh women, for whom braids are the essential means for maintaining their *kesha* (long hair). The diaphanous and flowing waters of the northern Indian Bein draw us to a female space. They form the placenta in which the Sikh religion was initially lodged. The *Janamsakhi* relates the Sikh *gesta*, the primal sacred act, and meets Eliade's definition of a myth as "always an account of a 'creation'; it relates how something was produced, began to *be*."[4]

In a very meaningful way, the tenth Sikh guru returns to this primal moment of Sikhism and opens it up into the future through his inauguration of the *amrit* initation at Anandpur on Baisakhi Day 1699. The "beginning" of Sikhism, embodied in the private, individual, and mystical experience of the first guru culminates in a public, social, and institutional ritual of the tenth. In the final analysis, the historical rite of passage initiated at Anandpur is a visual and dramatic reconstruction of Guru Nanak's metahistorical experience. The tenth guru unleashes the force of Guru Nanak's mythic narrative and brilliantly choreographs it into a *fixed* and *enduring* ritual for the present and future of his community. In Eliade's words, "By virtue of the continual repetition of a paradigmatic act, something shows itself to be *fixed* and *enduring* in the universal flux.... [R]itual abolishes profane, chronological Time and recovers the sacred Time of myth."[5]

By grounding the Khalsa initiation in the primal moment, the apodictic value of the *Janamsakhi* is reconfirmed, and in turn, Guru Gobind Singh's ritual is endowed with significance and authenticity. The vigor of Nanak's *amrit* is extended into perpetuity: the metahistorical drink becomes an enduring and integral part of the daily life of the Sikh community. Guru Gobind Singh recreates the *Janamsakhi* narrative as a vital ritual act and accomplishes Malinowski's goal of lifting myth from its "existence on paper" and placing it "in the three-dimensional reality of full life."[6]

Specialists in the study of myth and ritual have shown the two as parallel phenomena. With its preterpunctual and eternal events, myth is distinguished from ritual, which consists of punctual and immediate events. Whereas myth expresses a situation in its ideal, transcendent aspect, ritual is an actual event taking place in historical time and involving everyday people. Although they are two distinct processes, anthropologists, sociologists, and psychologists have claimed that there is a powerful connection between them. *Mythos* leads to *ethos*; stories control moral and social behavior. Malinowski, the pioneer in functional anthropology, inspired the study of the practical result of myth in a living society. His research on Melanesian culture and his voluminous contributions to the study of ritual elaborate his thesis that "an intimate connection exists between the word, the mythos, the sacred tales of a tribe, on the one hand, and their ritual acts, their moral deeds, their social organization, and even their practical activities, on the other."[7] Malinowski's theoretical formulations are valuable to us, for they enable us to understand the cultural force of Guru Gobind Singh's undertaking. As the 1699 initiation rite moves into the past, it gains great force and momentum, building a sense of continuity, stability, and direction for future generations. Time and the timeless, history and myth, are blended together in the potent *amrit*.

For millions of Sikhs the two events are an indelible part of their past, and their historical veracity is not questioned. Both of them lie mingled in some remote part my own subconscious self. They have great personal value for me, for these are the earliest narratives I recall hearing from my parents, and they constitute a most precious part of my past that I want to pass on to my daughter. Like Baisakhi 1699, Guru Nanak's revelation in the river is remembered by generations of Sikhs as an irrefutable fact, and carries a profound significance.

The reason why the two events have not really been linked in Sikh memory is that there seems to be a rupture between the alchemical *amrit* made by Guru Gobind Singh and the cosmic *amrit* tasted by Guru Nanak. The first and the tenth Sikh gurus are recollected as being very different from each other. But if Guru Gobind Singh is perceived as a contrast to and deviation from Guru Nanak, how can we appreciate the identity of their drinks? A recent study on the institution of the Khalsa enumerates modern historians who continue to reiterate Toynbee's view that the tenth guru wrought "a process of transformation for the Sikhs from a pacifist fraternity into a militant political community."[8] As a crusader against tyranny and oppression, the tenth guru is seen as opposed to the peace-loving Guru Nanak.

Even in popular imagination, the two are perceived very differently. In most Sikh paintings, Guru Nanak is portrayed in dress that combines Hindu and Muslim elements. He wears a patched cloak with arabesque designs, and his spherical turban has a rosary on it. He is rapt in contemplation, with his right palm imprinted with his message of "Ikk Oan Kar" (One Being Is). In contrast, Guru Gobind Singh, as we have been noticing all along, is richly dressed and ready for action. Instead of a rosary placed on a flat turban, he is decked out with a jeweled crest upon a lofty, cone-shaped turban. He is either standing erect or seated on his horse and armed with various weapons, including a bow and a quiver of arrows, a sword, a discus, a shield, and a spear. He is shown riding handsome bluish-gray horses, with white hawks around him. Professor G. S. Talib captures Guru Gobind Singh's popular portrait: "In contradiction to the other preceptors of the Sikh faith, he is thought of as the warrior, the hero with a resplendent, knightly figure fighting against tyrants and evil-doers, somewhat like Saint George of the Christians."[9]

Of course, Guru Gobind Singh fought batttles, and we looked closely at how courageously he fought them (chapter 1). Moreover, he wanted his people to have a body of warriors to defend them against enemies who attacked. So he ensured there were excercises to strengthen their athletic and military skills. He had the Ranjit Nagara (Drum of Victory), too. But that was not the essence of his personality or his message: *He did not want all Sikhs to fight all the time.* It was just during crises that they were to take up weapons, as he declares in his *Zafarnamah*: "When the matter is past all other remedy, / It is but lawful to take up the sword" (*Zafarnamah* 22). They were never to be aggressors; battle was to be the last resort for himself and his Sikhs. He knew well—in fact, from Guru Nanak—that greed is the cause of wars. Lamenting the assault of Babur on the Lodi sultanate, Guru Nanak offered a timeless insight: "[I]t is greed that divides brother from brother" (GG, 417). Having failed in his conquests in the direction of Khurasan, the Muslim Babur from Kabul turned against his Muslim brothers, the Lodis in Delhi. It was pure greed for the treasures of India that drove Babur into war. Guru Gobind inherited Nanak's view and saw battles and wars as superficial incidents that were caused by greed, pride, and lust; they were not "holy" by any means. That is why he could record them in those playful tones we heard in his *Bicitra Natak*. War and conflict are to be used only when circumstances demand. That deep down, we are one family, with one progenitor, was the ardent belief of the gurus. The tenth lived his life just as the first did: intimately remembering and celebrating the Infinite Reality, and like Nanak, Gobind exhorted his peers to savor That One while living fully in our variegated world. Indeed, he extolled the virtues of peace and love. He did not possess, nor did he want his Sikhs to imbibe, the spirit of a crusader or mujahedin. War was peripheral, not central, to Guru Gobind Singh's life and mission.

For his part, the "peace-loving" Guru Nanak was boldly engaged in the affairs of his society. He loudly challenged social hegemonies. He strongly criticized degrading and exclusive cultural norms. Heroism was important for him, too. Babur's incursions into India were devastating for the country and her people. In poignant poetry recorded in the Guru Granth, Guru Nanak narrates how the innocent and the defenseless were slaughtered, women raped, and princes trampled in the dust. There is a powerful protest in Guru Nanak's depiction of Babur's brutality. The Sikh guru found Babur's Western concept of "oneness" in conflict with his own experience of "oneness." As a continuation of the Jewish and Christian traditions of the West, Islam penetrated India with the concept of the "One God." But the Western idea of oneness could not accept the polyphonic imagination of Hindus, Buddhists, or Jains. Guru Nanak vehemently denounced the exclusivity of the Muslim conquerors. When Allah was projected as the only way to reach the Divine, or the Qur'an as the only sacred text, or the mosque as the only sacred space, he reacted strongly. In a feminist voice Guru Nanak harshly rejects those who force their way on others, those who reduce the richness and variety of routes by imposing their own narrow path.[10] His protest becomes a manifesto, a call to action.

Guru Gobind Singh therefore has much more in common with Guru Nanak than with St. George! The comparison, however, is very interesting, for St. George was originally a simple Christian who was martyred around 300 CE. Centuries later, he began to appear as a knight in the minds of people and was eventually made the patron saint of England. Similar distortions hide the real personality and motivations of the Sikh guru who aspired to crystallize Guru Nanak's vision of the One Reality. It was to be a feeling of peace and harmony within and without; not war and discord. The tenth guru passionately wanted men and women in his society to feel the transcendence that the first Sikh guru felt in his veins, and it is from this very transcendence that he draws his alchemical *amrit*. When we get stuck on contrasts and contradictions between Guru Gobind Singh and his predecessor gurus, we overlook the powerful message of continuity and tradition at the heart of the Sikh religion. The polarized images of the first and the tenth guru keep us from enjoying the intrinsic unity that constitutes the *amrit*, and they keep us from utilizing their combined strength. Such preoccupations lead to historical aberrations, and they deflect us from understanding the liberating process inherent in the *amrit* initiation.

In his autobiographical *Bicitra Natak*, as we found, Guru Gobind Singh is very proud of his past, and confident that his own ideology, poetics, and practices are rooted within an existing structure. In an essay on the theory of influence, the contemporary critic Harold Bloom explores the anxiety that writers and poets feel about their literary heritage. Bloom comments, "Every major aesthetic consciousness seems peculiarly more gifted at denying obligation as the hungry generations go on treading one another down."[11] But Guru Gobind Singh is in no way reticent about acknowledging his indebtedness to Nanak and his successor gurus. He celebrates his rich legacy and even exhorts us to recognize the oneness of their form—*ek rup* (*BN*, 5:10). So if the tenth guru identifies himself totally with Guru Nanak, and the Sikh community affirms a continuous identity of the ten gurus in their liturgical prayers, why should we be carving out differences and contrasts between them?

The polarized stereotypes of them are wrong. And they are detrimental to the community. They have made the Sikh psyche and society schizophrenic. An exclusive reliance on the "warrior" and "knightly" figure of the tenth guru distracts us from the maternal and feminine dimension of his personality and undertakings. This overemphasis has led us to view *amrit* initiation primarily as a hypermasculine event, which was not Guru Gobind Singh's intention. Performed by men, for men, and through men, it somehow ends up being more of a military action than a spiritual transformation. It seems to me that the interrelationship between the first and the tenth Sikh gurus illuminates the full meaning of the Sikh rite, and gives us a taste of the peace and the freedom and the newness that each sip carries for all members, high and low, male and female. In our re-memory, the motherly waters of the River Bein function as the primordial womb from which the Khalsa *amrit* is made; the waters in which Guru Nanak had his divine encounter constitute the material substance of Guru Gobind Singh's *amrit*.

This chapter commemorates the two vital moments of Sikh history—namely its origins and its crystallization—and how they flow together into the fluid *amrit*. We search the past to make use of it in the present. So with the help of the phenomenological reflections of Mircea Eliade and Martin Heidegger, and the anthropological structures of Bronislaw Malinowski and Victor Turner, let us try to recognize how the first guru's mythic drink in the River Bein is re-created by the tenth guru and feeds generations of Sikhs. My goal in remembering the past is to recover the possibilities and potentialities of the nutritious *amrit* so that we may create a more egalitarian and liberating future. Memories incubate and memories animate. I want us to remember the vital ingredients of selfhood and autonomy supplied by Guru Nanak and Guru Gobind Singh, so that we can retrieve the full force of Sikh identity sipped in the *amrit*—for both men and women. A Punjabi proverb recited frequently by my mother rings in my ears: "1 and 1 together are not merely 2; they are endowed with the potential of 11!" We must keep our gurus together.

Mythic Inheritance

The origins of the Sikh religion are traced to Guru Nanak's epiphanic moment in the waters of the River Bein recorded in the *Puratan Janamsakhi* (number 10).[12] *Janam* (birth) *sakhis* (stories) are short narratives depicting the birth and life of Guru Nanak. I find the *Janamsakhis* particularly significant for introducing the earliest women in Sikhism. Whereas Sikh scholarship scarcely mentions them, the *Janamsakhis* tell us about Mata Tripta, who gave birth to Nanak; about the Muslim midwife Daultan, who brought the child into the world; about his sister Nanaki, who befriended her little brother; and about Sulakhni, Nanak's wife and the mother of their two sons. The narratives do not fully develop the individual characters of these women, and reveal them only insofar as they are related to the guru. Yet even in their rudimentary presentations, the authors highlight the subtle awareness that these women possessed. Mata Tripta is a noble woman who understands her son and can see into his unique personality—much more so than can his father, Kalu. The midwife Daultan is struck by the extraordinary qualities of the child she delivers. Just as Mary Magdalene was the first person to have witnessed the resurrection of Christ, so Nanak's sister Nanaki is the first person to recognize Nanak's enlightenment. Only Sulakhni's role is ambiguous, as if the authors did not quite know how to deal with her. As the wife of the founder of the Sikh religion, where was she? What was her relationship with her husband? How did she feel when he left her with their two sons and went on his long journeys? How was their reunion? Their life together in Kartarpur?

Guru Nanak's close association with his mother (Tripta), sister (Nanaki), and wife (Sulakhni) was crucial in shaping his social and religious consciousness, which was then carried on by his nine successor gurus. The fact that a Muslim midwife took care of the pregnant Tripta shows the trust that Nanak's family had in people of "other" faiths. The women from his family must have raised Nanak's awareness about gender inequities in his milieu. Nanaki, after whom Nanak was named, must have been especially significant, because he spent a lot of his formative years with her, and even went to live with her in Sultanpur after she got married. Guru Nanak's condemnation of the beliefs in purdah (segregation and veiling), sati (upper-class women obligated to die in the funeral pyre of their husbands), and pollution (associated with menstruation and childbirth) must have emerged from his close relationship with and respect for the women in his life. Their reverberations had to be felt by his successor, the tenth guru.

Some of the *Janamsakhi* scenes were illustrated by Shrimati Phulan Rani for Guru Nanak's Fifth Birth Centennial in 1969. Sponsored by the Indian Sahitya Academy, she illustrated the life of Nanak in a series of forty remarkable paintings. Phulan Rani's eyes caught the presence of women in the first guru's life. Not only does she show us the female relatives of the guru but also women from his village and town—women who saw Nanak go to school, and women who attended his various rites of passage. There is one that strikingly captures the sister and brother walking together in the serenity of nature.[13] The older sister has her left arm lovingly around her little brother, who in turn is holding on to it as it gently rests on his shoulder. Both are wearing loose and rather similar outfits. Both are in a contemplative mood: while he looks down at the ground, she gazes far into the distance. She bends over him, seeming to protect his head with its halo, and they together form a beautiful whole. Nanaki and Nanak, the sister and brother, female and male, are physically and psychologically integrated. In this picture of oneness and harmony, Nanaki gently leads her little brother forward into a new world. *Her* love, guidance, and togetherness at the core of the Sikh tradition flow into the bowl of *amrit* prepared by Guru Gobind Singh and Mata Jitoji.

The *Janamsakhis* dwell on the illustrious advent of Nanak's birth. The prophets told the Buddha's father, King Sudhodhan, that his child would be a great king or a great ascetic. The Three Wise Men followed a bright star to honor the baby Jesus, born in a stable in Bethlehem. And just as that stable was lighted by the bright star of Bethlehem, the humble mud hut in which Nanak was born was flooded with light at the moment of his birth. The gifted and wise both in the celestial and in the terrestrial regions rejoiced in the momentous event and bowed to the exalted spirit that had adopted bodily vesture in fulfillment of the Divine Will. But unlike the "virgin" births of Sakyamuni and Jesus, the birth of Nanak was a normal one. In the Buddhist tradition, Queen Maya dreams that a white elephant enters her womb. She later miraculously gives birth to the future Buddha, with the child emerging from Queen Maya's right side as she stands in a grove of trees in Lumbini. In the Christian tradition, Mary becomes pregnant by the power of the Holy Spirit, and Jesus has no biological father. In contrast, Nanak has a biological father, Kalu, and Mata Tripta carries Nanak in her womb, generates him from her being, and bodies him forth. The midwife Daultan attests to Tripta's regular pregnancy and birth. The validation of both female and male creativity is reiterated in the *Bicitra Natak*, for Guru Gobind Singh recounts his birth as a consequence of the spiritual devotion and physical union of his father and mother. *The Janamsakhis* show us Tripta happily holding the baby in her arms, while Daultan proudly reports that there have been many children born under her care, but none so extraordinary as the baby Nanak. Affirmation of female sexuality and the powers of conception, gestation, and birth underlies their rejoicing.

The *Janamsakhis* provide wondrous and miraculous details of Guru Nanak's entire life. They depict scenes in which dreadful and dangerous elements of nature either protect him (like the cobra offering his shade to a sleeping Nanak) or are controlled by him (with his outstretched palm Nanak stops a huge rock hurled at him). They depict his divine configuration: at his death, only the shroud is left. Flowers are found instead of Guru Nanak's body, and both Hindus and Muslims carry away the fragrant flowers—to cremate or bury according to their respective customs. These stories also show the human side of Nanak: his conflict with his father, Kalu; his closeness with his sister, Nanaki; his unhappiness with formal education; and his denunciation of formal and empty ritual. In one of the accounts we find Nanak sprinkling water from a jug across the village. He makes the point that if water sprinkled by priests could reach the dead ancestors, surely his would reach the fields down the road. The narratives describe the rites of passage he went through (like his marriage to Sulakhni), and those that he refused (like the Upanayana ceremony). Many of the stories of vivid events also serve as a stage for his sublime verse. But rather than literally and factually transcribe Guru Nanak's life, the various authors try to present their moral and theological interpretations of the events in his life.

The *Janamsakhis* may not be objectively accurate. But these are myths with tremendous power. They are the animating forces that open our imagination, our view of the world, our horizons. As Eliade has constantly reminded us, myths constitute sacred history, and hence a "true history," because they always deal with *realities*. So the ahistorical *Janamsakhis* are very important historical sources for the Sikh religion. Their simple and vigorous style of narration lent itself easily to oral circulation, and they became very popular. They have also been painted and brightly illustrated. They typically provide the Sikhs with their first literary and visual introduction to their heritage, and continue to nurture them for the rest of their lives.

It is these *Janamsakhi* accounts that the tenth guru must also have heard, read, and seen; to borrow Victor Turner's phrase, Guru Gobind Singh had an "existential encounter" with them. Whether they were factually true is irrelevant. Though Guru Nanak's initiation in the River Bein is not specifically mentioned by Guru Gobind Singh, he was deeply aware of it at some level. He was the tenth guru to succeed Nanak, and as he inherited his precursor's history, he inherited his metahistory as well. According to Anil Chander Banerjee, the tradition of the *Puratan Janamsakhi* was quite well known in Guru Gobind Singh's time.[14] The reference to Guru Nanak's revelation in the Bein is even found in the work of Nand Lal Goya, a leading poet in Guru Gobind Singh's literary entourage: "Thus spoke God unto Guru Nanak: Thou, My Son, art the true Guru (Enlightener) / Go, reveal My Light to the world."[15] *Janamsakhis* had become quite popular by the time Gobind was born. "Myth," as Ninian Smart perfectly said, "is the food which feeds our sense of identity,"[16] and so the stories of the birth and life of the founder of the Sikh religion became an essential part of his successor's self-construction. Guru Gobind Singh uses these narratives from the past to structure his own worldview and give it meaning.

As Guru Gobind Singh both intentionally and subconsciously reaches back to his predecessors, there is a constant interrelation between him and Guru Nanak: in Gadamer's sense, there is a "fusion of horizons." Surely, Guru Gobind Singh does not simply repeat and reproduce the mythical account, for it is not a mechanical output. Guru Gobind Singh is creative and innovative, and his is an authentic development and reformulation of his predecessors' voice and action. His tendency toward the dramatic gives a new fervor to the *amrit* ritual that he initiates on the historical Baisakhi Day. As we know, Guru Gobind Singh was a superb poet himself, and his artistic sensibilities would have absorbed the paradigmatic myth and developed it into a new creation of his own. Martin Heidegger reminds us, "All creation, because it is such a drawing-up, is a drawing, as of water from a spring. Modern subjectivism, to be sure, immediately misinterprets creation, taking it as the self-sovereign subject's performance of genius. The founding of truth is a founding not only in the sense of free bestowal, but at the same time foundation in the sense of this ground-laying grounding."[17] By returning to the earliest moments of Sikhism, Guru Gobind Singh draws up layers of meaning, sustenance, and experience from his tradition's past and mingles it with the *amrit*. When we recognize that their philosophical, social, and aesthetic horizons are fusing together, we experience the full power and dynamism of the *amrit* drink. Many symmetrical relationships and fascinating parallels emerge in our analysis. The Khalsa initiation becomes an exciting hermeneutic opening for Guru Nanak's vision—revealing Guru Gobind Singh as a perfect fulfillment and certainly not a "contradiction to the other preceptors of the Sikh faith."[18]

Deconstructing Tradition

First of all, the *amrit* given to the newly born Khalsa is a uniquely Sikh phenomenon that debunks centuries-old rites and customs. A radical departure from traditional rites of passage such as the *upanyana* ceremony or circumcision that were practiced by the Hindus and Muslims of his times, the *amrit* initiation is grounded on Nanak's initiation into the spiritual stage. The paramount significance of initiation rites has been discussed by Eliade in his comparative work *Rites and Symbols of Initiation*. He begins by delineating three categories: puberty initiations, which establish sexual identity and adult status; secret initiations, which establish membership in a secret society; and voluntary or involuntary initiations, which give one a higher religious status.[19] Eliade focuses upon the first type, which is an essential rite for all communities, and elaborates its various patterns. His extensive study unfolds the construction of male superiority and dominance as the standard outcome of such rites.

The *Janamsakhis* show Guru Nanak boldly rejecting the rites practiced in his society. We get a specially vivid picture of Nanak refusing to participate in the *upanyana*, the important rite of passage in his own father's and grandfather's biocultural life cycles. All upper-caste Hindu boys perform this rite, by which they are "reborn" into their caste identities. Only after the *upanyana* initiation does the boy achieve his caste status, and only then is he allowed to read the sacred scriptures. The boy is given the *janaeu* (the sacred thread) which marks him off from the low-caste Shudras. The ages for initiation differ for each of the castes. The Savitri hymn is recited in different measures by the boys of different castes. The color and texture of the garments that the neophytes wear, and even the length and wood of the staff that they are given, vary in each case. These differences that systematically draw on and underscore the qualities peculiar to each caste have been studied by Brian Smith. In his essay "Ritual, Knowledge, and Being" Smith explains how the *upanyana* ritual reinforces caste and sex differences and hierarchies.[20] The ritual also marks the point in time when a boy has his last meal with his mother and leaves her world behind.

The *Janamsakhis* show an eleven-year-old Nanak (his age fits into the Kshatriya pattern) disrupting this crucial rite of passage that had prevailed for centuries. Guru Nanak's critique ties in well with feminist aspirations for securing for all people equal access to all rights, all responsibilities, and all aspects of life. The privileges and exclusive rights reserved for upper-class men had to be dismantled. The youngster's harsh denial is framed within an elaborate setting. Nanak's father, Kalu, the accountant for their village, makes extravagant arrangements for his son's initiation. A large number of relatives and friends are invited to his house. Pandit Hardyal, the revered family priest, officiates at the ceremonies. Pandit Hardyal is seated on a specially built platform purified by cow-dung plaster, and the boy Nanak is seated across, facing him. Pandit Hardyal lights up lamps, burns fragrant incense, draws beautiful designs in flour chalk, and recites melodious mantras. When the priest proceeds to invest Nanak with the sacred thread, he interrupts the ceremonies, questions him as to what he was doing with the yarn, and categorically refuses to wear the *janaeu*. At this point, the narrative juxtaposes Nanak's vehement criticism of the handspun thread to his ardent proposal for one that is emotionally and spiritually "woven by the cotton of compassion, spun into the yarn of contentment, knotted by virtue, and twisted by truth" (GG, 471). Rather than being draped externally, the *janaeu* becomes an internal process. "Such a thread," continues Nanak, "will neither snap nor soil; neither get burnt nor lost." Nanak's biography and poetry are thus blended together by the *Janamsakhi* author to illustrate his rejection of an exclusive rite of passage. The soft-spoken Nanak is, after all, not that temperate! Even as a child he questions his elders, he challenges authority, and goes so far as to interrupt an established ceremony in front of a large gathering in his father's house. His daring and defiant character is somehow forgotten in Sikh memory, but it emerges clearly in the *Janamsakhi*, and is subtly, most poignantly remembered in the Khalsa initiation.

On Baisakhi 1699 Guru Gobind Singh enacted a ritual that visibly shattered all differences and hierarchies. Though born in different castes, the Five Beloved were enjoined to sip from the same bowl—discarding all differences of temperament, occupation, caste, class, or religion. As we explored in length in chapter 2, each of them recited the same set of verses and each went through an identical ceremony. Each received the same name, the same outfit, and the same five symbols. The birth into the Khalsa order represented the "annihilation of their family" *(kul nas)* and the "annihilation of their hereditary profession" *(krit nas)*. Guru Gobind Singh's Baisakhi reversed the rebirth into the ranks of the twice-born Aryans; it destroyed the particular qualities intrinsic to each caste. By drinking the *amrit*, the Five Beloved equally became the Khalsa, and through the five, the entire Baisakhi gathering—from left to right, front to back—was declared as his Khalsa by Guru Gobind Singh.

Guru Gobind Singh's own words at that moment are recorded by a Persian source and are quoted extensively by historians: "I wish you all to embrace one creed and follow one path, rising above all differences of the religion as now practiced. Let the four Hindu castes, who have different dharmas laid down for them in the Sastras, containing the Institutes of Varnashrama dharma, abandon them altogether, and adopting the way of mutual help and co-operation, mix freely with one another. Do not follow the old scriptures . . . but all should cherish faith in the teachings of Guru Nanak and his successors."[21] The tenth guru articulates a deliberate discontinuity with the ancient past, and supports direct continuity with Guru Nanak. The age-old notion of Dharma, contingent on each person's caste or complexion and stage of life (*varnashramadharma*), was abandoned for the teachings of Guru Nanak and his successors. In spite of their different social backgrounds, the single path of mutuality and reciprocity is set forth for all the members of his newly created Khalsa. Nanak's disruption and dismissal of the exclusive rite of passage so neatly orchestrated by his father, Kalu, and Pandit Hardyal is replayed amid a huge gathering in Anandpur. Nanak made this bold refusal when he was just a child, and Guru Gobind Singh re-creates his defiance and makes it a communal response. The backdrop of the Khalsa initiation is the protest of Nanak, a protest anchored in his belief in human equality. Baisakhi 1699 shatters those social inequities Nanak denounced during the rite of passage his father so elaborately arranged, and conducts us to his primal experience of Unity in the depths of the River Bein.

A New Construction

Instead of a puberty rite, the *Janamsakhi* literature presents Nanak going through another type of initiation, one which would correspond to the third category enumerated by Eliade—the transition to a higher religious status. The passage does not establish his social identity or adult status; it is simply a transition into a liberated and liberating mode of existence—a new mode open to men and women. We learn that Nanak in his early years was a contemplative person who spent most of his time outside, tending the family herd of cattle, conversing with wayfaring sadhus and Sufis, and devoting his time to solitude and inward communion. Later, at the invitation of his sister, Nanaki, and her husband, Jai Ram, he moved to Sultanpur, where he worked in the Muslim nawab's *modikhana* (grain stores). It was at Sultanpur that Nanak went through a critical transformation. This was his personal rite of passage, a symbolic birth that redefined Nanak's social and spiritual identity, and it becomes the starting point of the Sikh religion. As the tenth successor to Guru Nanak deconstructs established social borders and reconstructs new formations, he models his momentous Khalsa initiation on Nanak's rite of passage. Guru Nanak's ideal of eradicating sociopolitical hegemonies is fulfilled in Guru Gobind Singh's Khalsa initiation. Guru Nanak's new identity and Guru Gobind Singh's Khalsa initiation conform to the archetypal tripartite pattern of rites of passage: separation, liminality, and reincorporation. But these two critical events in the Sikh religion are not just rites of passage; they are also rites that make the passage to feminist concerns and values.

Separation

The first stage of initiation in both cases is marked by death. Nanak goes for a bath in the river. He leaves behind his clothes, indicative of his previous set of codes and signs; he leaves behind his attendant, indicative of his home, family, and society at large. He now possesses nothing. Nanak has stripped off his cultural conditioning and divested himself of society's structures. His concomitant identity is left behind. He disappears in the Bein for three days. His Muslim employer summons the fishermen, has nets thrown into the river, and has his men search everywhere in vain. Nanak is nowhere to be found, and Nanak's employer leaves dejected, thinking how good a worker Nanak was.

Just as Guru Nanak was considered dead in the River Bein, Guru Gobind Singh's five devotees are also assumed dead by the Baisakhi gathering in Anandpur. Across cultures, the theme of death is used to anticipate dynamic new beginnings. In the Katha Upanishad, Naciketas discovers true living after his encounter with Yama, the god of death. Closer to our own times, Malinowski writes, "And he who is faced by death turns to the promise of life."[22] Nanak's true vocation began after his "death" in the River Bein. The realistic perspective of death in the *Janamsakhi* narrative becomes the template for Guru Gobind Singh's re-creation of the initial stage of separation. Turner observes that the segregation of the initiates in different cultures is similar to death, and he compares it to the womb, darkness, bisexuality, and a lunar or solar eclipse.

But rather than being "likened to death," the initiates in both of the Sikh instances are depicted as being literally dead. Guru Nanak is searched for and ultimately declared dead by his contemporaries. Guru Gobind Singh emulates Nanak's crisis by "making up"—in the sense of Aristotle's *poiesis* (crafting)—the death of the Five Beloved. In order for the Khalsa to enter a new womb, death was necessary. How else could the Khalsa be born into a new family? How could the Khalsa have new parents? A new name? A new personality? A new residence? Nanak's accident in the River Bein is metamorphosed into a deliberate act. The natural and silent hazard recounted in the *Puratan Janamsakhi* changes into a willful and audible requirement during Guru Gobind Singh's ritual re-creation of the event. Whereas Nanak "disappears" in the *Janamsakhi* account, death during Baisakhi 1699 blatantly appears and reappears through Guru Gobind Singh's crimson sword dripping with warm blood. The guru asks for the lives of five of his devotees; five times the audience hears a thud and sees a flow of blood.

Blood and water are cast as the agents of death: the river current for Nanak, the flowing blood for the Khalsa. In both discourses, the fluids are not represented; they exist in actuality and create real dramatic scenarios. Both retain an element of mystery, for the transparent waters reveal nothing about Nanak, nor the blood anything about the five devotees who offered themselves to the guru's sword. Their spectators remain equally bewildered. The vital fluids lead us to the concealment of the mother's womb where the menstrual blood and the amniotic fluids fuse together to feed and sustain the embryo. The light, white, and life-giving water of the *Janamsakhi* account does not form a contrast with the dark, red, and life-taking blood of the Baisakhi celebration. The tenth guru rends the goats during the Sikh *aqedah* in such a fashion that the blood flows like a river. Most likely the Sikh guru shared Empedocles' view of blood as "the perfect substance, containing all elements united in equal measure" for him to reveal it so openly![23] We recognize the crimson flow as a visual celebration of the life-giving powers of blood shed by women. That fertile flow ultimately weaves tissues in the womb, and ultimately creates limbs, organs, mind, consciousness, and spirit. Through the guru's performance, the frightening and dangerous fluid acquires the primacy and sustaining power of the waters of the River Bein. Rather than an end to life, the red elixir becomes the blood that nurtures and sustains the germination of the Khalsa. It becomes both life and life-giving, and as Trumbull termed it over a century ago, an "analogon of life," a "means of inspiration."[24]

Death is definitely an element in Guru Nanak's mythic account as well as in the ritual enactment of the Khalsa initiation. Yet both instances emphasize that we must acknowledge the finitude of life. In the case of Nanak, men and women realize that he was drowned in the river and accept it as a natural phenomenon. It is noteworthy that in the Baisakhi congregation women stayed and witnessed the Sikh *aqedah*. Feminist scholars remind us that Socrates' wife, Xanthippe, was banished from his presence during his last hours: "[A] reminder of gender, birth, and embodied life, . . . her presence cannot be tolerated while Socrates practices the philosophical life. . . ."[25] And in the Jewish *aqedah*, we noticed, Sarah is left at home while Abraham goes by himself to sacrifice Isaac. During Baisakhi 1699, women with their male counterparts receive the guru's call, and both alike witness the graphic scenes of death. Women are not excluded.

The acceptance of death has been a central concern for feminist scholars. Philosophers equate our society's obsession with death to its obsession with women's bodies; they trace the denial of death and efforts to master it to a deep-seated misogyny."[26] Rita Gross envisions that for the postpatriarchal transformation of religion, an affirmation of death and our embodied condition is essential. In *Feminism and Religion*, she discusses the different ways in which Rosemary Ruether, Carol Christ, Sally McFague, Naomi Goldenberg, and she herself, who writes from a Buddhist perspective, condemn the dualism of death and life, finitude and transcendence. Feminist thinkers universally argue that such a dualism carries dangerous consequences for humanity and the earth: "Women are identified with the despised body that constantly changes and finally gives evidence of its finitude by dying, and the entire natural world of change and decay is also rejected in favor of the spiritual, other worldly ideal."[27]

Instead of idealizing release from bondage to the mortal body, our accounts accept a natural cycle of birth, growth, and death. Just as the feminist scholars claim, death is not a punishment, and guilt is not attached to being human. In either case, eschatological joys are not offered as an antithesis to life, for there are no scenes celebrating any paradisal existence of beauty or bliss in contrast with life here on earth. The *Janamsakhi* does not extol the end of Nanak's suffering and entry into a beatific world; in fact, the khan returns dejected for having lost a good worker in Nanak. In the same vein,

Guru Gobind Singh does not promise a life of joy after death: he demands the supreme *gift of life* from his devotees. That death is not to be feared, that death is not to be mastered by miraculous deeds, that death does not lead to some wonderful world beyond, but rather that death simply is—all this comes out vividly in both discourses. The tenth guru repeats the first guru's return to a transformed mode of existence here on earth. Guru Gobind Singh did not put his beloved Sikhs through the torturous ordeal to prepare them for some distant world, but rather to usher in an authentic mode of existence for them *here and now*. In both our mythic and ritual discourses death is a part of life, not the opposite of life, and in both instances, it leads to new life in this world, with the full experience of being human in and through the body.

Betwixt and Between

The ambiguous and paradoxical stage in both of the Sikh discourses conforms to an archetypal pattern. Features from Turner's study of the "Betwixt and Between: The Liminal Period" apply to our myth and ritual. In their "inter-structural situation," Guru Nanak and the Five Beloved are "at once no longer classified and not yet classified."[28] As Guru Nanak is ushered into the realm of the Divine, he is no longer the store employee, nor is he yet the guru who would attract millions to a new world religion. Similarly, when Guru Gobind Singh ushered his five devotees out of the congregation, they no longer had their social cultural identity, nor were they yet the Khalsa. Each of them was at a dynamic threshold where the past borders were gone and future possibilities were not yet come.

During the three days that he is deemed drowned, Guru Nanak has a numinous experience. The reader is drawn into the depths of the river where Nanak has a vision of the Transcendent—to an opening of infinite possibilities. The waters are the womb in which Nanak gestates. For three days he is in that germinative ocean that is carried within the body of every woman. The *Puratan Janamsakhi* narrates a sequence of events that take place in the fecund and fertile waters. The events that take place in the womb of the Bein lead up to Nanak's religious status of guru.

1. In the multilayered mythic account, Nanak is ushered into the divine presence and hears the words "This *amrit* is the cup of my Name."[29] Enclosed in the waters of the Bein, Nanak receives the drink of immortality—*amrit* (literally, *a*=not + *mrit*=death). The voice he hears does not come from some high mountaintop, but from the inside of the river. Drink is our most basic and primal need: upon entry into the world we first drink our

mother's milk. The account validates a basic human process. The divine command *pio* (drink) substantiates the human body with its capacity to drink and taste and grow and be nourished, and its capacity to produce the elixir as well.

What Nanak received was *nam ka piala*—the cup of Name. *Nam* (the cognate of the English word "name") is the identity of the Transcendent One. This elemental process constitutes Nanak's introduction to the One: by sipping the universal drink, Nanak gets to *know* the Ultimate Reality. Sikh scripture posits *amrit* as the one reality of the universe: "[T]here is only one *amrit*; there is no other *amrit*" (GG, 1238). Several passages from the Guru Granth expand on its creative and restorative powers. "*Amrit* is the name of the Divine, by drinking it thirst is quenched" (1283); "[L]isten, O guru oriented, the Name is immortal; whosoever eats it, will not be hungry any more" (GG, 1250). The Immortal Name is the cure for all physical, psychological, and ontological suffering.

The dynamic unity, interrelationships, and nourishment provided by *amrit* resonate with those of the amniotic fluid described by a contemporary feminist ecologist: "Before it is drinking water, amniotic fluid is the creeks and rivers that fill reservoirs. It is the underground water that fills wells. And before it is creeks and rivers and groundwater, amniotic fluid is rain."[30] *Amrit* is the universal phenomenon shared by our planet and therefore no different from the maternal fluid that is the basis of all life. Immortality is not a renunciation or end of life; rather, it is the full intensity of the human experience in which the sharp dichotomies between subject and object, transcendent and immanent, spirit and body, are completely dissolved. The transcendent name constitutes the somatic self, and all the wondrous divine treasures are savored by our sensuous body. "The multitreasured drink of the divine Name/Rests within the body itself" (GG, 293). The immortal drink that Nanak receives and drinks is the sapiential experience of the Transcendent One in his body, which in turn is a precious repository of divine treasures. *Nam* and *amrit* are declared as synonymous, and so by tasting the elixir all treasures are found, and all thirst is quenched. In the River Bein Nanak enters the depths of his own being and recognizes the Divine Reality. Ninety percent of our body is, after all, water. Nanak's vision is a vision of his own Self—the infinite and transcendent experienced by his finite and innermost body.

After being given the cup of *amrit*, Nanak is asked to go and instruct others. But there is also the implication in the *Janamsakhi* narrative that he is put through a test. Before he departs—he has made his salutations and stood up—Nanak is ordered to illustrate his method and technique. "How does one praise my name? Recite!" Guru Nanak responds with a hymn that was his song—and proof—of praise. We find here a striking affinity between *kahu* ("recite" in Punjabi), the command that Nanak receives, and *kun* ("recite" in

Arabic), the order given by God to the Prophet Muhammad through the Archangel Gabriel. While the Prophet Muhammad hears the Word in the caves of Mount Hira, Guru Nanak hears it in the River Bein. Neither was previously known for his poetic genius, but after passing through the feminine spaces, each of them becomes the matrix for a voluminous and momentous and most artistic text—the Qur'an and the Guru Granth, respectively.

2. Guru Nanak passes the test through poetic syntax and is accepted by the Divine. The hymn he recites (GG, 14) is an excellent testimony of his psychic and spiritual power (its melody is unstruck), and of his artistic sensibility. Nanak becomes a poet. He explodes human language. He uses poignant similes and analogies and metaphors to describe That which is utterly ineffable. Feminist philosophers have shown the contrast between the abstract, intellectual, and patriarchal theology and the feminist thealogy that is "the reawakening of sensitivity to the forgotten dimensions, to the spheres of the senses, the psyche, the body, the imagination."[31] Through his poetic outpouring Guru Nanak implements a feminist reawakening of sensitivity into the very foundations of the Sikh faith. Hearing Guru Nanak's poetic outpour, the Voice spoke: "Nanak, you discern My will." The *Janamsakhi* thus attests to Nanak's success. He has passed his divine examination; in fact, he has triumphed in his praise of the formless One. Nanak then recites the Jap. Although the *Janamsakhi* does not cite the entire text of Guru Nanak's hymn, it specifies that Nanak "concluded the Jap." Recited at this particular juncture of his spiritual encounter, the Jap becomes an expression of Nanak's acceptance and gratitude. The Jap constitutes the core of Guru Nanak's metaphysics, and forms the opening text of the Guru Granth.

3. In the third phase of his sacred liminality, Guru Nanak is given the dress of honor (the *sirpao*, more commonly known as *saropa*). As the *Janamsakhi* continues, "The Voice was heard again: 'Who is just in your eyes, Nanak, shall be so in mine. Whoever receives your grace shall abide in mine. My name is the Supreme One; your name is the Divine Guru.' Guru Nanak then bowed in gratitude and was given the dress of honor from the divine court. A sonorous melody in the Raga Dhanasari rang forth. . . . Arati. . . . " Nanak is thereby initiated as the guru. He is endowed with a new status and identity. The *sacrum* or physical object that marks his special dispensation is the *sirpao*—the dress of honor. Nanak receives it from the divine court. Literally, it is a piece of material that goes from head *(sir)* to foot *(pao)*. But the dress does not carry any male or female connotations. It is not tailored for one or the other sex, and could be worn by both men and women. Immediately following his conferral, the guru rapturously recites Arati, a hymn in which he celebrates the transcendent light permeating every being. *Joti*, the insubstantial light, is the feminine dimension of the Ultimate One.[32] Contained by the fecund waters of the River Bein, Nanak recognizes the

ontological basis of the universe and is called upon to disseminate what has been vouchsafed to him.

Nanak's initiation does not establish his sexual status, and if anything, his rite of passage shatters the construction of a male identity. Although it was a son, brother, and husband who entered the river, the mythic initiation endows him with his essential humanity. Located in the amniotic waters, he goes through the process of physical drinking that gives him the metaphysical insight into the feminine *joti*. He responds in a sensuous, poetic outpour, and receives a gender-inclusive piece of clothing from the divine court. The space, the process, the revelation, the result, and the gift all pulsate with female imagery and activity. Through them, Nanak recovers the fullness and intensity of the human experience, and is called upon to enlighten others.

The symbolic form of the *Janamsakhis* is inherited by the tenth guru and is realized and materialized in his ritual event. Guru Nanak's initiation in the River Bein serves simultaneously as a "model of" and "model for" Guru Gobind Singh's Khalsa initiation. According to Clifford Geertz, this double aspect is important, because only through the two senses—an "of" and a "for" sense—do cultural patterns give meaning to "social and psychological reality both by shaping themselves to it and by shaping it to themselves."[33] The leitmotif of death, and the liminal experience of drinking *amrit*, reciting sacred poetry, and robing recounted in the *Puratan Janamsakhi* was historically transmitted to the tenth guru; it was his "system of inherited conceptions." And in a most subtle and artistic way, the first guru's mythic experience became a "model of" and "model for" Guru Gobind Singh's enactment of the Khalsa initiation.

The sequence, however, differs. Guru Gobind Singh first gives an extremely difficult test, and only after that does he offer the drink of *amrit*. We discussed how Sikhs had gathered in Anandpur from far and wide for the annual Baisakhi celebrations in 1699. We tried to imagine what the audience must have felt when their revered guru addressed them with sword in hand, asking for a head. His particular demand would hold great meaning for Guru Gobind Singh. As mentioned, "head" had personal resonance, since his own father's head had been demanded by political rulers. But it would also carry cultural connotations. His call could have been motivated by his goal to sever social verticalities. The head serves as a strategic symbol for delegitimizing and decapitating the traditional hierarchical orders denounced by Guru Nanak. Guru Gobind Singh's creative genius directed him to take up the dramatic sequence. He had to go through the dismemberment process before he could restore a sundered unity. Theoreticians have argued that discourse holds the capacity to shape and reshape society through the "paired instrumentalities—ideological persuasion and sentiment evocation. . . ."[34] Guru Gobind Singh was well aware of the power of his dramatic discourse; by replicating the ultimate "gift of life" in a sensational style, he could lodge his community in a creative new womb out of which new potentialities and possibilities could be constructed.

When a volunteer comes forward, he is taken away by the guru. The devotee enters a womblike dark and mysterious world, utterly unknown to the audience outside, and so Guru Gobind Singh re-creates Guru Nanak's disappearance in the Bein. Separated from his Baisakhi congregation, separated from his social role and rank, the volunteer is left in an ill-defined marginal space. He has made his passage into a liminal sphere, which Turner shows is full of positive and active qualities. Meanwhile, the guru becomes the recipient of the ultimate gift: his devotee's life.

He returns triumphantly with his sword dripping in blood with the demand for yet another head. The tough test is repeated five times. Each time the guru puts his Sikhs on trial—examining their courage, endurance, love, and devotion. Altogether, five men end up being taken away from the congregation into a sacred liminality. But the five—like Guru Nanak—return splendidly. Just as both men and women witnessed Guru Nanak stepping out of the Bein, so the Baisakhi congregation witnesses the five returning with the guru. The joy of the men and women is boundless. Women were not hidden or invisible in either of the events. They are "seers" who are active agents in the history-making process. Standing by the river seeing Nanak reappear after three days, or sitting in Anandpur seeing the Five Beloved reappear after they were taken away by the guru, the women and men alike gain insight into vital moments of their religion. The Sikh gurus wanted women to witness these events, because the gurus had complete confidence in their spiritual capacities. There is a striking example of this confidence in the Guru Granth when Nanak admires the beautiful eyes and features of a woman and asks her, "Have you seen the One, my sister?" (GG, 1257). This is not a rhetorical question but an expectation and trust that women have the ability to know the unknowable One. The gurus may not have been women, and neither were the Five Beloved, but women did participate in Sikh history in an essential way.

After their severe test, the Five Beloved receive *sacra* from their guru. In Turner's theoretical formulations, the conferral of the *sacra* constitutes the crux of liminality. Guru Nanak and the Five Beloved are communicated the typical three *sacra*: exhibitions (what is shown), actions (what is done), and instructions (what is said). However, Turner's overall premise that the liminal *sacra* are imbued with secrecy does not quite fit in with the Khalsa initiation, for Guru Gobind Singh brings Guru Nanak's encounter out from the depths of the River Bein onto the lofty stage at Anandpur.

The cup of Divine Name that Guru Nanak drank in seclusion is drunk by the Five Beloved in front of the huge gathering on a bright Baisakhi Day. In contrast with Turner's observation, no "great importance is attached to keeping secret the nature of the sacra,"[35] and a liminal period, like that of the Swazi wherein people become one only in darkness, silence, celibacy, and in the absence of merriments and movement,[36] does not hold true for the Khalsa initiation.

Actually, we find the Heideggerian strife between the earth and the world at the heart of the Khalsa liminality. According to Heidegger, art is created from the conflict between the grounding, founding, and sheltering "earth" and the open, flamboyant, and soaring "world." In his unforgettable essay "The Origin of the Work of Art," Heidegger explains that the relationship between earth and world is not an insipid and vacant coming together of opposites, nor is it a destructive relation of any sort. Rather, there is an intimacy with which the two belong to each other: "The world grounds itself on the earth, and earth juts through world."[37] In his creation of the Khalsa, the tenth guru discloses and preserves the historical grounding and founding of the first Sikh guru. In his artistic projection, Guru Gobind Singh draws the liminality of Guru Nanak from under the waters and sets it openly and firmly upon the ground. Baisakhi 1699 is a wonderful work of art that brilliantly illuminates Heidegger's aesthetic principle: "Art is history in the essential sense that it grounds history."[38]

When Guru Gobind Singh ushered his Five Beloved back into the Baisakhi congregation, the first object he asked for was water from the river flowing by. Water thus forms the starting point of the Khalsa initiation. We are struck by the formal simplicity of Guru Gobind Singh's *sacra*. His simple request takes us through the waters of memory to Nanak's experience two hundred years earlier. The *sacra* become an expression of the tenth guru's desire to capture the fluidity of time for his community. What had been creatively flowing needed to be held together and formulated into an everlasting ritual. He had to safeguard the event from generation to generation. The water put in an iron bowl and held in the guru's hands revokes chronological time and recovers mythic time. Its placental nutrients form the intrinsic self, the very ground of the Khalsa's being.

The quintessential sacred action of the liminal stage is the drinking of *amrit*. Guru Nanak received the bowl full of nectar and heard the command: "Nanak! This *amrit* is the cup of Name-adoration. You drink it. Then Guru Nanak paid his respects, drank the cup. . . ." During Baisakhi 1699, Guru Gobind Singh actively prepares the *amrit* that Guru Nanak directly received from the Divine: after getting the water from the river, he stirred it with his double-edged sword while reciting sacred poetry. Mata Jitoji added sugarpuffs to the mixture.

The recipe for Guru Gobind Singh's *amrit* is in fact provided by Guru Nanak. In our mythic account, Guru Nanak does not witness the preparation of *amrit*, but is aware of its contents. The final stanza of the *Jap*—which the *Puratan Janamsakhi* explicitly states he recited in full in the Bein—specifies the ingredients and the procedure for the ambrosial compound. During Baisakhi 1699, Guru Gobind Singh reconstitutes the very fusion of physio-chemical and spirito-psychological elements that were proposed by the first guru:

> Let smithy be the continence, patience the goldsmith;
> Let anvil be wisdom, knowledge the hammer;
> Let bellows be divine fear and fire be inner control and heat;
> In the crucible of divine love, let the ambrosial gold flow,
> In this true mint forge the transcendent word.
>
> (Jap, stanza 38)

The tenth guru does not make strict use of the smithy setting that the first guru used to underscore the importance of Divine Love. Perhaps by restricting himself to the fires of a smithy, Guru Gobind Singh would only have confused his people and misled them into thinking about the ascetic heat, and he would have reinforced current rituals and practices that restrained the natural flow of senses, emotions, and thoughts. Eliade discusses how in both Hinduism and Buddhism, and especially in their schools of tantrism, heat and fire represent magico-religious power. He provides several important examples: Prajapati generates the world by heating himself up to an extreme degree of asceticism, Buddha burns with heat because he practices asceticism, Kundalini arouses an intense heat in the yogi, and tantric texts transmute sexual energy into magical heat. As he says, "all over the world shamans and sorcerers are reputedly masters of fire, and swallow burning embers, handle red-hot iron and walk over fire."[39] Rather than ascetic heat, or fiery magic, or a transmutation of the sexual energies, the cool waters of the river, essential to life and living, dominate Guru Gobind Singh's configuration.

And yet, by his innovation, Guru Nanak's metaphor of the goldsmith seated in his smithy with his anvil and bellows and hammers forging *amrit*, the immortal gold, is made into a reality by Guru Gobind Singh. In front of the Baisakhi gathering he performs a metallurgical and chemical operation: he stirs the iron bowl of water with his double-edged sword and recites sacred verse while Mata Jitoji adds sugarpuffs to his mixture. Just as the ambrosial gold flows in the goldsmith's crucible, so the ambrosial Nam flows into the guru's iron bowl. The receptacle in both instances is made of Divine Love, but the metaphorical container of the goldsmith is concretely held in Guru Gobind Singh's hands. The metaphorical motion (*phora*) across (*meta*) the metallic toward the spiritual, which Guru Nanak introduced, is practically accomplished by his tenth successor. The first guru's words contained in the myth are transformed into deed.

The guru then offers *amrit* to his five initiates. Anthropologists and sociologists have repeatedly remarked that commensality leads to the formation of *societas*: "Of all human behaviors, there is none more conducive to the integration of society than the ritual sharing of food."[40] Guru Gobind Singh extended Guru Nanak's individual drinking of *amrit* to all of his five initiates. The tenth guru's act signifies that Nanak's initiation was not just reserved for a chosen one but was meant to be a wide opening for his entire society. The spirit of unity and mutual belonging underlies the communal sipping. The five initiates came from different castes and professions, but by drinking the *amrit* together all societal conditioning and divisions were eradicated; together, they were bound in the new family of the Khalsa. While the elixir tied them together through bonds of sentiment and obligation, it also gave the members a new life, a new birth into freedom and authenticity. They did not take any vows or oaths; theirs was a purely somatic experience.

What Guru Nanak experienced by drinking the ambrosial cup transformed him forever. This sacred historical account was exemplary for the tenth Sikh guru, who wanted a similarly radical transformation for his community. Eliade's theory about mythology that "not only does it relate how things came to be; it also lays the foundations for all human behavior and all social and cultural institutions" comes true.[41] The tenth guru's aim for his Khalsa was to taste what the first Sikh guru had tasted. In the River Bein, Nanak did not see the Divine in any form, male or female, god or goddess: the cup of *amrit* constituted the medium of his revelation. The *Janamsakhi* describes him drinking the ambrosial cup and rejoicing. How could Guru Gobind Singh's initiates resee Guru Nanak's revelation? How could they reexperience the joy of Nanak's vision? Like Guru Nanak's own experience in the Bein, which I termed "aestheticontological" in an earlier work,[42] the Khalsa initiation is intrinsically a rejoicing in Divine Beauty and wonder. Drinking the ambrosia signifies the sapiential quality of the Divine. By drinking *amrit*, senses are heightened, and the infinity of the One is recognized. The utterly simple yet most viable and enlivening encounter of Guru Nanak with the Transcendent is reaffirmed in the Khalsa rite.

Guru Gobind Singh's *amrit* initiation reinforces the feminist emphasis on the union of mind and body. This central Sikh rite restores the coexistence of sensuous knowledge, which involves hearing the word, holding the *amrit*, and drinking it, and Absolute Truth, which is insight into the Infinite One. Likewise, feminist aspirations find fruition in the element of delight that comes with the drink. Nanak is absolutely delighted to receive the cup of *amrit* in the waters of the Bein; the ecstatic poetry that he bursts into is a testament to this. So are the Five Beloved when they are given the *amrit* by their guru and exclaim *waheguru*. We may recall that Guru Gobind Singh is also delighted to receive the *amrit* from his Khalsa. His joy is so expansive that he embraces the entire Baisakhi congregation! For the first and the final Sikh guru, *amrit* is an entry into the realm of pleasure and *jouissance*, for in each sip come together the joy of the Transcendent One and the joy of humanity.

Reincorporation

After their radically new liminal experience, the protagonists in both our mythic and ritual discourse return to society: the former as the Guru; the latter as the Khalsa. In their new status and role, they had gained a new awareness of their self, and were constructed in a profound way. Unlike other initiation rites there are no additions to or subtractions from the body: tattoos, circumcision, or scarring did not mark the transition of either Guru Nanak or the Khalsa. In each case, their new identity was marked by the unity of *bana* (outfit made of sacred material) and *bani* (poetry consisting of sacred verse), body and mind, exterior and interior, *sirpao* (dress) and *nam* (word).

As they reincorporate into society, "antistructure" became the mode of existence for both Guru Nanak and the Khalsa. The first Sikh community that developed with Guru Nanak at Kartarpur fits in with Turner's description of "antistructure," because the neat horizontal divisions and vertical hierarchies of society were broken down. Three important institutions of Sikhism—*seva* (voluntary service), *langar* (community meal), and *sangat* (congregation)—evolved in which men and women formerly from different castes and religions took equal part. Together they listened to and recited the sacred hymns, together they cooked and ate *langar*, together they formed a democratic congregation without priests or ordained ministers.

These institutions were intended to open up a window of opportunity for all women, irrespective of their caste, class, or marital status—married and single, widows and wives, were equally validated. Women were no longer confined to homes, but could now freely participate in *sangat* wherever it met. There were no more rules for them to eat apart or after their men: in *langar* they could sit along with men, cook and serve with men, and eat with them. No longer were menstruation or childbirth stigmatized as pollution; they were regarded as essential natural processes. No longer were women rejected as temptresses to be left behind (as Buddhist monks or Hindu celibates might do); they were celebrated as vital partners in spiritual growth. The Hindu ideal of *pati yoga*—in which the yogic discipline of restraint, purification, concentration on a single point, equanimity, and desirelessness is exercised by the woman for her husband (*pati*) and his family—was discarded: the sacred word opening her to the Transcendent became the sole focus of her life. These institutions established in the first Sikh community at Kartarpur were a practical and existential consequence of Guru Nanak's mystical experience recounted in our *Janamsakhi*.

But since they lived within the parameters of an overwhelmingly patriarchal society of northern India, things did not change much for Sikh women. Conditioned for centuries to accept their physical, spiritual, and emotional confinement and inferiority, they were unable to utilize the antistructures introduced by the Sikh guru. Undoubtedly there would also have been androcentric and misogynist predecessors of men like Chaupa Singh who would have twisted Guru Nanak's antistructures back to the old norms. As we found, even half a century after Guru Gobind Singh, Chaupa Singh insisted that a Sikh woman's religious duty was "to know her husband as god," and she was to keep fasts for the sake of her husband—changing Guru Nanak's egalitarian new patterns back to the ancient norms that harshly discriminated against women.

I would imagine that with the establishment of the Mughal empire life became even more oppressive for Sikh women. They were now caught between two patriarchal systems instead of one. To the long list of ancient Hindu codes of woman's duties were now added the Islamic values of honor and chastity coming from societies beyond the Indian peninsula. As Riffat Hassan notes, "Since women's sexuality is so vitally related to men's honor and self-image in Muslim culture, it becomes vitally important in Muslim societies to subject women's bodies to external social controls."[43] Many forms of oppressive control (including segregation of the sexes, veiling, and confining women to the innermost quarters of the home) penetrated the evolving Sikh community. Women did not become equal partners in the liberating new institutions set up by Guru Nanak.

Almost two centuries later, Guru Gobind Singh's *amrit* initiation dramatically staged the antistructures introduced by Nanak. *Seva* (voluntary service) is epitomized in scenes of the Five Beloved offering their lives one by one to their guru. *Langar* (community meal) is quintessentially represented in people from different castes sipping *amrit* from the same bowl. *Sangat* (congregation) is best pictured when the guru embraces the entire Baisakhi gathering, upper and lower castes, men and women, as his beloved Khalsa. Guru Gobind Singh's new rite of passage shattered traditional social and religious structures by which people were divided and stratified, and brought forth the family of the Khalsa in which all of them were to have the same last name, the same parents, the same birthplace, and even the same physical format—*kesha, kangha, kirpan, kara*, and *kacha*.

Guru Gobind Singh marked the internal transformation of his newly constructed subject with the five *Ks* which are patterned on the *sirpao* that the first guru received in the River Bein. For me it is absolutely essential that Guru Nanak's *sirpao* is the paradigm for the code of dress that the Khalsa wears. The *sirpao* was the symbol of divine honor bestowed on Guru Nanak—"sirpao baba dargaho milia" (Nanak received the fabric from the divine court), and the five *Ks* are also a symbol of honor and respect for both men and women. Guru Nanak received the *sirpao* after he passed his test; the Five Beloved received the five *Ks* after they passed their severe examination. Corresponding to the open and expansive *sirpao* that Nanak received from the Transcendent One, the five *Ks* are to be worn by people from all classes, castes, and ages. Indeed, they are external signs that each member of the Khalsa wears as a mark of self-respect and respect for one another. They carry on and illuminate the legacy of the divine gift that the first Sikh guru received in the Bein.

Sadly, history has emphasized their masculine and militaristic definitions. The stereotyped "tough guise" image of the tenth guru is carried over into his five symbols, with the result that a crusader or jihad mentality governs their understanding. That their design is based on Guru Nanak's *sirpao* goes unnoted, unseen. Carried away by their particularity, Sikhs neglect the affinity that the five *Ks* have with the open and universal dress of honor received by Nanak. The *sirpao* is a material with the potential to be stitched and tailored into many creative patterns and forms. The only exception is that it cannot be designed into any exclusionary or ostracizing shape (like that of *janaeu*—the sacred thread exclusively for upper-class Hindu males—which Guru Nanak loudly denounced). The Sikh community has yet to recognize the primal pattern of Guru Nanak's *sirpao* in the five *Ks*. How do they endorse self-respect and dignity for *both* men and women? How do they impart value to the individual? How do they articulate the body as resource for and object of significance and power? How can they be worn other than as patriarchal symbols?

The outer mode is linked with the interior. In his new role Guru Nanak was commanded "to go and recite the Divine Name and teach others to recite it as well." Sacred poetry was the medium and object of Guru Nanak's mission that the tenth guru inherited and fully absorbed. His own hymn called Jaap is born from the Jap Nanak uttered during his initiation in the Bein. Guru Gobind Singh's Khalsa is required to recite it and live in accordance with the verses of the Sikh gurus. In fact, *amrit* is prepared and drunk in the sight and sound of their sacred poetry. Through the Divine Name the Khalsa is born, through the Divine Name the Khalsa is nurtured. It is not simply that the body must be dressed in the five *Ks* *(bana)* and the mind must think about the hymns *(bani)*; Guru Gobind Singh brought about a real fusion of the external self with the internal into his formulation of Sikh identity.

Very much like the *sirpao*, the Divine Name is open and inclusive. It is not confined to any structure or format but directs the individual to the Transcendent in a kaleidoscope of concrete images and multivalent symbols. That One is both male and female, father and mother. In the five hymns of the Khalsa, love and heroism are appropriated as the emotions that expand the self and stimulate intimacy with that infinite One. Sikh Gurus do not opt for either-or: the "peace-loving" Nanak does not choose love and the "warrior guru" does not choose heroism. Both love and heroism are essential to enter a life of freedom and to experience the Transcendent in and through the human body, as we will explore in our final chapter.

Fused with his own sociohistorical horizon, Guru Gobind Singh's interpretation and transcreation of the *Puratan Janamsakhi* discourse has the energy to produce more new and powerful phenomena. Eliade's theoretical views make a lot of sense: "Though the myths, by presenting themselves as sacrosanct models, would seem to paralyze human initiative, actually they stimulate man to create, they are constantly opening new perspectives to his inventiveness."[44] The primal myth so inspired Guru Gobind Singh that he created his own "dramatic breakthrough"; in turn, it can stimulate and empower generations of Sikhs into entering exciting new horizons. The origins of their faith and the energetic actions of their heroic past are crystallized in the alchemical *amrit*. Whatever part of the world Sikhs may be in, the *amrit* brimming in the cup held in Nanak's hand, or in the bowl in Guru Gobind Singh's hand, brings meaning to their lives, linking their personal experience to that of their ten gurus. "Meaning arises when we try to put what culture and language have crystallized from the past together with what we feel, wish, and think about our present point in life."[45] Most of the time, rites of passage underscore the biological and physical makeup of the person and demarcate gender roles that the initiates are to follow for the rest of their lives. Guru Nanak's aspiration to deconstruct such exclusionary rites, and to reconstruct an emotional and spiritual rite of passage, is accomplished in Guru Gobind Singh's *amrit* initiation.

But the real transformative power of his rite of passage has yet to be fully reclaimed. As June O'Connor says, "[O]versight as well as insight marks human knowing," and in our instance, the horizon that the historical Baisakhi could have opened for women remains overlooked.[46] It is important that we remember the *amrit* made on Baisakhi 1699 flows from the maternal waters of the Bein. The moral vision of Guru Nanak was formed by his relationship with his mother, sister, wife, and midwife, and of course with other members of his family and society; this vision grows organically, continuing existing currents that are poured into the bowl of *amrit* given to the Five Beloved. Mary Midgley has correctly said that "Moral insights are not explosions, interrupting all previous thought. . . . However startling they may be, they always arise from a community, and they always aspire to go on and influence a community."[47] Indeed, Guru Gobind Singh's rite is a passage to the wellsprings of history, conjoining the first and final moments of Sikhism. As each sip goes into the bloodstream, the individual is connected with the Sikh community, with fellow humans, and with the cosmos at large. The *amrit* is not divisive; it is not a circumscribed mode of existence. Rather, it is a living out of the infinity that the first guru experienced and that the tenth retained and re-created. To return to the words of a modern feminist ecologist and a verse of a Sikh Guru:

> Before it is drinking water, amniotic fluid is the creeks and rivers that fill reservoirs. It is the underground water that fills wells. And before it is creeks and rivers and groundwater, amniotic fluid is rain. . . .
>
> Sandra Steingraber

> There is only one *amrit*; there is no other *amrit*. . . .
>
> (GG, 1238)

When we remember Guru Gobind Singh's action we must remember that he himself remembers the first guru, and we too must keep alive their shared experience of transformation and liberation.

Chapter Four

The Five Ks and the Accoutrement of the Khalsa

> [E]ven traditional symbols can have revolutionary consequences. For, symbols can invert as well as reinforce social values . . . , if traditional rituals can evolve to meet the needs of new participants . . . , then old symbols can acquire new meanings, and these new meanings might suggest a new society.
>
> —Caroline Bynum, in *Gender and Religion*

The internal transformation of the Sikh rite of passage is marked by five external *sacra*, all beginning with the letter *k*: *kesha* (long hair), *kangha* (comb), *kirpan* (sword), *kara* (bracelet), and *kacha* (underwear). Sikhs firmly believe that during Baiskahi 1699 Guru Gobind Singh introduced a new physical identity for his community, and no matter what part of the globe they may migrate to, Sikh men and women proudly continue to maintain their five *Ks*. Just as Sikh men can be easily distinguished by their topknots and turbans, so Sikh women can be distinguished by their distinctive braids and coiffures, and their long sheer scarves (*dupattas*). The five *Ks* are the *bana*, the "dress" of all Sikhs. Whether they were fully established by Guru Gobind Singh or finally codified by later Sikh reformers, they have definitely become as McLeod says the "immutable code" of the Sikhs.[1] Their widespread usage and significance is recapitulated by another distinguished Sikh historian Dr. Ganda Singh.[2] His research spans three centuries and incorporates various genres, including Guru Gobind Singh's commandments recorded in his *Hukamnamas*, later Sikh sources such as the *Gurbilas* and *Rahitnamas*, British testimonies, and the discourse of twentieth-century Sikh theologians. Providing us with important historical evidence, Dr. Ganda Singh effectively conveys that on Baisakhi 1699, Guru Gobind Singh asked all Sikhs to adopt a special dress code that would make them immediately recognizable. The five *Ks* thus instantly identify the wearer as a Sikh, but they also move the wearer to participate in a deeper universal reality. They are signs and they are symbols.

The five *Ks* are therefore a way of cultivating the self. Michel Foucault defines such cultivation as the art of existence: "It is this principle of the care of the self that establishes its necessity, presides over its development, and organizes its practice."[3] According to Foucault, the activity devoted to the self "constituted, not an exercise in solitude, but a true social practice."[4] Foucault has discovered that "the cultivation of the self" is a major force in Western philosophical systems, and his exploration takes us into the moral reflections of Plutarch, Epictetus, Marcus Aurelius, and Seneca. This cultivation of the self is the goal of Guru Gobind Singh. The five *Ks* of the Khalsa format are basic to the construction of the individual subject: they serve as a means of defining one's physical and psychological identity. The five *Ks* constitute a social practice, and are a means of intensifying social relations. They are concerned with forming an ethical citizen situated within an active social, political, and religious world. Thus, the cultivation of the self is practiced within a vibrant social context. The five *Ks* become public symbols with a variety of socially significant meanings. They give rise to relationships between individuals, and thereby promote the crystallization of the Sikh community.

In spite of their importance and their uniqueness, they have not caught the attention of scholars outside the field of Sikh studies. The five *Ks* have been ignored in the phenomenological and theoretical discussions of Mircea Eliade and Paul Ricoeur, and by scholars in the field of religion in general. They have not held much attraction for cultural anthropologists, either. Refreshing exceptions are Patrick Olivelle and Bernard Cohn, who have shown an interest in Sikh identity. In his study of the social significance of hair in South Asian traditions, Olivelle considers the meaning of *kesha* in relation to the shaven head of male Hindu ascetics.[5] Bernard Cohn's chapter "Cloth, Clothes, and Colonialism: India in the Nineteenth Century" examines Sikh turbans and how they get wrapped up with the British in India.[6] We hope others will follow suit and pay more attention to the Sikh symbols. Future studies will, of course, have to include the female side: the turban is primarily a male item of clothing, and the symbol of *kesha* must not be limited to the long hair and beard of Sikh males.

Olivelle and Cohn are simply following the trend of Sikh scholars, who have approached the five *Ks* entirely in male terms. From the traditional codifiers of the ethical manuals to contemporary theoreticians, Sikh scholarship has erected them as markers of male Sikh identity that show Sikh men off and apart from men of other faiths. When they are implemented merely as antitheses of Hindu and Muslim prescriptions, the five *Ks* end up importing the patriarchal hegemonies of these neighboring faiths into the Sikh way of life. If Sikh *kesha* is an inversion of Hindu *mundan* (the shaving of heads for boys), or the *kacha* is an abandonment of the Brahmin's dhoti (worn by Hindu priests), or an antithesis to Muslim circumcision, the symbol of male hierarchy changes but that hierarchy itself still survives in all its potency. Such inversions or substitutions are divisive by nature, and they do not encompass the new identity encoded in the five *Ks*.

Indeed, Sikh identity has been blatantly monopolized by the male gender, for it is the Sikh man, with beard and turban, who is "positioned on book covers, as frontispieces, and within texts—to stand in for all Sikhs," as Brian Axel remarks. The same Western scholar continues, "Within a peculiar, yet seemingly quite banal, logic of signification, 'Sikh' and 'Sikhs' have come to signify Sikh men. . . ."[7] Axel's observations are accurate. The braids of Sikh women and their *dupattas* have not received any attention. No matter what discipline or lens the *Ks* are examined from, male scholars such as J. B. Singh Uberoi (sociology), Kapur Singh (cultural history), Sahib Singh, Teja Singh, and G. S, Mansukhani (theology) and Ravi Batra (military history) have entrenched Sikh interpretation in male experience. As a Sikh woman, I have to admit that I am most disappointed by the contemplative expositions of Puran Singh, "the Walt Whitman of the Sikhs."[8] Growing up in the Punjab as a teenager I was so taken by his poetic muse and his cross-religious interests that I did not notice consciously that his interpretation of the guru's *Ks* was such a blatant construction of "brotherhood," "fraternity," and "knighthood." But the effect of what I now realize was its strident machismo must have done a lot of damage to me and my Sikh sisters, who wore braids and *dupattas*. A wistful Puran Singh writes, "Each Sikh wears the hair and beard of Guru Gobind Singh. We are moulded in His own image. We.... the brothers of the Tress-Knot of Guru Gobind Singh."[9] The "we" is, of course, exclusive of the sisters, who don't have beards and wear braids instead of topknots. It is taken for granted that Sikh heritage belongs to men alone. As we have said, the Sikh tradition originates in the Bein—in a woman's braid,[10] not a man's topknot. But this is utterly forgotten. The wonderful force of female currents remains lost to the community.

Some other writers flaunt the supposed masculinity of the five *Ks* even more openly. In *Handbook on Sikhism*, S. S. Johar goes into great detail to prove the "manliness and virility" of the five *Ks*. He has an interesting collection of male paradigms from East and West that substantiate their masculinity. In his cross-cultural exposition, Samson's long hair and that of nameless Indian ascetics gets curled up in the Sikh *kesha*. He eulogizes long hair as a sign of masculinity: "Being nature's gift preservation of Keshas gives their wearer a look of sagacity, scholarship, bravery and manliness. With Keshas man looks like a lion and thunders like him. The custom of keeping long and unshorn hair is, therefore, among the most cherished and distinctive signs of an individual's membership of Khalsa brotherhood . . . a symbol of manliness, virility, honor, and power. . . . In the end, we conclude that Keshas are a symbol of masculinity and strength."[11]

Johar's androcentric thesis is carried on by Ravi Batra, who claims that the five *Ks* are a typical military outfit designed to bring about a "war-like" transformation in the entire personality of the wearer. Batra's emphasis on the militant puissance of the five items is perfectly natural, since he is, after all, a colonel in the Indian army. Surprisingly, however, his views are shared by all sorts of Sikhs. Batra's work has been published by the governing Sikh executive body, the SGPC. It teaches Sikhs in contemporary times that the five *Ks* are designed as a "military uniform" for men: "Each individual was characterized by the possession of Kacha, Kara, Kirpan, Kesh and Kangha at all times. Basically, it was to remind him that without these he was incomplete and to bring war-like change in his entire attitude and personality. Also, it was the most impressive means to provide the cheapest uniform to his Khalsa army. With the apparent symbols, the Khalsa could not hide his identity and thereby had no chance of survival if he managed to evade the enemy in the battlefield."[12] The image of Guru Gobind Singh's character embedded in the minds of the Sikh community is mirrored in their understanding of his five *Ks*. They remember their guru in hypermasculine images, and that is how they see his legacy. Even a great liberal historian like Khushwant Singh emphasizes the maleness of the Sikh symbols: "Within a few months, a new people were born—bearded, beturbanned, fully armed, and with a crusader's zeal to build a new commonwealth."[13] Half the Sikh people, the half that are not turbaned or bearded—are simply forgotten!

Ironically, even contemporary Western women writers echo these conventional Sikh interpretations, and continue to reinforce men's experiences as normative. In *Religion and the Body*, Eleanor Nesbitt reads the five *Ks* as employing a male grammar that demarcates the Sikhs from Hindus and Muslims.[14] Malestream views of Sikh scholars are carried over to those outside of the tradition, and the five *Ks* of the Sikh faith are being studied and perpetuated solely in male terms. How they emerge from our deeply human dimension, how they connect male and female, or Sikh, Hindu, and Muslim, how they fashion Sikh metaphysics, how they may speak directly to a woman—these vital reservoirs remain untapped.

As symbols, the five *Ks* fulfill the classic religious functions outlined by Eliade. Each of them is "multivalent," "paradoxical," "sacred"; each reveals "an inner pattern," "a perspective in which diverse realities can be fitted together," and "translates a human situation into cosmological terms."[15] No categorization can embrace all the semantic possibilities, as Ricoeur would say, and they are, to use Turner's qualification, polysemic. And yet, when we do look at the five *Ks* closely, we find that their multiple qualities and semantic richness have been reduced and contracted; they have ended up becoming mere signs of male dominance. The unifying force at the heart of Guru Gobind Singh's symbols has been broken and diverted into sharp and narrow dichotomies, their liberating and buoyant power calcified into heavy weights and burdens.

Instead of symbols of self-respect and mutuality, as Guru Gobind Singh intended them to be, the five *Ks* operate as tools of male domination, with women excluded as the "other." They have, in effect, codified a division between male and female roles based on a stereotypical identification of gender characteristics. The five *Ks* have come to dictate who is to soldier and who is to submit, who is to demand and who is to give, who feels superior and who feels inferior, who expresses anger and who suffers in silence, who inherits the father's land or business and who is left out, who is a credit and who is a debit, and ultimately who is rejoiced over in birth and who is aborted. The macho interpretations of the five *Ks* uphold macho moods and motivations and make the man who wears them expect to be strong, virile, and aggressive. These traits determine his overall behavior, which he carries over from the "battlefield"—the public world of work, politics, and power—and they especially determine his relations with women, whom he has to protect in the private world of the home. The five *Ks* make men the upholders of the code of honor for their families. While men courageously guard the sexuality of their wives, daughters, sisters, and nieces, women have to submit to and depend upon and assist their men with all their physical and spiritual might.

The double standards of strength and courage in Sikh life come into play from the moment of birth and are reinforced throughout life. Girls are indoctrinated with their duty to staunchly guard their virginity; women, to be deeply committed wives and to honor their husbands; daughters-in-law, to serve their husband's families energetically and steadfastly; mothers, to be devoted in bearing and rearing children; and widows, to remember their heroic husbands faithfully till the day they die. The woman wears the same five symbols of strength that he does, but in her case they work against her; the very symbols that empower him nullify her through silence, invisibility, and oppression, and sometimes even lead to her murder or suicide.

The range and subtlety of the male interpretations are bewildering. I was born in a household in which a daughter's birth was actually celebrated—my mother and grandmother told me over and over again how thrilled my brother was to have a baby sister and how he joyously distributed sweets (a glaring anomaly in that part of the world). I came to the West on my own to attend a girls' preparatory school, and I have lived in the West since I was a teenager. I went to an all-women's college. I have taught courses on feminism at a liberal arts college in New England. And yet, it is only now that it has occurred to me that the Sikh symbols I wear could belong to the female realm! My intellectual training and cultural codes had trained me so well in the male and militant meaning of the five *Ks* that I could not even imagine that long hair, combs, bracelets, underwear, or swords could be viewed from a female perspective. The thought of their being female never crossed my mind!

But what sounds so radical is in fact the most natural. Indeed, what could be more commonsensical than the idea that long hair, comb, bracelet, underwear, and even the grammatically feminine *kirpan* (sword) have a female identity? If symbols that are intrinsically paradoxical and multivalent can be masculine, why can't they be feminine as well? While Sikhs were resisting political oppression, it may have made sense for some men to view them as part of their army uniform. But to divest them of their human significance, and invest them completely with "militancy," "virility," "soldierly hygiene," and divisive sentiments for all Sikhs for all times is a grave distortion. Sikhism is not a military resistance movement. It is a religion. It is a faith grounded in a love and a heroism that are rooted in the experience of the Divine One. The *Mulmantra,* prologue to Sikh scripture, characterizes the Infinite as *nir vair*—"without enmity." The world was not a battlefield or a war zone for Guru Gobind Singh. He certainly carried his weapons and fought his battles at certain times and in certain places, but the world was full of the Divine that he so loved and enjoyed. In his person flowed the harmonious life-current of the universal reality that was "codified" in the five *Ks.* To think of them as combative instruments goes against the spirit of Guru Gobind Singh.

Thinking is a fluid and expanding process, and we must expand our interpretation so as to retrieve the radical force of Guru Gobind Singh's five *Ks*. Carolyn Bynum's insight (this chapter's epigraph) is most valuable, because new meanings of these symbols can create a new society for us. We really need to think of ways in which the five *Ks* can help us reconstruct our human subjectivity rather than leave us weak, angry, or alienated. Military and male outfits do not tally with all lifestyles. They are partial and selective to the extent that they articulate male experience as human experience, and are projections of patriarchal tendencies and functions. Their sheer virile and military bearing keeps us from utilizing their real power in the day-to-day affairs of our lives. The monopoly of male analysis is detrimental not only for women who are severed from what they wear, but also for men who have to live up to those "tough-guise" expectations, and it is especially harmful to their relationships with one another. For our own mental and physical health, we need to balance our asymmetric interpretations. We remember the guru giving the five *Ks* on the dramatic stage of Baisakhi 1699 so that they would empower all his Sikhs for all times to come. He intended them to have revolutionary consequences for the wearer. It is in keeping with the guru's intentions that we tap into their female matrix and retrieve the new sensibility, the freedom from gender demarcations, and that heightened awareness of the Divine brought by his *Ks*. And this is how we rediscover the essence of Sikh identity.

As we slip into our feminist re-memories, we immediately discover that *kesha, kangha, kirpan, kara*, and *kacha* ontologically blur with the female accoutrements enshrined in the Guru Granth. The male gurus and poets of the Sikh sacred text identify with women, and express their search for the Divine in female tones and in the women's mode of dressing up. The five *Ks* suffused with spiritual significance flow freely in their rhythmic verses. Their meaning is restored by the relationship between the paradigmatic female and the Divine. "Meaning," says the psychoanalyst Nancy Chodorow, "is an inextricable mixture of the sociocultural and historically contextualized on the one hand and the personally psychodynamic psychobiographically contextualized on the other."[16] The everyday articles from his culture—something so simple and common as a comb, a bracelet, long hair, underwear, a sword—had great personal meaning for Guru Gobind Singh, because they were laden with spirituality in a text that constituted his psychodynamic and psychobiographical being. The tenth Sikh guru grew up on the sacred utterances of his predecessors, which formed the core of his daily routine. That he would endow their words with guruship in the final hour of his life manifests the profound motivational significance they had for him. In my re-memory, the metaphysical ideals cherished in his sacred text coincide with the simple items in his sociocultural environment, and their "coincidence" leads to Guru Gobind Singh's construction of the five *Ks*. That is why we find a perfect valence between *bana* and *bani*, between what Sikhs wear and what they recite. Outward objects, they take us into our deepest interior.

But as they send us gliding into sacred scripture, the five *Ks* connect us across cultures. Guru Gobind Singh had to be a great artist to create unique and distinct Sikh symbols, which yet are "set in the heart of the universal." Rabindranath Tagore's question for the artist, and his response to it, have relevance for the Sikh guru. "How does he do it? Not through the peculiarity which is the discord of the unique but through the personality which is harmony."[17] Guru Gobind Singh's *Ks* open us to a harmonious zone where we can befriend one another. Because they reveal the full range of our human response to our Divine One, these external representations construct the identity of the Sikhs. Guru Gobind Singh's five symbols are thus both representations and revelations, and function as ligaments that join us across religions and cultures, linking us with the Hindu Durga-Kali, with the Christian Mary, with the Shinto Amaterasu, and so on. Instead of pitting Hindu, Sikh, and Muslim against one another (Sikh *kesha* vs. Hindu *mundan*, Sikh *kacha* vs. Muslim circumcision, or Sikh *kacha* vs. Hindu dhoti), our feminist re-memory ushers us towards our common humanity, down the waters of the Bein to the *sirpao* that Nanak received. "Memory and recollection" may have been supervised and managed by male elites, but they are, as Fatima Mernissi brilliantly says, "the dawn of pleasure; they speak the language of freedom and self-development."[18]

k-kesha

The five *Ks* are equally important, and we could start our analysis with any one of them. Since hair or *kesha* is the most visible, we begin with it. But as soon as we take up the significance of hair in world religions, we are bombarded with phallic interpretations equating long hair with the male genitals. In the volume *Hair: Its Power and Meaning in Asian Cultures,* Alf Hiltebeitel concludes his fascinating chapter on the hair symbolism of the Alis, the Tamil-speaking eunuchs: "Flowers like snakes, hair like flowers, snakes like hair: all like penises: they are what Alis have had to offer."[19] In discussing Western religious practices, Charles Berg uses psychoanalytic theory to prove the identity of hair with the phallus. For Berg, tonsure, the shaving of heads by monks, and other such public rituals of cutting hair, unconsciously represent castration. Even the daily shave and daily hair brushings are an expression of castration anxiety. Berg claims that the average person "dealing with hair so remote as that of his face and head . . . is unconsciously dealing with a phallic substitute."[20]

Berg may be a blatant case of a man who ignores the fact that women have hair, too. But the overall unconscious male primacy and premises, and the male identifications that we encounter in his study, permeate even contemporary Sikh notions about hair. A Sikh writer, Dalip Singh, for instance, calls the trimming and cutting of hair "chronic castration suicide."[21] In his study of the Khalsa, he extensively argues that the cutting of hair leads to the loss of man's potential and sexual virility.

Hair is becoming an important subject of research, and specialists are studying it as a key semiotic device to understand the way people think and behave in different societies. Cultural norms influence the length of hair, the style it is groomed in, whether it is bound or unbound, and the techniques of decorating it. But in these various studies, there is barely any mention of the Sikh tradition in which long hair is a crucial religious tenet. Even the substantial volume on the topic of hair in Asia does not devote any chapter to this essential *k* of the Sikhs. Patrick Olivelle is the only contributer in it who introduces a Sikh perspective, yet he too concentrates on the male Sikh and *his* symbol. Olivelle observes how the uncut hair of the Sikh male has become a "condensed symbol . . . that is a symbol so powerful that it encapsulates all the diverse aspects of the symbolized, which under normal circumstances would require separate symbolic expressions."[22]

Olivelle's analysis of Sikh male hair follows the structuralist approach of J. P. Singh Uberoi in which *kesha* is interpreted as an antithesis to Hindu initiations and institutions.[23] Olivelle extends the Hindu parameters to ancient India, and highlights how the *kesha*—uncut but groomed—signifies a simultaneous renunciation of society and immersion in it.[24] He persuasively brings out *kesha* as a marker of a full-fledged participation in society, and his recent reflections provide an interesting perspective on the theoretical inversion that Uberoi articulated decades ago: "The meaning of being unshorn, in particular, is thus constituted by the 'negation of the negation:' It signifies the permanent renunciation of renunciation."[25]

It is urgent that we move beyond such binary perspectives, which discount women both in theory and practice, and are bent on dividing Sikh from Hindu. In Indian culture, women have always had long hair. But somehow, the long hair of *sanyasis*, yogis, and *bairagis* dominates the scholarly imagination in its approach to *kesha*. Even Buddhism is dragged in. Kapur Singh, for instance, finds parallels between Sikh *kesha* and Buddha's *ushnisha* (topknot): "The iconographical representations of the Buddha, therefore, rightly show a tress-knot of uncut hair on his head, precisely like the one which the Singhs are enjoined to keep by Guru Gobind Singh."[26] But he soon gets lost in the similarities between the youthful and beardless faces of Buddha and Alexander, and their contrast with the mature and bearded faces of Sikh men—losing his female readership completely. Woman is not the concern of our thinkers. The anomaly of male long hair has drawn so much attention that it has obscured the essential feature of the long hair of women in everyday life, of Hindu goddesses, Buddhist *yakshis*, and Muslim houris, and it has obscured the memory of female mystics, heroines, queens, nautch girls, and attendants in the Hindu, Buddhist, Jain, and Muslim societies that formed Guru Gobind Singh's cultural horizon. The one-sided attention given to male long hair continues to eclipse our full understanding of Guru Gobind Singh's "condensed symbol" and stifles its meaning and value. How can a Sikh woman consider it as the guru's gift to her when she is barred from any meaningful relationship with it? How can she feel confidence in herself when she has been conditioned to believe that it is *his* long hair that really constitutes *kesha*?

So we move beyond the "inversion" theories, and re-member that in the religious, cultural, and artistic framework of Guru Gobind Singh's life, there is an "equation" between long hair and women. For me this equation plays out in three important areas: (1) Long hair expresses a female mode of spirituality in his sacred text; (2) long hair was the social norm for women in his milieu; (3) long hair is strikingly associated with a female protagonist in his poetry. These three areas show that in Guru Gobind Singh's consciousness long hair was essentially female. So when he chose *kesha* as an identifying symbol for his newborn Khalsa, he was choosing something that characterized women in his worldview. He obviously valued this female quality and "condensed" *her* multidimensional energy into his Khalsa symbol. If we recognize the female roots of *kesha*, we can thereby give it—and receive from it—its full human value.

Scriptural symbol. Over and over, the Guru Granth evokes the figure of the bride and her dressing up, which makes the Divine accessible to the human experience. Woman is "privileged" in Sikh scripture because she is the one who is psychologically and spiritually honed. Her various bodily adornments are imbued with great significance. Her hair is neatly braided (GG, 558), and *her* braids are held together by embroidered tassles *(dor)* (937). The long hair of women is an expression of the sanctification of the human personality in the Sikh holy writ. Clearly, it is *her* braids and not *his* topknots that are so highly valued in the Guru Granth. She is ever the *suhagan*, the "fortunate wife" who is never abandoned. Her hair is not shorn, for that was a cultural mark of the "unfortunate widows" (*duhagan*). As Olivelle observes, the shaving of a widow's head was the sign of her ritual pollution, of her inauspiciousness, and of her unmarriageable state.[27] The *suhagan* has her hair long, which signifies her proximity to and rapture with her Divine Lover. She embodies the central scriptural message that the relationship between the individual and the Divine is tightly braided.

In Guru Nanak's discourse on Babur's invasions, the shorn hair of women is a poignant synecdoche for the rape and victimization of innocent people. In a haunting scene, Guru Nanak describes the ripping apart of Hindustan through the brutal shearing of women's hair: "With luxuriant hair, and partings filled with crimson vermilion, they suffer now the shears of brutality"(GG, 417). His descriptions are graphic. We see the long healthy hair of young women brutally clipped. What a ferocious application of mechanical instruments against nature's gift! Nanak's compassion expressed in the sections of the Guru Granth called "Babur Vani" extends equally to all the female victims: Hindu or Muslim, upper or lower castes, Turks, Bhatts, or Thakurs.[28] The image of their clipped hair, which hit Guru Nanak at a visceral level, must have been absorbed by his tenth successor. What was violated had to be restored. Guru Gobind Singh reacts to the political repression in his own times by reconstructing tragic memories into triumphant hopes: his people ever more were to keep their hair long, untouched by any scissors. The physical identity of Sikh men and women that Guru Gobind Singh gave to them is a mark of strength and confidence against political repression and brutality. Rather than borrowing its significance from the uncut hair and beard of the forest hermit, the Sikh symbol has its prototype in the poignant poetry of the Guru Granth, where it is women who have long hair.

Long hair is not only a female feature; it is also a feature of the Transcendent One. Beyond space and time, the ultimate reality is imagined palpably in the Guru Granth: "You have alluring eyes, dazzling teeth, lovely nose, the One with long hair!"(GG, 567). That One is beautiful, and That One has long hair. The Divine frequently envisioned as *kesav* (long-haired) is extolled as "the worker of enchanting actions" (1082); "the long-haired gets rid of all conflict" (829). In another instance, the image of the long-haired One is set in between its formless characteristics:

> Needs no food, the long-haired, has no enmity!
> (GG, 98)

In their ardent attempt to feel the Transcendent, the gurus avail themselves of numerous attributes, and the image of long hair is definitely a part of their polyphonic imagination. However, Sikh exegetes rely on the conventional meaning and identify *kesav* as Vishnu, the popular Hindu deity.[29] In this way they not only limit and mold the infinity of the Divine, but they also confine it to a masculine figure. The Transcendent that is both male and female is torn in half. The male god Vishnu is not threatening for the Sikhs; they easily identify with *him*. In fact, they drag him into the text even when he is not explicitly mentioned by name. In *his* case, they raise an adjective ("long haired") into a reference to Vishnu. But if and when a female heroine is clearly named in a text, there is an entirely different response![30] Sikh scholars have no problem importing and sticking to traditional figures if their long hair happens to be male. The Guru Granth includes models from both genders; the *kesha* is a divine attribute of both male and female representations of beauty. And this fundamental unity conceived in his spiritual text shaped and enlivened Guru Gobind Singh's Khalsa symbol.

We also notice that *kesav* in the above verse goes with *nirvaira (nirhari kesav nirvaira)*. Evidently, the long-haired (*kesav)* is devoid of enmity (*nir*=without + *vair*=enmity). Denounced here are "weaponlike" notions of *kesha*, and actually, "the long-haired One gets rid of all conflict." Factions and divisions, hostility and belligerence, could not possibly be characteristics of the long-haired *One*. Enmity toward others poisons the arteries. It shrivels the self, stunts the natural growth of the body, and deprives the spirit of the joy of kinship and expansion. In light of the Guru Granth, *kesha* does not position us for war.

If anything, *kesha* is a vivid expression of the process of cultivating humility and overcoming the ego. It serves in Sikh scripture as an external symbol of a serene interior, an interior purified from the defilements of conflict, aggression, and arrogance. In a very imaginative way, Sikh gurus picture *kesha* as a whisk that fans their intense devotion. Guru Arjan says, "I dust the feet of the Enlightener with my hair" (GG, 387). "My only objective in life is to dust the feet with my hair as your slave" (500). In another verse the guru says, "I make a fan out of my hair to wave it over the saint" (745). For those of us raised in the pre-modern Punjab, fans conjure up images of soothing female hands. In the blistering hot months, it was the mothers, aunts, grandmothers, and older sisters who lovingly fanned their young ones to sleep. Beautifully embroidered fans were an important part of a Punjabi bride's dowry. Artistically, innovatively, Sikh Gurus draw upon the feminine image of the fan to show that even a male guru must turn his *kesha* into a woman's fan before he can use it to demonstrate his spiritual love. Certainly long hair for them does not characterize the Samsonian strength so idolized by our malestream exegetes!

Ultimately, "hair" is utilized as a passionate expression of the closeness with the Divine. The Guru Granth celebrates that One abiding in us—"In every pore lives the Divine!" (GG, 344). The metaphysical being is sensuously felt in every bit of our bodies. There is no body-spirit division, and the Divine flows out of the pores of our flesh—male and female alike. The varied connotations of *kesha* in the Sikh sacred text do not pump us up to fight an enemy with a "crusader's zeal." Rather, they lead us to spiritual enjoyment here and now. In our feminist memories of Guru Gobind Singh's *kesha*, the organic fibers constitute our crucial link with the Transcendent One. Their lasting effect is that we respect our long hair, and every pore of our bodies, but as a result we will inevitably have to respect the body of the *other*—male or female, black, yellow, brown, red, or white, Sikh, Hindu, or Muslim.

Social norm. If we were to look at Guru Gobind Singh's pan-Indian sociocultural horizon, long hair again is a key aspect of female beauty. Throughout India's visual and aural art, women have been depicted with long dark tresses. Widows are an exception, because they have to shave their head in mourning for their husbands. Hindu goddesses including Durga, Parvati, Sita, Laxmi, and Sarasvati are all portrayed with long hair. Interestingly, in the *Markandeya Purana* account of Durga's creation, her hair comes from Yama, the god of death. Durga is created from the combined energies of the male gods: while her face is from Shiva and her arms from Vishnu, her hair is from Yama (*Devi Mahatmya*, 2:13). It is a most logical progression, for hair is a part of the body that does not die! Created from the god of death, her hair serves as a matrix for the coexistence of life and death. These paradoxical forces are lodged in the luxuriant hair of Indian goddesses and heroines.

The pattern of long hair that Guru Gobind Singh adopted for his Khalsa seems to have been the norm only for women in his milieu. In ancient India, men sometimes had long hair, with different types of coiffures to distinguish their gender. In literary and iconographic sources from ancient India, male hair can be either short or long, whereas women in sculptures from Barhut, Sanchi, Amaravati, Nagarjunakonda, and Mathura, and in paintings from Ajanta, invariably wear their hair long.[31] By Guru Gobind Singh's time, it was customary for men from all religious traditions to have their hair cut and beards trimmed or shaved, but women—Hindu, Muslim, Sikh, Buddhist, or Jain—had their hair consistently long. The Sikh guru's configuration of the *kesha* symbol, the uncut, untrimmed hair, is clearly rooted in the style typical for women.

Valuable insights into the latent sexual and religious energies of female hair across cultures are coming out in recent scholarship. Gary Ebersole's illuminating study of hair symbolism in Japanese popular religion reveals the auspicious nature of female hair, and how it was used for offerings in temples and shrines, for amulets, and even for making ropes in sacred precincts. Through the ropes made out of female hair in temples and shrines, large beams could be lifted, but more than for its practical tensile strength, Ebersole writes, the "religious purpose was to contribute the life essence of these women to the good works of these religious institutions and to build good karma."[32] Japan may be geographically and linguistically quite far from India, but the efficacy of female hair elucidated by Ebersole carries beyond her islands. His essay brought back a host of memories from my own childhood in rural Punjab, where Hindu, Muslim and Sikh customs and beliefs fluidly crossed over between neighbors and religions.[33] I remember hearing about amulets of hair from pregnant women being worn by women who could not conceive. Just as in Japan, women in the Punjab regarded female hair as a repository of the powers of life and fertility. Through hair collected in an amulet, female potency could be carried and transferred from one woman to another. My own grandmother was very cautious about gathering each strand of our fallen hair. She would never let a single strand of hers or mine be caught by anyone else, lest our personal powers were usurped by an *other*. The similarities in practice between Japan and India at the popular level disclose the universal power of female hair.

But what I now recall is her feeling of fear and trembling. Somehow Granny did not have access to the empowering process of our fibers. Guru Gobind Singh's symbol of *kesha* that aspired to put each of us in touch with ourselves resulted in pulling my grandmother away from herself, away from her experiencing her true womanhood. What she did with her hair was more out of fear than out of rejoicing. Male Sikh voices fed her with convoluted reminders that Guru Gobind Singh wanted a Sikh woman to keep her hair long not because of its intrinsic female power, but because male ascetics in India had worn their hair long and this was the symbol of their holiness. So her long hair became a token of holiness demanded by men rather than an expression of herself. On the other hand, the very same voices told her that her long hair—unlike that of the Hindu ascetics—had to be combed and controlled so that she would behave as a proper female member of the Sikh social fabric. So her hair became a token of conformity rather than release of the energy of the *suhagan*, the ideal female enshrined in her own sacred scripture. It only carried the holiness of the Hindu male ascetics so removed from her religiously, culturally, and gender-wise. Such contrived notions only served as a pair of scissors that cut off her and her daughters and her granddaughters from the natural female potency of their hair, leaving them confused and fragmented, and even frightened to share their psychic world with other Sikhs lest they be denounced as "Hindu," or "Muslim," or simply "superstitious"—certainly *not* "Guru Gobind Singh's daughters." Only by opening up to the intrinsic human potency of hair that transcends Hindu and Muslim, Indian and Japanese, mythic and social, male and female, do we discern and experience the deeply personal transformative power and beneficence of wearing the *kesha* mandated by Guru Gobind Singh. At that point its power is not transferred to others; it is experienced by each individual for himself or herself. Thus we genuinely follow the unique models of the *suhagan*, the guru, and the Long-Haired One embodied in the Guru Granth.

Artistic embellishment. Long hair surfaces frequently as an artistic embellishment in Guru Gobind Singh's own poetry. He wanted to instill heroism in his dejected and listless society, and what symbol would function better than the potent female hair? With his fascination for the powerful goddess Durga-Kali, Guru Gobind Singh must have remembered the paradoxical and multivalent powers of *her* hair. Yama's gift of hair to Durga from the *Markandeya Purana* would not have gone unnoticed. That her long hair impinged on his artistic sensibilities shows up in his Punjabi and Braj compositions.

When he praises her triumphs in the *Akal Ustat*, for example, Guru Gobind Singh describes the goddess repeatedly as the one with the "beautiful knot of hair" (*rama kapardan*):

> Victory, victory shall be to the vanquisher of Mahikhasur
> With the beautiful knot of hair, you are the protector of earth 211
> Victory, victory to the vanquisher of Mahikhasur
> With the beautiful knot of hair, you are the primal power 212
> Victory, victory to the vanquisher of Mahikhasur
> With the beautiful knot of hair, you are the conqueror of demons. 213

In each verse, her beautifully arranged hair intertwines with her primal powers. K. Krishna Murthy explains *kapardan* as a type of coiffure, arranged in the form of a conch shell, that dates back to the Vedic period. In those days young women wore their hair in four *kapardas*, forming a crown-shaped coiffure, which was patterned on the four corners of the altar.[34] Guru Gobind Singh reaches far back into his Indian literary heritage, repeatedly describing Durga's *kapardan* hairstyle, and qualifying it as beautiful (*rama*). In her striking feminine form, his heroine is both the destroyer of demons and the protector of the earth.

In another verse from the Akal Ustat we get the image of the goddess with her hair open: "with eyes swifter than arrows, with hair speedier than a steed..." (line 221). In the guru's imagination her hair has such velocity that it surpasses the speed of horses. He also uses compelling analogies in *Candi Caritra* to describe her flowing hair: "Her face like the moon, she annuls all pain; her locks like Shiva's garlands, her radiance conquers all..."(CC I, verse 88). We can picture Durga-Kali's locks (*alikai*) hanging like the serpents that garland Shiva's neck. The image of black serpents surrounding a luminous moon creates a powerful artistic effect. But this analogy works out philosophically as well, for her hair—like the hissing and slithering black snakes—shares with them the qualities of shedding and renewing!

The energy of Durga's hair extends even to the lion she rides. In this instance, too, Guru Gobind Singh expresses his awe at the beauty of hair. The sharp Kantian distinction between the sublime and the beautiful disappears as he visualizes the mane of Durga's lion through a kaleidoscope of contrasting similes. Deadly weapons and life-giving nature combine to portray the force of the lion's hair: "The mane is like deadly arrows, growing like trees on a yellow mountain..." (*Candi Caritra* I, verse 26). In a second simile the lion's mane is compared with "a group of black wasps surrounding yellow jasmines" (CC 1, verse 26). Like its rider with her moonlike face, the lion has a delicate jasminelike face. The black wasps encircling the pretty yellow jasmine flowers evoke the energy, the fear, the poison, the grace, and the quick motion of the dark serpents around the luminous moon. A plurality of images and meanings are shared by hair in his compositions.

But not all hair has the same potency. In the following instance Guru Gobind Singh is talking about long hair in specifically male contexts.

> Their hair unbound, the demons lay unattended
> asleep like matted-hair ascetics intoxicated by hemp.
> (Var Durga Ki, verse 17)

Not only does he dismiss male hair rather hastily, he also expresses it negatively. For the guru the unbound hair of the demons in a story is no different from the matted hair of the ascetics. Neither holds his attention. Male hair belonging to the "good" and the "bad" remains equally listless and lusterless.

He rejects the long hair of the demons in the same vein as he rejects the long hair of the ascetics. Female hair, on the contrary, dominates his artistic canvas. As the repository of *her* élan vital, female energies are splendidly displayed in her hair by the Sikh guru. It is in those positive roots of *her* hair that we discern the origins of our symbol. The *kesha* of the Sikhs germinated in dignity and confidence, and carries positive qualities in each of its long strands. We must remember these positive associations and recognize them in the long hair of our daughters, sisters, mothers, and wives.

It is a pleasant surprise to find that a very keen understanding of *kesha* is shown by the acclaimed Dutch–Sri Lankan novelist Michael Ondaatje. Ondaatje's Sikh protagonist Kirpal Singh (in *The English Patient)* maintains the Khalsa format. We recover a strong female energy in his long hair. Ondaatje describes his unshorn hair many times in the novel: "He will sit up and flip his hair forward, and begin to rub the length of it with a towel."[35] With his hair open, the masculine body of the soldier becomes for Hana (his Canadian lover) an Indian goddess holding "wheat and ribbons." The "gnats of electricity" in Kip's hair are analogous to the lightbulbs attached to the wings of the angel in the damaged Church of San Giovanni. The peace, security, and vitality that come with the lighting up of the bulbs on the angel in the church parallel Hana's emotions as she lies besides Kip with his hair charged with electricity in his dark tent. Kirpal even puts his head back, spreading "his hair like grain in a fan-shaped straw basket" so that the sun can dry it. The fan-shaped image of his hair from Ondaatje's novel artistically encircles the verses we cited above from the Guru Granth. It brightly illuminates for us the symbolic grammar of *kesha*: a human cultivation that joins the male with the female, sexuality with sacrality. The Sikh community rightly honored Michael Ondaatje with the Seva Award for his superb gift of Kirpal Singh to our global society.[36]

The Guru Granth, the vast Indian mythological world, Guru Gobind Singh's own literary compositions, and the cosmic associations are all indicative of a strong female impulse behind the Sikh practice of wearing long hair. The female energy of *kesha* informed the guru's subjective consciousness, and his inner reality was also in congruence with the social norms for women in his period. Olivelle quite rightly says that "an individual is unable to produce an entirely new symbolic value of hair from his or her own subjective consciousness and still be able to communicate with the rest of that society."[37] The Khalsa was Guru Gobind Singh's new institution, and a meaningful communication with its members involved speaking in a language that they were familiar with. When he formulated *kesha* as a construction for his Khalsa, he appropriated the symbolic grammar that defined and identified hair in his society, and this symbolic system is entirely feminine. So the male *sanyasis*, male yogis, and male *bairagis* are tangential. The beautifully cultivated long hair was a female feature prevalent in Guru Gobind Singh's spiritual, cultural, and mythological world, and in our re-memory, the guru condenses *her* long hair, her uncut hair, her untrimmed hair, into a public symbol for the future of his Khalsa members, men and women. In words attributed to Guru Gobind Singh—"*eh asadi mohar hai*: [this is our seal],"[38]—the guru's seal bears the strong imprint of female patterns.

k-kangha

The second *k* also belongs typically to the female space. The *kangha* or comb is used to groom the hair, which is neither to be cut from its natural source in the human body, nor let loose and unkempt. Like the *sirpao* that Nanak received from the Divine, the hair is a divine gift, and combing is the technique for maintaining its dignity and beauty. Patriarchal interpretations encode *kesha* and *kangha* as a "unitary pair" of polar opposites. For Uberoi, their mutual association explains the full meaning of *kesha* as distinct from *jata*—the uncombed matted hair of the ascetics. Since it performs the function of constraining the hair and imparting an orderly arrangement to it, the *kangha* symbolizes the "orderly assumption" of social citizenship, while the uncombed *jata* (or the shaven head) symbolizes its renunciation.[39] Underlying Uberoi's thesis is the nature-culture dichotomy: although hair is natural, it must be controlled, ordered, and fashioned by the manufactured and "man-made" comb. Without the comb we are left with *jata*, the long unkempt hair, which is a symbol of the unruly phallus. Along the same lines, Olivelle concludes his thesis that the combing becomes the sign for an "*individual's participation in social structures within a publicly defined role and that individual's submission to social control.*"[40]

These sophisticated analyses are very interesting, but they leave me dissatisfied. For not only do they obliterate any memories of the comb as a female accessory, they also discount its artistic and philosophic dimensions. Far too removed from Sikh spirituality, they do not allow us to get to touch the teeth of the guru's comb.

The comb carries a particular association with women—though it has been used by both men and women. Durga-Kali's beautiful *kapardan* hairdo, which the guru repeatedly compliments, is indeed the artwork of the comb. Instrumental to inventive hairstyles, the comb has the capacity to unfurl the creative surplus in us all. Guru Gobind Singh's aesthetic sensibility has picked up on the artistic dimension of the comb. In his cultural milieu, combs were a part of women's *sringar dan* (something akin to our modern "vanity cases").

In form and function it bears a special reference to women's dressing up. From time immemorial women have used combs to style their hair, and for Indian women braiding their hair has been a typical style for millennia. The braid—*veni* in Sanskrit—is a vital part of woman's identity, and a comb is used to create a *veni*. In the *Mahabharata*, Draupadi is disrobed by the villainous Duhshasana, but the worse insult to her is when he undoes her braid and drags her by the hair. Witnessing Draupadi's ultimate humiliation, the hero Bhima swears that he will one day kill Duhshasana and drink his blood. When he fulfills his threat, Draupadi's hair is braided back again! Combing the hair is therefore not a game; it is the essence of selfhood. But most interestingly, the *veni* is also vital to the construction of Nanak's identity: we have seen how he goes into the River Bein and acquires his authentic selfhood. As we demonstrated in chapter 3, the river that carries the birth of the Sikh faith is the same word as *veni*, braid.[41] In the flow of the Bein the first Sikh guru is braided with the Transcendent One. The identity mandated by the tenth guru on Baisakhi 1699 evolves from the identity that Nanak established within the natural female currents. The braid is not controlled. It flows as freely as a river. The comb promotes the natural growth of our bodies, and allows hair to take their course rather than "controls" them as our structuralists theorize. There is no nature-culture split in the harmonious *kesha-kangha* relationship.

For the ancient culture of the Arapaho, combs also had a cosmic female significance. The combs were made with porcupine tails, and in the oral literature of this indigenous North American people, they were specified as female.[42] The porcupine-tailed females were lured by an animal that happened to be the moon. Thus, the porcupine-comb relationship with this lunar animal led to the menstrual cycle. The lunar and female menstrual cycles have been well-known facts, but this Native American insight forges an organic relationship between women and combs. Clearly, the role of combs recollected in this Native American *Weltanschauung* is an opening to the cosmos, rather than a submission to social control.

In the Japanese context, Ebersole's study discloses the comb not just as an instrument for fashioning hair or representing social participation, but a repository for a woman's life force. Considered a memento of a dead woman, the comb—through ritual means—could become the repository of her life force.[43] Ebersole discusses the case of Empress Ototachibana-hime, who sacrificed herself by drowning in the ocean to save the life of her husband. Her comb was substituted for her corpse. The comb was washed ashore seven days after she drowned herself; it was then taken by the people and placed in her tomb. The comb embodied the deceased empress: "She is present in the comb and in that form receives the ritual honors due her."[44] Yet again, a woman is honored for sacrificing herself to her husband!

I feel the most important factor contributing to the construction of the comb as the special *k* for the Sikhs is the religious significance it receives from the Guru Granth. The Sikh scripture assigns regularly a transcendent value to female activities and accoutrements. Throughout the text, female toiletry is highly valued: women's necklaces, ribbons, jewels, clothes, cosmetics, and perfume are all imbued with spiritual significance. The woman is extolled for the mental tenacity with which she uses her items. We can see the comb in her hands as "*dhiraj dhari bandhavai kaman* [the woman with patience gets her braid knotted]" (GG, 359). The poetically charged alliteration of *d*'s evokes a rhythmic application of the comb, its teeth turning and returning, smoothing and arranging her hair. Only after she combs her hair can it be knotted together. Her contemplative patience (*dhiraj*) she shares with mother earth (*dharti*), for the etymological root *dhr,* "that which holds" (common to *dhiraj, dhari,* and *dharti*), ties together her physical and religious activities. Another verse from the Guru Granth further qualifies this: "It is with Truth that the woman braids her hair" (GG, 54). The quintessential philosophical ideals of Sikhism are reproduced in this daily female activity. The Truth with which she braids her hair is not an abstract mathematical conception; it is not a "reified noun" out there, as Mary Daly would say. Truth is a dynamic activity. It is a subjective and existential engagement with the ultimate reality that pours out organically into our self-understanding, and our relationship with our families and society. Profoundly captured, Truth is the woman's hands holding her long hair, and with the help of her comb, weaving the different strands together. The harmony and wholeness of immutable Truth is re-created daily by her combing and braiding.

Guru Gobind Singh absorbed these images from his revered text. Since the item used commonly in his society held a profound philosophical meaning for his tradition, it had to have registered in his mental eye. In order to "knot" his community together, the tenth guru did not have to rely on any controlling masculine devices. He had the scriptural paradigm there before him, and so the female mode of cultivating the self—*dhiraj dhari bandhavai kaman*—becomes the model for his newborn Khalsa. Her female accessory is appropriated by the male guru and is made a requisite for both men and women. The guru incorporates female sensibilities into the daily life of his Sikhs. The *kangha* is not an antithesis to the *kesha*; there is a synchronicity, a close relationship between them. Both together release, redesign, and retrieve infinite human potential. The comb is the instrument for attending to oneself, and so combing the hair becomes a self-reflective process that leads to a life of beauty, imagination, and Truth for both men and women.

k-kirpan

The *kirpan* is not only worn on the body; it is mentally evoked in Ardas, and it is visibly used in Sikh rites. Ardas, the Sikh liturgical prayer recited daily, individually or communally, begins with the remembrance of the feminine sword: "having first remembered the sword."[45] She has a major place in the daily memory of the Sikhs. The sword is then physiologically partaken both in the *amrit* sipped by the Khalsa and in the *karahprashad* eaten by the Sikh congregation. We discussed how vital a role the double-edged sword plays in the churning of *amrit*, but even *karahprashad,* the warm and delicious Sikh sacrament, cannot be distributed to the congregation until it is sanctified by her touch. The sword therefore exerts tremendous influence in the daily life of the Sikh community.

Obviously a weapon, it is narrowly understood as a device for crusades or jihad, and so its rich symbolic significance is not tapped into; its double-edged body with the potential of stirring our deepest human emotions is not embraced. There are Sikh scholars who have highlighted its etymology from *kirpa* (compassion), and G. B. Mansukhani elaborates upon it as an instrument of compassion, used "to protect and safe-guard dignity and honour of others."[46] But this is rare. For the most part, Sikhs understand and apply it as a weapon of male heroes. Such androcentric inscriptions foreclose any possibility for women to establish a meaningful identity with the sword they wear, the sword they remember, and the sword they partake in the *amrit* they drink or the *karahprashad* they eat. By excluding the female from the symbolism of the sword, women—and men—are left bereft of its power in the psychological, social, and public realms.

In our re-memory, the *kirpan* is the guru's item for cultivating divine knowledge, inner courage, and, to reiterate Mansukhani, the virtue of compassion. In the opening chapter we analyzed its thealogical conception in Guru Gobind Singh's autobiographical *Bicitra Natak*. Here I want us to explore how this *k* of the Khalsa sustains scriptural values, and how it retains a female identity. The tenth guru did not introduce a "new metaphor"; he dived into the depths of his religio-literary inheritance and resuscitated a beautiful slender and shining item to adorn his newborn Khalsa with. In fact, this item is embedded at the root of Sikh history. As the Sikh sacred text reads, when Nanak passed his succession to Angad, he gave him a "powerful sword" (*kharag jori*). This sword "constructed out of divine wisdom" (GG, 966) was the mode of transferring spiritual vigor from the founder guru to his successor. At some subconscious level, the tenth guru followed Nanak's precedent, and on that Baisakhi Day imparted his spiritual inheritance to his Khalsa by this *k*. Like Nanak's sword, the *kirpan* of the Sikhs is not an external male instrument of military power. It is a reservoir for spiritual growth.

The prototype for the sword is distinctly found in the Guru Granth where the sword is made up of literally "divine wisdom" (GG, 235, 938, 1072). Paradoxically, this sword of transcendent texture is concretely held in the hands of men and women: "[I]n the hand we hold the sword of divine wisdom." *Dharana* (to hold on) is a contemplative activity. Rather than a phallic weapon, the sword is in fact a medium for grasping the One Reality of the universe. In another Granthian passage, wisdom is conceived in the form of a "mighty sword"—"[K]nowledge we receive from the Divine is a mighty sword" (GG, 1087). A "symbol is not an arbitrarily chosen or created sign, but presupposes a metaphysical connection between visible and invisible," said Gadamer.[47] In the symbol-making process of the Guru Granth, the intangible and infinite illumination coincides with the visible and tangible sword. The picture of the sword is eminently suitable, for as it pierces through dense darkness, dualities, and distortions, it generates light, joy, and harmony. Even its adjective—*karara*—carries connotations of "spiciness": in daily usage, *karara* is used to describe food that is piquant and zesty. The scriptural expression thus indicates the sapiential quality of knowledge and shares the life-giving characteristics of *amrit*. Divine knowledge is not knowledge in the patriarchal sense of an Absolute Truth or a God removed from us; it is an awakening of our senses and consciousness so that we can relish the Reality that is with and amid us. It is a holding to the sword.

From Gadamer's perspective, by concentrating on symbols we too come into contact with what is represented,[48] and so the sword in the Guru Granth serves as an avenue for both men and women to attain the infinity that it represents. According to Guru Nanak, "[L]ike the sharp edge of a sword, it is an extremely narrow lane" (GG, 1028). With our mind (in the Sikh sense of *man* "which combines the functions of mind, the emotions of the heart, and the qualities of the soul"[49]) concentrating fully on its sharp edges, we walk away from all selfish hostilities toward the divine presence permeating our cosmos. The path of the sword is no different from the love for the Divine: "Sword and armor constitute divine worship" (312).

Actually, the "peace-loving" Nanak spells out a host of weapons. They are used as symbols for moral virtues by which we live harmoniously in this world: "quiver, arrow, bow, spear, sword and scabbard are the essence of virtue" (GG, 16). The sword (or the rest of the weapons) is not deployed to attack others out there; it is deployed on oneself. It is visualized, walked on, held in the hand, and utilized inwardly to tear away the duality of subject and object, and connect us back with our essential Self. "Arrogance, attachment, and the sense of 'mine' and 'yours' are annihilated by the path of the sword" (534).

This sword vital to the construction of our true identity is given as the physical symbol to the Khalsa. Throughout the Guru Granth it is conceived as an essential instrument for the development of human consciousness. And, importantly, the paradigmatic person utilizing the sword in the Guru Granth is a woman. In a lyrical passage from Rag Maru, the female subject heroically fights against her inner propensities: "[B]y taking up the sword of knowledge, she fights against her mind and merges with herself" (GG, 1022).

Sikh scripture greatly values the female for her strength and finesse, because she is the one to direct us to the authentic self that lies beneath all our superficial differences and conflicts. Not only does she know how to wield the powerful sword, she also triumphs over her hostile opponents. She is a crucial model in Sikh epistemology. By following the way *she* carries and uses her sword, men and women alike can get to know the unknowable One. The female *mansa* permeating Nanak's scriptural writings recurs in Guru Gobind Singh's autobiographical narrative when he acknowledges *mansa mai*, the mother, as a vital figure in his intellectual and moral self-construction.

It is also intriguing how the Guru Granth joins the sword with both "hair" and *amrit*, and thereby provides us with some memorable preludes to the five *K*s of the Khalsa. The Sikh practices of wearing long hair and carrying the sword are brought together by Guru Amar Das (Nanak 3, the third Sikh guru) as he urges us to "know this path as sharper than a double-edged sword and finer than hair" (GG, 918). The path of the sword is a popular metaphor in Hindu and Muslim piety (and in Buddhism as well, for Buddha Maitreya carries the sword of knowledge), but its kinship with hair has a uniquely Sikh import. Both the sword and the hair that Sikhs maintain as their visible symbols share the qualities of sharpness and refinement, and together they underscore the honing of human faculties (*ghariai*) enumerated by Guru Nanak in the Realm of Beauty, to which we shall return in our final chapter.[50]

Equally fascinating is the Granthian ideal for relishing *amrit*: "After drawing the mighty sword of divine wisdom, we get rid of venom bit by bit, and enjoy the drink" (GG, 1324). Clearly, wielding the sword does not lead to any outward victories. There are no territorial battles to be won. The mighty sword of wisdom is applied to cutting down various sorts of egotistical and dualistic poisons so that an inner space is created where joy and plenitude can be savored—*pijai* (drink). The sword performs its task meticulously: it minutely pierces (*chhedi chhedi* ["bit by bit"]) lethal substances that clog our somatic and spiritual circuits. In our scriptural testimony, Guru Angad only receives Nanak's spiritual sword after he has "sipped the *amrit* of divine praise" (GG, 966). The Guru Granth repeatedly celebrates it as a most relevant and creative instrument. It is very clear that the double-edged sword was not "arbitrarily chosen" by the tenth guru to prepare *amrit* on that historic Baisakhi Day.

These Granthian archetypes with their strong implications must have deeply influenced Guru Gobind Singh's feelings, thoughts, and modes of response. His compositions draw upon the fundamental scriptural significance of the sword and carry it forward—sometimes seriously, sometimes playfully. With his fascination for the dramatic, Guru Gobind Singh personifies the sword as a woman and has her enact her role of minute piercing *(chhedi chhedi)*. In keeping with the female paradigm of the Guru Granth, he even takes up the Durga myth, and illustrates her actions in great detail. It was natural that the female sword of Durga—rather than weapons of male gods—would enter his aesthetic consciousness. Just as the goddess Athena springs forth her father Zeus's head fully armed with a spear in hand as the guardian of Athens and protector of civilization, the goddess Durga-Kali in the Hindu tradition brandishes her sword to curb evil and restore justice in the world. Guru Gobind Singh imports the image of a benevolent sword, and reworks it graphically in sensational scenes. We remember these scenes as his artistic devices to "make visible" for his readers the epistemological and ethical values enshrined in the Guru Granth.

In his Durga compositions, the sword is personified as a female figure who appears in a variety of forms, combining princess, goddess, and lioness. Divisions and verticalities between the human, divine, and animal realms are erased as figures from each of the three unite to personify her. In a way she, the female sword, is the heroine of his composition, for he claims, "The story of the sword will be remembered for many time-cycles" (*Var Durga Ki*, 19). Though the setting of his story is primarily a battlefield, the guru imaginatively presents his heroine in different psychic and geographical landscapes. When she disposes of the demons and comes out bloodred, the poet with his inward eye sees her "descend gracefully like a princess dressed in a crimson sari." Paradoxically however, the crimson outfit reveals her naked body: "Drenched in blood, the naked swords appear like goddesses bathing together in the Sarasvati" (40). With the analogies to princesses and goddesses, the sword emerges as a fluid character, endowed with a status that is both secular and divine. Blood and water also come together to reveal the coexistence of her procreative and destructive dimensions. Her royal bloodred sari turns into the transparent waters of Sarasvati, the goddess of knowledge and learning. The female sword coalesces with literary texts and musical instruments. And the crimson sari that conceals her is the one that reveals her, too! Through a "curiously indeterminate quality" of his poetics, Guru Gobind Singh imparts a distinctly female personality to the sword.

He describes her performance as well, unraveling her fierce movements *(chhedi chhedi)* that ring in the Guru Granth. In a way his own artistic style replays the poignancy of the sword's actions, the alacrity of her movements, and the confidence and grace of her "lioness-like" demeanor. Following the scriptural precedents, the movements of Guru Gobind Singh's sword are directed toward the interior landscape. She gets rid of all that is dead and dull within the self, stirring up our innermost senses and emotions. By recounting her accomplishments, Guru Gobind Singh "pointedly" replays the message of the Guru Granth, the triumph of knowledge over ignorance. The coincidence between the Guru Granth and Guru Gobind Singh is perfect.

Just as the goddess's sword penetrates the kidneys and liver of the massive demon and destroys ignorance and violence, it delves into the very heart and mind of the poet and gives birth to love and creativity. Durga and her sword are interchangeable. *She* is the matrix that biologically generates the universe, and the inspiration that motivates poets, philosophers, and artists.

> Virtues dark and white, you are maternal love, you are humility
> you are poetry, pierced deep into the being of the poet.
> You transform stone into gold in the world
> your touch has the power of the philosopher's stone.
> (CC 1, verse 4)

The guru addresses her in images and tones that we heard in the *Bicitra Natak*. So these compositions are obviously from the same pen, as Sikhs have always believed. Together they artistically fuse many of the goddess's functions with that of her weapon. She is *mamta* (maternal love)—the source of emotional and mental cultivation. She is *namta* (humility)—the requisite for spiritual development. She is *kavita* (poetry)—the artistic surplus vital to our moral and spiritual sensibility. Our essential humanity, so treasured in the Granth, is generated by the female caress. Emotions and intellect, morality and spirituality, are sharpened by her, and like a philosopher's stone, whoever she touches (*chhuhi*), is transformed. By touching the innermost part of the person, the sword provokes us to intuit the immensity of our being, and to sense the inexhaustible mystery of our universe. For us today Guru Gobind Singh's sword becomes the mother who gives birth to poets, artists, philosophers, and scientists.

Her touch excites us to delve into our collective memories where we rediscover her across cultures. This Sikh *k* is not confined to an Indian goddess; it embraces the primal female power embodied in such figures as Greek Athena, Catholic Mary, Japanese Amaterasu, a power that recalls our five *Ks*. The Shinto tradition celebrates three imperial regalia: the mirror, the jewel, and the sword. Amaterasu, the heavenly ancestor of the Japanese royal house, gives her mirror, her jewels, and her sword to her grandson Ninigi and sends him to rule the earth. While the mirror symbolizes the brightness of the Japanese matriarch, and the jewels her cosmic abundance, the feminist sword stands for her justice, resolution, and wisdom. Through this sword Amaterasu enables her descendants to follow her as defenders of the nation and as just and wise rulers. The justice, strength, and wisdom of Amaterasu's sword are qualities shared by the swords of Durga and Athena.

Christianity offers us yet another significant female identification. In his study of the goddesses from East and West, David Kinsley brings our attention to a frame at Notre Dame in Paris. It shows the Virgin Mary threatening the devil with a sword. In this visual narrative of the Theophilus legend,

Mary uses her sword to rescue her devotee from the negative forces, and thus upholds righteousness like Amaterasu, Athena, Durga, and the female archetype in the Guru Granth.[51] The sword represents courage and sympathy, passion and compassion, heroism and tenderness.

The metaphysical symbol for the wellspring of life power and creativity in the hand of the female archetype in the Guru Granth was made into a physical symbol by Guru Gobind Singh so that his beloved Sikhs could wear it close to their bodies. Touch was a vital sense for him, because like a philosopher's stone, it brings about a metamorphosis. The sword on the body of his Sikhs was to transform and refine them at their deepest level. In the guru's aesthetic imagination, the sword itself dazzles like lightning, and since her luminosity overshadows the sun, it can surely enlighten those who wear her on their person.

Ultimately, the *kirpan* is about following the scriptural precedent of the female who cultivates spirituality and is committed to living the different dimensions of life with strength and sensitivity. Guru Gobind Singh's own compositions dramatically choreographed the female identity and function of her sword that is sustained in the Guru Granth. The guru's *k* is a remembrance, a reinforcement, a repository of the virtues enshrined in the Guru Granth. It is not an instrument for male glorification of conquest and dominance. His construction of this *k* draws the female into Sikh aesthetics, religion, and rituals in a very meaningful way. In her various modes, the sword pulsates with the finest of human qualities. For Gadamer,

> The representational function of a symbol is not merely to point to something that is not present. Instead, a symbol manifests the presence of something that really is present . . . it makes the past itself present again and causes to be recognized. Only because it thus presents the presence of what it represents is the symbol itself treated with the reverence due to the symbolized.[52]

We give the guru's *k* its due reverence not by the size of a sword we wear *on* our bodies, but by experiencing the female presence that really is present *in* it, and therewith participating in our common humanity.

k-kara

Kara, the fourth *k* of the Sikhs, is a simple bracelet, but it is forced to play some commanding roles by our male exegetes. For Kapur Singh, Buddhist and Hindu symbolism is codified in the *kara*: "The iron bangle on the right wrist, is the *Dhammacaka* (*dharamcakra*) of Buddhist symbolism and the wheel (*cakra*) the Hindu symbol of the Universal Monarch (Cakravartin Raja)."[53] Thus the *kara* is a reminder for sons and monarchs of their dominant status.[54] Though Kapur Singh tries to give it a cosmic signficance, the *kara* is normally interpreted as some form of weapon of control and self-defense. Uberoi's theory that "the steel bracelet imparts the same orderly control over the sword which the comb does the hair"[55] continues to carry force in contemporary scholarship. As Olivelle says, "[T]he comb controls the power of the hair, the steel bangle controls the power of the sword."[56] The *kara* is perceived as a twin of the sword, and in Batra's words, "It was supposed to give inherent protection to the right arm; the master arm against enemy's sword lash."[57] "Worn on the right hand as it is, it also provides protection to it when wielding a weapon," writes Dr. Ganda Singh.[58] Professor Sahib Singh, another eminent commentator on Sikhism, defines *kara* as a specific marker of Sikh identity that sets the wearer apart from Hindu society. He defines the *kara* as Guru Gobind Singh's warning to his Sikhs against the "Brahmanic trap" of superstitious beliefs. In the *kara* he hears the guru proclaim "that every Sikh should wear an iron bangle as reminiscent of their victory over the superstitions."[59] "Overall, he sees the *kara* as an invitation to masculine qualities: "The Iron Bangle inspires us of sternness and constraint."[60]

That it is a bracelet, a form of jewelry typically bedecking the arms of women, does not surface in male Sikh thought. Their androcentric interpretations cannot imagine a female ornament as part of the Khalsa dress code. Gender is so polarized in its patriarchal framework that Guru Gobind Singh's vision of transcending biological essentialism, and positing a female style for both men and women, is simply beyond their ken. For generations, Sikh men and women have been conditioned to accept the *kara* they must wear for their entire life as some type of male insignia of monarchical power, or male equipment of self-defense, or a male device of control or warning.

In our re-memory, Guru Gobind Singh's steel *kara* evokes the female ornaments and mode of dressing up treasured in the Guru Granth. The articles so idealized by Guru Nanak and his successors in the Sikh sacred text are crystallized into three-dimensional requisites by the tenth guru. The *kara* worn by men and women is but another endorsement of the scriptural expression of spirituality through women's activities and embellishments. As we noted before, women's jewelry, cosmetics, and activities retain spiritual significance throughout Sikh holy text. The gift of the body is adorned by ornaments. Like the *kangha* that styles and dresses up what grows naturally, the bracelet enhances the contours of the body. Gliding on the wrist, moving between the arm and the hand, the *kara* caresses that part of the self which is constantly in action.

Sensuous poetry and sublime philosophy delineate the Granthian precedent for the Khalsa's bracelet. Like the sword, its material substance is the Divine. As Guru Nanak says, "[B]y wearing the bracelet created by the Creator, consciousness is held steady" (GG, 359). The bracelet (*kangan*) is a symbol of dynamic action, and the word "action" (*kar*) recurs constantly in this line: her bracelet is made (*kari*) by the creator (*karta*) and worn around her hand (*kar*). It is artistically set in the midst of her many spiritual adornments. Guru Nanak's entire passage vividly illustrates the highest cultivation of the self through the female mode of dressing up. Sound and sense together describe her activities as *she* opens up the divine for us all. All of the female articles and movements are imbued with the sacred, and morality is gained by attending to the physical self. Since the texture of her bracelet is literally the divine creatrix, by wearing it on our bodies the chasm between the material and the divine is suspended. The bracelet around our wrist lays our consciousness still and bare—ready for a passionate experience with the Transcendent One. All narrow, discriminating, self-centered, self-serving actions, and all heavy-handed masculinist operations, are discarded by the hand that wears this bracelet. The *kara* formulated by Guru Gobind Singh for his Sikhs is modeled on this Granthian bracelet.

Wearing necklaces, bracelets, and rings, putting on vermilion and eyeliner, and dressing up in silks add to the expression of the body. They exemplify ways of sharpening mental and spiritual sensibilities, and include the functions of the sword. *Kara* and *kirpan* are not antithetical; the *kara* does not control the *kirpan*: they are united in revealing the female body as the nexus of all human experience. *She,* with her items, leads to a most sensual union with the Divine. Supreme knowledge is integrated with her sexuality; the transcendent light, with her corporeal self. The *kangan,* by which she focuses and holds her mind together, touches the *kara* of the Khalsa in a profound way. The sheer beauty of this passage of the first guru must have left a deep imprint on the religio-aesthetic worldview of the tenth guru. Its poetic alliterations and its description of *her* articles of adornment constituted his psychodynamic and psychobiographical context, and they eventually made their way into the daily life of the Sikhs. The bracelet made up of the divine material in Guru Nanak's metaphysics was refashioned in steel/iron by Guru Gobind Singh for his beloved Khalsa.

Another beautiful scriptural verse expresses the intimacy between the individual and the Transcendent through a gold bracelet: "Between you and me and me and you what difference can there be, like the gold and the bracelet, the wave and the waters?"(GG, 93). Just as the outward shape cannot be distinguished from the essential substance of the bracelet, nor the wave from the water, so the very specific marker of Sikh identity given by the Tenth Guru cannot be distinguished from the wearer's essential Self. The bracelet enables us to experience That One physically and proudly.

The *kara* also brings to mind the touching metaphor of the Divine as a bangle-seller. Since this may be a foreign figure to Western readers, let me explain. The Guru Granth imagines the Ultimate as a vendor who goes from neighborhood to neighborhood selling glass bangles to women. The scene depicted in Guru Nanak's verse is that of life in rural Punjab, in which the bangle-seller was a familiar figure. Women were confined to the space of the home, but his visit with a basketful of colorful glass bangles during the late afternoon would bring them out of their homes together into a neighborhood spot. His visit would mark a joyous occasion. As the bangle-seller, the Divine is incorporated into the daily life and rhythm of Punjabi women: we can see him deftly slipping delicate and multicolored ornaments around the wrists of women from different stages of life, and around the wrists of women from different castes and classes. In this, the scriptural stream of consciousness, the *kara* that Sikhs wear is brought in the basket of that divine Bangle-Seller first envisioned by Guru Nanak.

We recollect yet another Nanakian prototype for Guru Gobind Singh's *kara*. In North Indian culture, ivory bracelets from the maternal side of the family are worn by the new bride. Just like the wedding band in the West, these bracelets are a mark of her rite of passage, of her new role and status. When Guru Nanak witnessed the brutal rape of India by Babur and his men, he depicted the tragedy through the abuse and carnage of women from different religious and cultural backgrounds. With a radically feminist consciousness, Guru Nanak describes the shattering of women's bracelets, the shearing off of their long hair, the tearing off of the veils of Muslim women, and the suicides committed by Hindu women. Guru Nanak gives a lot of narrative space to women, and the marginalized objects of medieval Indian society become very significant subjects in his poetry. Their tragic situation is captured hauntingly. The brides who once arrived "ceremoniously seated in palanquins with ivory bracelets adorning their arms" are now being smothered and mutilated (GG, 417). The brutality is painfully remembered through woman's body—through the loss of her hair, of her ivory bracelets, of her ornaments, and of her rituals. The rape of women is not just a symbol for the conquest of Hindustan, but of that and more.

The lamentations of Guru Nanak must have lingered in the psyche of Guru Gobind Singh. The bracelets made of ivory *(dand khand)* should never be broken. The hair should never be shorn. The tenth guru found himself in a similar political and social milieu: the Mughal empire launched by Babur was now at its zenith under Aurangzeb, and non-Muslims were oppressed and taxed heavily under his dictatorial regime. The guru wanted to instill courage in his people, and so the delicate ivory bracelets from his culture are given a new syntax; they are converted into a steel/iron bracelet to be worn forever. The bracelets symbolizing a bride's transitory phase from daughter to wife were made into the *kara* to be worn by both men and women, from birth to death. The temporary moment of entering a new family by the bride was given a permanent status of belonging to a new religion on that Baisakhi Day. Like his predecessor, Guru Gobind Singh was pained by the humiliation suffered by his contemporaries. He shared Guru Nanak's empathy for the downtrodden, and thought of creative ways to change the situation.

With its circular wholeness, the *kara* invests the wearer with strength and resolution. Just as the ivory bracelets were a marker of the bride's new status and identity, the *kara* became a marker for the identity of Guru Gobind Singh's newborn Khalsa. Like the ivory bracelet, the *kara* was a sign of membership in a new family. The expansion of the bride's psychic and emotional range denoted by her ivory bracelet fully chimes with that of the *kara* worn by Sikhs, but this time the music lasts beyond the honeymoon.

The fragile ivory bracelet transformed by Guru Gobind Singh into the steel *kara* partakes in the identity and function of the sword. It does not "control the power of the sword," and it does not "protect the master arm against the enemy's sword." Rather, the bracelet joins with the sword. The two *Ks* come together on the body of the wearer to expand the horizon of openness and freedom even more. And like the hair that was never to be shorn, the bracelet could never be broken. Guru Nanak's plea for the raped, abused, plundered Hindustan embodied in the pain and subjugation of mothers, wives, sisters, and daughters was heard by his successor. For Nanak, women were the most important part of the *mother*land, and the healing process was to come through *her* expression and accoutrements.

The process of fusion between the first and the tenth Guru is continually going on in the symbols of the Khalsa. From Gadamer's hermeneutic position, the Granthian paradigms of the first guru unite with the material *Ks* that were constructed by the tenth guru into "living value, without either being explicitly foregrounded from the other."[61] It is in their fusion that the full sacrality of the Sikh symbols opens up, radiating wholeness and illumination to our fragmented selves. When we realize that the concrete *kara* worn by Sikh men and women is identical with the bracelets worn by women in the Guru Granth, we feel its true human significance. Rather than a male weapon of defense, the *kara* is an adornment of beauty, harmony, and healing. As such, it brings male and female together, overcoming the alienation, that brings so much pain in our lives. With each person deprived of the other half, the wholeness of human nature is violated. But remembering the bracelet of divine material worn by Guru Nanak's paradigmatic female figure, the wearer of the *kara*, male or female, can gather his or her fragmented bits of self together. Men and women can integrate with themselves, and unite with each other in their lives. Thus, they will go beyond themselves to change society. The gurus were longing for the identity of symbol and action, an identity that contemporary thealogians like Carol Christ are still longing for: "Instead of a discontinuity between symbols in the deep mind and desired social change, there will be continuity and reciprocal reinforcement."[62]

With neither a beginning nor an end, the circular bracelet is a reminder of the Infinite One. Like the sword, it is a means of centering the self as the person is engaged in various activities; like her, it is not a means for high-handed aggression. Worn around the right wrist, the *kara* participates in all physical functions and gestures, thereby reminding men and women that the timeless moment touches upon each moment, that sacred action touches upon every action. Dressing up, hugging, cooking, reading the holy book, working in the farm or at a computer—all actions are equally validated by the *kara*. When the Khalsa first put it on, all hereditary professional attachments, divisions, and hierarchies were melted away in its metallurgical construction by Guru Gobind Singh. *Kara* is the sign par excellence of *krita nasa*—an annihilation of all occupations that determined one's place in society. The sacred enters into every action because the *kara* around each wrist is made up of the divine substance, "[B]y wearing the bracelet created by the Creator, consciousness is held steady."

k-kacha

The final Sikh *k* is the *kacha* or underwear (sometimes called *kacchera*, and usually translated as "breeches"). Whereas the other four *Ks* are publicly visible, *kacha* constitutes intimate apparel. Garments covering private parts of the body scarcely ever form part of religious discourse. That an undergarment like that would be such a critical item of identity for the Sikhs is a unique phenomenon in the history of religion. Our "mind"-exalting scholars would of course ignore an item that would be so close to the body, but even recent studies on "body," "gender," "sexuality" have not paid any attention to this Sikh item. During my informal discussions with community members the *kacha* appears to be an "embarrassing" topic that is hastily brushed aside. Since childhood I have known *kacha* means "breeches"—i.e., short informal male trousers—and left it at that. Why Guru Gobind Singh gave this *k* to his beloved Sikhs was never seriously questioned.

Only recently with my research into a feminist understanding of the five *Ks* have I become more daring. So last summer I broached the topic with Professor Witzel at Harvard, and I am very grateful to him for his insight that *kacha* is etymologically related with *kacch*, our underarm. Now we can understand the guru's logic better. There is a parallel between the "upper" and "lower" parts of the body: they are not hierarchical or divided. The body, like the *kara*, is a complete and harmonious unit, and by mandating the *kacha* he wanted his Sikhs to pay full attention to their entire body. In Punjabi, the expression *kachh vicu varna*, literally "stuck to an armpit," is used frequently to denote closeness between couples. The fifth *k* of the Sikhs brings our attention to a garment that not only remains close to one's own body, but that also draws another into the folds of the self. Since it has ramifications both for the individual and for his/her intimate partner, the *kacha* becomes an extremely vital construct of Sikh personality. Guru Gobind Singh's religious worldview focuses on individuals and their deepest interactions with others. The *kacha* outlaws male dominance and binds Sikhs in love: it resonates with principles of *herethics* that are important to feminist philosophers.

In order to realize the meaning of our final *k* it is crucial that we deconstruct and displace all conventional interpretations that have codified it as a masculine symbol. The normative androcentric views have automatically taken the male body as the standard, and assumed *kacha* entirely for themselves without giving it any significance for women whatsoever. A wide range of masterly works narrowly relay the *kacha* as a male outfit, useful for "male protection," "soldierly duties," "control of the penis," as a "makeshift tent," and as a way of abandoning "effeminate submissiveness" or "Hindu customs and superstitions. . . ." According to Batra, "The form of *Kacha* was not like what it is today. It was meant to be of thick, coarse cloth with lot of folds, especially toward the front, in order to provide a little cushion and consequently protection to the most vulnerable part of the human body from any blow of the enemy in hand to hand combat. Also, it served the purpose of half riding breeches. In addition, when hung on a lance or a bamboo, it looked like the hoop of a tent from a distance under which, a few soldiers could rest. Therefore, it had the inherent element of deception."[63]

In the same vein, S. S. Johar says, "By adopting the small underwear, it was intended to symbolize the spiritual and mental breakaway from traditional dress and thought. The mind was freed from the bonds of superstition and the Sikhs were thus to be released from immature and effeminate submissiveness. They were destined to become mature, solid, brave and courageous soldiers. They were to be self-controlled, chaste and chivalrous."[64]And more recently, Olivelle writes that the *kacha* controls the penis."[65] Professor Sahib Singh analyzes this *k* as an antithesis to Hindu customs. His thesis reads: "In Vedic texts performance of certain sacrificial rituals through [the] hereditary priestly class, Brahmans, is prescribed. The Vedic texts forbid those persons to perform the rites who have not undergone the ceremonial purification and are not clad in 'dhoti,' an untailored piece of cloth used in place of [a]pair of trousers. Kachera is, therefore, a symbol of abandoning of the Brahmanic ritualism and the creed of sacrificial offerings."[66]

Professor Sahib Singh's analysis is in line with the eminent cultural historian, Professor Kapur Singh, who writes: "[W]earing of a *kacha* would, in practice, amount to abandonment of the rituals of the Vedic religion and the practices of Brahmanism."[67] Kapur Singh makes an extensive and interesting analysis, including a parallel with the "use of fig-leaves which Adam and Eve first made on achieving social awareness of each other."[68] He concludes that the *kacha* is a badge of civilization and of the concept of duty, and thereby, a clear repudiation of "the ascetic ideal based on the Sankhya system."[69]

Though more briefly, G. S. Mansukhani and S. S. Kohli offer similar views. "The Guru did not like the loose *Dhoti* or *Pajama* or *Salwar* worn by the people. The shorts symbolizes this freedom from traditional dress and thinking. It stands for the dynamic life of a man of action."[70] The list could go on. Totally absorbed in the "dynamic life of [the] man of action," "malestream" Sikh scholarship has not given any thought to women or their clothing.

With all their elaborate commentaries, the patriarchs have only covered up the significance of the *kacha*. Even for their own purposes they have neither discerned nor utilized its real power. In their normative hegemonic discourse the value of the *kacha* has been camouflaged as a tent or a tool of some sort. As a device to deceive the enemy, or a device to protect against the enemy's blows, or a device to control the male member or an agent for repudiating traditional rites, practices, and thinking, the *kacha* has been used to bolster male identity and erect a masculine subjectivity. But since they are based on an alienated male experience of power, their androcentric notions and commentaries have handicapped men from constructing their full identity, and by effacing women, they have made them worthless, invisible, and quite—the Other. Both men and women have lost out on the guru's gift. Its transcendent material and rhythmic stitches are not valued at all.

We are so programmed to hearing the master's voice that we have never questioned its importance from a woman's perspective. Isn't it just as natural for Sikh women to wear the *kacha*? They are obliged to wear it too, after all. Like the rest of the *Ks*—the bracelet, long hair, comb, and even sword—*kacha* fits in with typical female norms and patterns. When we look at it through a feminist lens, we retrieve in the *kacha* a powerful *human* mechanism for cultivating sexuality, and so the guru's *kacha* enables us to gather our humanity rather than divide male from female, Sikh from Hindu or Muslim. The South Asian feminist Nita Kumar rightly says that even "the slight displacement of a symbol from its conventional positioning is enough to codify completely different, opposing meanings for the subject."[71] From our angle the *kacha* is a visible investiture of reverence for the power of fertility and generation *for both* men and women. The "intimate apparel" intimates the mystery and joy of sex and procreation. Like the rest of the *Ks*, it is not repressive but a creative mechanism that generates natural forces and nurtures them.

Perhaps Guru Gobind Singh was far too radical for his message to be fully comprehended. The *kacha* requisite for his Sikhs makes a vital statement about human sexuality. Actually, it is this area in which we expect the most extreme differences between men and women, because sexual difference is the primary and only real difference between them. Genitals mark the two sexes at birth, and all other differences are socially and culturally constructed, and they are socially and culturally imposed. Scholars from different academic disciplines distinguish biologically marked "sex" from "gender," which is the way men and women are perceived, evaluated, and expected to behave.[72] Genitals make men and women different, and so they become the very origin of discriminations. Simply on the basis of their biology, boys from the moment of their birth are socially and psychologically empowered; girls are pathetically undermined. Sexism continues throughout their lives—with the most blatant form of discrimination being legitimized as just sexual difference.

The *kacha* required of both men and women rips asunder the binary categories that have been used to justify sexual inequality in our human history. Since Guru Gobind Singh charged both men and women to wear the same form of undergarment for their genitals, the *kacha* becomes a crucial symbol for the elimination of all other disparities. This is how we remember the guru's gift: the *kacha* is an outfit designed to dispense equality at the very source of inequalities. Clothes may seem unimportant, but as Virgina Woolf said, they mold our hearts, our brains, our language. "They change our view of the world and the world's view of us . . . it is clothes that wear us and not we them."[73] Clothes are indeed most effective signs of sexual difference. Therefore, by telling his Sikhs—both men and women—to each wear the *kacha*, Guru Gobind Singh, in a very basic and innovative way, eliminated sexual difference, the root of all differences. As a marker of Sikh identity, the *kacha* should tear apart those fabrications and constructions that have defined and confined women's roles, and controlled their destiny as daughters, sisters, wives, mothers, and nieces. But we have to recollect the *kacha* in its real sense, rather than its camouflaged versions, for only then will men and women reconstruct their authentic subjectivity.

In our re-memory the *kacha* is modeled on the metaphysical garments worn by the female figure in the Guru Granth. Not those "who take off their clothes and go naked like Digambaras" (GG, 1169), but she who "wears the clothes of Love" (54) is prized in the Sikh sacred text. As a covering for the genitals, *kacha* becomes a signifier of self-affirmation. Ascetics and celibates from different religious worldviews opt to wear nothing on their bodies as a sign of "mastering" their sexuality. The Granth rebukes the example of the Digambara Jains who for centuries have literally been "sky-clad." Kapur Singh even tells us that the sky-clad Digambaras were called naked philosophers, "gymnosophists," by the Greeks, who noticed them as early as Alexander's incursion into India.[74] This sect of Jains (different from the Svetambaras who wear only white—*sveta*) regard the sense of nakedness as a part of attachment to the body, and as long as one is aware of the nakedness of one's body, liberation or *moksha* cannot be attained. But according to the Guru Granth, "someone clad in wind would only be a proud fool" (318).

In the larger Indian context, Hindu yogis and *bhaktas* and Buddhist monks have also aspired to conquer their senses and practice total abstinence to gain full control over the self. The genitals and their processes are vehemently disparaged by the celibates. To feel nothing that the body feels is the ideal of the spiritually oriented saints. Our patriarchal exegetes rightly spotted the rejection of the ascetic practices in the guru's *kacha*. What we object to is that male critiques do not go far enough to recognize the positive and liberating sensations enfolded in the guru's *k*. They denounce celibacy and ascetic practices to announce their own anti-Brahmanic stance, their chivalry, their commitment to procreation. They view the *kacha* merely as a divisive garment that differentiates Sikhs from non-Sikhs, males from females. Stuck on *us vs. them*, the androcentric mentality fails to see its full human scope.

The Sikh gurus spurned asceticism not to instill anti-Hindu or anti-Jain or anti-Buddhist sentiments, but rather to expel antiwomen attitudes and customs against women—Hindu, Jain, Buddhism, Muslim, or Sikh. In *Sexual Morality in the World's Religions*, Geoffrey Parrinder comments that monks renounced "sexual intercourse as 'bestial,' and looked on women with fear and contempt."[75] According to feminist poet Audre Lorde, the ascetic aspires to feel nothing: "[T]he ascetic position is one of the highest fear, the gravest immobility. The severe abstinence of the ascetic becomes the ruling obsession. And it is not of self-discipline but of self-abnegation."[76] The Sikh gurus were familiar with the mores of their milieu in which the respect for asceticism went hand in hand with the devaluation of women. Patriarchal memory recites their criticism of asceticism, but forgets that it flowed from their compassion for and affirmation of the "second sex."

In fact, the poets of the Guru Granth empathize with Drapaudi's humiliation, and extol the Divine for supplying her with clothes when the Kauravas tried to strip her. The scene of her forced disrobing in the *Mahabharata* is captured twice in the Guru Granth. In the words of Nal,

> Again, O divine One, you protected Draupadi's honor:
> Just as her clothes were snatched, you adorned her with many more.
> (GG, 1400)

Through a plurality of voices and a variety of accents, the Guru Granth proclaims the wearing of garments as a sign of respect and reverence for the human body, male and female, Hindu and Sikh.

Rather than "smear the bodies with ashes, renounce clothes, and go naked" (GG, 1127), we must, enjoins the Guru Granth, "wear the outfit of divine honor and never go naked" (1019). The *kacha* given by Guru Gobind Singh is made up of "divine honor"—from the same spool of fabric as the *sirpao* that Nanak received in the Bein. The divine outfit is modeled by the woman who "dresses up in the silks of the highest One" (359). But we must be clear that she is no model like the ones flashed in our glossy magazines, because hers is not a flawed or "inferiorized" body. At some level we are all victims of this kind of manipulation by the media, but the feminist philosopher Sandra Lee Bartky has articulated it extremely well when she says, "A host of discourses and social practices construct the female body as a flawed body that needs to be made over," and so the media images that bombard us with overt glorification of female body are only covert operations that depreciate this body, making women feel deficient and ashamed.[77] In the Sikh scriptural instance, the female model is physically, morally, and spiritually wholesome, and her outfit fully matches her inner feelings. It is precisely because she is internally healthy and strong that the divine dress fits her female figure perfectly! With her rarefied senses, she can feel the texture of the outfit she wears close to her skin. The Guru Granth exalts her who "wears the clothes of Love" (54), and presents *her* as the paradigm to be emulated by both men and women. When the tenth guru invested the Khalsa with this *k*, the Granthian model was sure to figure into his worldview. Instead of a "cushioning" or "controlling device" for male genitals, the *kacha* is a garment of self-affirmation and honor for our bodies.

By wearing the Divine in the design of the *kacha* we join our corporeal and spiritual selves most snugly and securely. Our heroism, self-control, maturity, and all the other virtues spelled out by our scholars lie not in a "release from effeminate submissiveness" but in a realization of this vital *tan* (body)-*man* (mind/heart) conjunction. In contrast with self-abnegation, the *kacha* enunciates the metaphysical precept that there is no Cartesian duality between them. Our entire "body" with all its senses and organs is sacred; it is the home of the Infinite One; it is the source for attaining religious wisdom. How can we suppress and reject or hate that which houses the Divine? "Whatever lies in paradise beyond is found in the body here," says the Guru Granth (695). The body is our marvelous possession, and wearing the *kacha* indicates respect for our most intimate organs. The structure of our body is spiritual: "Body is the home of the divine One and by the divine One is the body maintained" (1059). How can we denigrate our physical selves when "all hope and wisdom *(mansa)* are this body, illuminated by the divine light?" The female figure of *mansa mai* in Guru Gobind Singh's autobiographical *Bicitra Natak* (14:5) issued from this body of the Guru Granth. In the tissues of the Granth, we find many different terms used for the body—*tanu, deh, kaia, pind*—but in each case it is made up of the Transcendent; after all, in every pore dwells the Divine! The integration of the physical and spiritual sides of the self openly expressed in Sikh sacred literature is enfolded in the *kacha* of the Khalsa.

Dressed up in her silks, our scriptural archetype enters a sensual relationship. She incarnates physical beauty and spiritual awakening, and she rapturously makes love with her divine lover! Says Guru Nanak again, "The woman abides in truth, and sleeps soundly locked in the Divine embrace" (GG, 843). Clearly the Granth posits women's sexuality as healthy and wholesome, which we find is sewn into every stitch of the *kacha.* All her desires materialize in her union with her Divine Lover: " [T]he young bride has her Husband; her hopes and wishes are fulfilled" (765). But in all parts of our world, and in all strata of society, women's sexuality is denigrated, and they are constantly victims of male fears, phobias, anxieties, and disgust. "Woman is always considered trash" says the Sikh novelist Ajeet Cour at the opening of her autobiography entitled *Kura Kabada* (*Trash and Garbage*);[78] "a sewer in which anal and urethral waste is poured," mourns the French philosopher Luce Irigaray. "The only words we have for women's sexuality are filthy, mutilating words."[79] *Kacha* is a protection against exploitation and victimization. We are not to fear or be threatened by sexuality; nor must we misuse the spiritual force of our physicality in any way. In the Granthian model, sensuality is fused with spirituality. If put on properly, Guru Gobind Singh's *kacha* should tear asunder patriarchal abuses and pornographic objectifications that deplorably rob women of their sexuality, their subjectivity. The wearer of the guru's *kacha* recognizes each body as the home of the Divine (*harimandir*), and not a battleground for domestic violence, economic deprivation, forced sterilization, forced pregnancy, female feticides, or honor killings.

As we noted at the beginning of this section, this marker of Sikh identity is a unique phenomenon in the history of religion. With our habit of studying our Subject in the heavens, it might give some scholars a pain in the neck to study something so close. But our analysis shows that the *kacha* draws our attention to our fundamental human identity in a most meaningful way. It really discloses an unusual foresight and wisdom on the part of Guru Gobind Singh, for the more I think about it, the more radical implications this *k* seems to carry for living our lives as men and women today. Whereas the other symbols attend to the construction of the individual and that of the communal identity, this *k* forces us to think about personal relationships between partners, be they man and woman, man and man, or woman and woman. Thus it even brings us toward an "*ethics of the couple*" desired by modern feminists. The place that Irigaray searches for between the morality of an individual (locked up in the family) and the morality of a whole people (*Sittlichkeit*), a place "where the two halves of the natural and spiritual world can be and change," is precisely the space of the guru's symbol.[80]

The *kacha* draws us to that intimate zone where we can bond with the partner we love and respect. It is the Sikh symbol for cultivating morality at a fundamental level. The *kacha* is linked with the virtues of modesty and sexual restraint. Guru Gobind Singh urged people to observe sexual morality within the context of normal family life instead of pursuing celibacy. Life is not to be renounced or rejected. Home, family, marriage, and children are a part of the natural life cycle and should be fully respected. The *kacha* continues to serve as the guru's reminder that couples come together in love, mutuality, honesty, and creativity—not in the combative spirit of the soldier. In the ethics of the couple, love and justice go together, and according to Carter Heyward, a committed lesbian feminist Christian priest and teacher, "where there is no justice/no love, sexuality is perverted into violence and violation, the effects of which most surely include rape, emotional and physical battering, relationships manipulated by control, competition, and contempt, and even war itself."[81] The *kacha* given to Sikh men and women as a code of their identity mandates that they cultivate the best of their human qualities so that they can share them with each other. It is only with an integration of their own sensations, emotions, intelligence and divinity that they reach out with intensity to their partner by their side. Thus they soar into ecstasy and illumination, and in the movement and rhythm of their bodies they choreograph the Granthian ideal, "they are called husband and wife who are one light in two bodies" (GG, 788).

To conclude our analysis, the *kacha* alliterates with the other four *Ks* both in its aesthetic form and in its spiritual significance because like the *kesha, kangha, kirpan,* and *kara, kacha* is all about a passionate experience of the Divine in our daily life. They all commence with the letter *k*, and they all consummate in and with the Infinite One. In our re-memory, the five *Ks* of the Khalsa belong to an interlaced pattern that is reproduced entirely from the Guru Granth. They are drawn from Guru Gobind Singh's own memory of his sacred text, and as they flow out and represent the ethical and philosophical values of Guru Nanak, they point Sikhs back to the origins of their tradition in the River Bein. Each of the five symbols is clearly a "coincidence of sensible appearance and suprasensible meaning," and this coincidence, Gadamer says, is the original significance of the Greek *symbolon*, "the union of two things that belong together."[82] As the five *Ks* unite artistically and philosophically with the Guru Granth, they reveal once again that the Sikh tradition is not fractured between the "peace-loving" Nanak and the "knightly" Gobind Singh. Rather, it is a single historical horizon. Because it fosters a strong sense of identity both at the individual and communal levels, wearing the five *Ks* conforms to Foucault's "true social practice." The art of existence is refined through them. As they enable each Sikh to cultivate his or her physical and psychological self, the five *Ks* intensify a communal identity among them. In this true social practice Guru Gobind Singh made the "past" of his Sikhs "present again" in a radically new and palpable way.

The memory of the "coincidence" between the five *Ks* and their scriptural prototypes is particularly important for women. The five *Ks* are foreshadowed throughout the Guru Granth in the hands and on the body of a female, the quintessence of womanhood. By recognizing the ontological equivalence between the items of the paradigmatic woman and the five *Ks* worn on their own bodies, Sikh women can reconstruct their lost identity. That they are not patriarchal symbols construed just for the bodies of men, but human archetypes revealed in their holy book by a woman, is most validating and self-affirming. The memory of "coincidence" is an empowering process that retrieves their sense of selfhood usurped from them. Women can ontologically share in the being of *her* physically and spiritually refined body; they can physically and psychologically receive the direct flow of *her* energy from *her* symbols to the five they wear on their own bodies. No longer does a woman have to mediate through fathers, husbands, uncles, or sons; the five *Ks* are hers as much as they are theirs. Guru Gobind Singh dispelled all conventional taboos against female pollution, menstruation, and sexuality by giving the five *Ks* to both men and women—without any exceptions whatsoever of widows or menstruating women, of women who are pregnant or in childbirth, or of single or married women. We need to remind ourselves again and again that the five *Ks* are symbols of sexual equality, and continually struggle to overturn their construction as symbols of phallogocentric subjectivity and spirituality.

My feminist interpretation of these five symbols does not in any way denigrate men. On the contrary, it enhances male strength and dignity. By remembering that what they wear has a female significance, men do not become "effeminate"; they only free themselves from the imprisonment of a gender polarization that has left all of us insecure, suppressed, homogenized, and painfully split. Once we acknowledge the female import of the five *Ks*, the culturally constructed divisions and categories disappear before our eyes, and we gain new power and confidence. Conventional weaponry interpretations do not speak for all people and for all times. They only represent an aspect, whereas the multivalence of the five *Ks* demands that we open them to both sexes so that we begin to actualize the human potential that we men and women possess together. The five *Ks* worn by Sikhs are a cultivation of our universal humanity. They give Sikhs a distinct identity, but they are neither religiously divisive nor gender-polarized. This is because they are essentially patterned on the *sirpao* that Nanak received from the Divine; it was open and inclusive, and therefore open to many different designs and forms. The five *Ks* are constructed from it, and as they join Sikh metaphysics with Sikh practice, they can join Sikh men and women together by joining together all the aspects of our lives—personal, psychological, institutional, and moral—that have been so badly ripped apart by our gender-polarized society.[83] It is only then that the five *Ks* will truly become the seal (*mohur*) of Sikh identity.

Chapter Five

Semiotic Poetry and the Reproduction of the Khalsa

> Says Nanak, the child, you are my father and my mother,
> and your Name is like milk in my mouth.
>
> (GG, 713)

Sikh identity wrought by Guru Gobind Singh is a fusion of the external and internal self, for just as the Five Beloved were endowed with the five *Ks* *(bana)*, they were endowed with the five hymns *(bani)*. If we return to Koer Singh's account of Baisakhi Day 1699 in chapter 9 of his *Gurbilas Patshahi 10*, we distinctly hear the following injunctions:

> Read the book daily, know *Jap, Rahiras, Kirtan* by heart.
> Combine your weapon with the guru's word,
> Always love *kacha* and *kesha*.
>
> (9:39–40)
>
> Know the Guru Granth ever present with you. . . .
>
> (9: 44)

Such proclamations recorded by Koer Singh are extremely effective in daily Sikh life. Wherever Sikhs may choose to live, they abide by these principles, which in fact affirm the fullness of the individual vital to our feminist understanding. The command is, literally, "always (*sada*) to know (*jano*) the Guru Granth with (*sang*) the body (*ang*)." The sacred text must never be apart from our bodies; its divine contents must be felt ever close to the flesh. The

Book (*pothi granth*) must always (*sada*) be read (*parho*) daily (*neeta*), and the hymns *jap, rahiras*, and *kirtan* (short for *kirtan sohila*) be memorized (*cita*). Through the process of memorization, *bani* is swallowed internally. Made a part of the unconscious self, it becomes the source of all conscious activity—physical, moral, and intellectual. It is required that Khalsa members combine their weapon (*sastra*), which is worn outwardly, with the word (*sabad*), which is remembered inwardly, and that they be emotionally attached (*sad prem*) to their hair (*kesha*), which is biological, and their underwear (*kacha*), which is tailored. Thus the identity of Sikhs lies in the ontological valence of *bana* and *bani*: body and mind, exterior and interior, natural and cultural, spiritual and sexual, daily and eternal, conscious and unconscious. The instructions attributed to Guru Gobind Singh are aimed at producing a complete and integrated personality.

Without jeopardizing the intrinsic unity of word and action in Sikhism, we must focus on the words of the Khalsa and examine how they are crucial to reproducing the Khalsa, for just as we explored *bana* in the previous chapter, we must now remember *bani* from our feminist perspective. In fact, *bani* has been crucial to our entire study thus far. When we look back, chapter 1 was really an amniocentesis of the autobiographical *Bicitra Natak*: was it not the pregnant guru's poetry that fed the embryonic Khalsa? In chapter 2, we witnessed the birth of the Khalsa take place in and through the divine word. In chapter 3 we recovered how the Sikh poetic imagination is crystallized by Guru Gobind Singh in the Khalsa institution, and in chapter 4 we found the five symbols of the Khalsa pulsate with motifs from the sacred poetry of the Guru Granth. Clearly, poetry constitutes the gestation, birth, inheritance, and adornment of the Khalsa. And as we begin to explore our next stage, poetry constitutes the reproduction of the Khalsa as well. How else is the Khalsa born? How does the family of Guru Gobind Singh and Mataji continue? Whether back at home in the Punjab or in diasporic communities across the world, Sikhs and non-Sikhs are initiated into Khalsahood through *amrit* prepared and drunk in the sight and sound of *bani*. Although about 15 percent of the Sikhs may formally be initiated into the Khalsa order, the *bana* and *bani* of the Khalsa are fundamental to all Sikhs.

Sacred verse is the only means for the procreation of the Khalsa. The ceremony takes place with the Guru Granth in the center. This holy text was compiled by Guru Arjan, and made guru by Guru Gobind Singh just a day before he passed away. Jap, Jaap, Swayyais, Chaupai, and Anand are the five hymns recited during the *amrit* initiation. Two of them are from the Guru Granth: the Jap by Guru Nanak and the Anand by Guru Amar Das. The Jaap, Swayyai, and Chaupai belong to Guru Gobind Singh's compositions, and as the title indicates, his Jaap is born from Guru Nanak's Jap. Thus the philosophical vision of the first guru is carried through and underscored by his successors and ultimately drunk in the *amrit* prepared by the Five Beloved. This particular repertoire of the five *banis* for the Khalsa initiation is also incorporated into the daily routine of the Sikhs. While the Jap, Jaap, and Swayyai constitute the morning prayers for all Sikhs, the Chaupai and Anand are incorporated into Rahiras, the evening prayer. The five hymns are a means of daily tuning and refining the inner dynamics of the Khalsa, and like the outward wearing of the five *Ks*, they are essential to Sikh identity. Even those Sikhs who are not formally initiated into Khalsahood are nurtured and matured constantly by these hymns, and so even if the ritual of *amrit* initiation occurs only once in a lifetime, it is replayed daily in Sikh life, and Baisakhi 1699 resonates constantly.

The ritual is based on Guru Gobind Singh's Baisakhi 1699: it involves the preparation of *amrit* by five chosen members of the Sikh community. Each of these Five Beloved recites one of the five prescribed hymns in turn, while stirring water and *patasas* (sugarpuffs) in an iron bowl with a double-edged sword. The initiates, fully bathed and groomed with the five *Ks*, remain in attendance, listening to the sacred verse. When the recitations are completed, the *amrit* is given to the initiates, one by one, in their cupped hands. Five times they take the drink and say, "Khalsa belongs to the wonderful guru, victory belongs to the wonderful guru!" The Five Beloved then sprinkle the *amrit* five times on the eyes and hair of the initiates. The remaining drink is sipped from the same bowl in turn by each of them, signifying their new birth into the Khalsa family. The preamble to the Jap is repeated five times, and the new members are reminded to abide by the Sikh code of conduct. The recitation of Ardas (liturgical supplication while the congregation stands), reception of the Vak (reading of the passage from the Guru Granth as the book is opened at random), and partaking of Karahprashad (the Sikh sacrament) culminates the ceremony.[1]

This central Sikh rite of passage is open to men and women. Regardless of nationality, religion, caste, or sex, anyone who is prepared to accept the rules governing the Sikh community has the right to receive *amrit* initiation. In fact, the Sikh Rahitmaryada mentions the candidacy of women even before that of men: "[E]very woman and man has the right to take the *amrit*."[2] No particular age is prescribed for Khalsa initiation. It may be as soon as a boy or a girl is old enough to be able to read the scripture and comprehend the articles of the Sikh faith. Or it may be later in life—some people even wait until their own children are grown up. The same pattern of initiation is followed by both men and women.

While women's right to receive *amrit* is clearly articulated, their right to administer the *amrit* ceremony is covertly denied. Equally and alike, women cross the threshold from the "outside" into the "inside" of the Khalsa community; however, they do not initiate the Khalsa, and so they are born into the family of the Khalsa but they do not reproduce it. Although Sikh tradition holds that the Khalsa initiation can be conducted by any five Sikhs who are already members of the Khalsa, women are usually excluded from taking on this special role. In this instance, the words of the Rahitmaryada are not as welcoming, either. When they are to be administered the rite, women are eagerly spelled out first, but when they are to administer the rite, the code states that "women may *also* (*bhi*) be included amongst them" (my emphasis).[3] The hesitation that we sense in the wording of the Sikh ethical code translates into an outright discouragement in the practice of this central rite of passage. We do not find women holding the privileged position of the Five Beloved. The recitation of the five *banis* during the preparation of the elemental drink is withheld from them. Women are tacitly barred from fusing the semiotic verses with the placental waters, their voices from chiming with the rhythm of the double-edged sword, their hands from caressing and sprinkling the verbally energized waters. They are distanced both from their rich literary text and from their vibrant ritual inheritance.

Like the five *Ks* of the Khalsa, the five hymns unite male and female, but just like the five *Ks*, they have been limited by a one-sided androcentric exegesis. The liberating verses of the Sikh gurus, meant for men and women, have been taken over by men. They have been taken over by men both in meaning and in praxis. Their human and universal meaning is primarily understood from a male point of view, leaving women with the feeling that to be universal is to be not female. Public worship is also dominated by men. Male hands drape the holy book in silks and brocades, male lips recite the sacred verses, and male lenses interpret the scriptural passages. Men have the privilege to touch and read the textual body during all forms of public worship. Since men conduct rituals and ceremonies, their voices and hands have seized the practical modality of the sacred word. Instead of a union of male and female, only male procedures are applied for the procreation of the Khalsa, and so the female biological and psychological mode underlying the birth of Guru Gobind Singh's Khalsa is lost. Just as women are shut off from the female vitality of the five *Ks*, they are shut off from the intrinsically female power of the reproductive process.

Women's absence from the human symbolic of the *bani* and its ritual application relegates them to a secondary position and reinforces their subordination in Sikh society. The result is their constant abuse, oppression, and victimization. The hegemonic structure reinforced by excluding women from the sacred verse is dangerous to society as a whole, because fathers, husbands, sons, brothers, and lovers suffer from the subjugation of women, too. It produces terrible effects in the daily lives of Sikhs rich and poor, and among all Sikh communities, whether they be in rural India or in metropolises of the New World. The emancipatory conception of the Khalsa germinated by Guru Gobind Singh is aborted, and sadly, a patriarchal structure is reproduced in the Sikh world.

It is imperative that a one-sided memory of Sikh sacred verse and its male application be rectified. We must hear the verses in their expansive and inclusive meaning, and we must utilize the female dimension in rites and practices. In the literature of the gurus, female images serve as vital reminders of the Transcendent One, and they are greatly valued for cultivating spirituality; but the minds of the Sikh community lack the ability to store this rich symbolic data. The mnemonic failures to recall *women's* engagement with the Divine have stultified and stratified Sikh society. If we can shift the invisible, imaginary symbolic, we can bring about a change in the visible, social, and political realms of Sikh life. Once we see *her* positioned equally with *him* through our mental eyes, we will likewise be able to see her in that very position with our physical eyes. In this final chapter of ours we want to recover *her* from the layers of sediment under which she lies buried. Borrowing Julia Kristeva's terms, our objective is to free the "semiotic" verses of the Sikh gurus from the oppressive "symbolic" that has buried them, so that all readers and reciters, male or female, can reconstruct their subjectivity and become full citizens.

In Kristeva's analysis, the "symbolic" does not pertain to symbolism in the poetical sense, but rather to a male way of using language. In fact we want to duly notice the true female sense of female symbols that have been forgotten, deleted, and even overturned in Sikh malestream exegesis. Following Jacques Lacan, the symbolic for Kristeva is the logical and signifying level of meaning in language through which we communicate with one another—a modality that follows the "Law of the Father." Kristeva distinguishes this male construction and codification of language from the primordial female "semiotic." While "symbolic" for her is a patriarchal mode of developing and structuring univocal terms of language, "semiotic" is the maternal basis of language—its sounds, cadences, tones, and rhythms.

Kristeva's usage of the semiotic is a valuable process for bringing out the feminist import of Sikh sacred poetry. Kristeva bases semiotic on the Greek atomistic philosophers' notion of *chora*, which Plato recalls in the *Timaeus*. In her evocative text, *In the Beginning Was Love: Psychoanalysis and Faith*, Kristeva explains it as "an ancient, mobile, unstable receptacle, prior to the One, to the father, and even to the syllable, metaphorically suggesting something nourishing and maternal."[4] By entering Kristeva's primordial realm we are ushered into the preoedipal state of language where male and female are united, and thus we enter the elemental power of the gurus' verses. We become sensitive to the sensuousness and sensuality of their spiritual poetry and reexpereince the full physicality, dynamism, and élan vital of their words. Kristeva's "semiotic" helps us realize that the female is not set aside in the male compositions of the Sikh gurus, and that "word" and "flesh" do meet in their expression of and quest for the Transcendent Reality.

Actually, from time immemorial ancient Indian philosophy has underscored the female dimension of language that Kristeva found in the early Greek concept of *chora*. Before Plato imposed the male *logos* on words, before philosophers restricted language to express Ideas alone, there was a maternal voice. This voice is also celebrated in the Vedic hymns. She is Vak, exalted as the goddess of speech. A passage from the Taittiriya-Brahmana strikingly unfolds Kristeva's definition of the semiotic modality of language quoted above: "Vak is endless; Vak is beyond all creation; she is immeasurable; all the gods, Gandharvas, humans, and animals live in Vak; Vak is *aksara* (syllable), the firstborn of Rta, the mother of the Vedas, the navel of immortality."[5] Ancient Indian seers eloquently predicted a contemporary French feminist's views! The infinite Vak by herself creates and sustains the divine, human, and animal worlds. All aspects of life live upon this powerful female potency. Vak as the "mother of the Vedas" is the progenitor of all that is "seen" and "known," for that is the meaning of *veda*. Its etymological root, *vid*, can be seen in the Greek *oida* (to know), the Latin *videre* (to see), and the English words *wit* and *witch*. In Indian philosophy, the mother Vak has to precede her creation, just as the premasculine *chora* precedes Being in Plato. Vak is indeed "prior to the One."

Whereas the West imposed a male *logos*, the Indian religious traditions have retained this female personification of language. The female appropriation of speech or utterance exalted in the ancient scriptural hymn has been applied practically in Vedic ritual in the form of mantras for centuries.[6] In later Hinduism, Vak is blended into Sarasvati, the goddess of eloquence and learning. In popular Hindu art, the beautiful goddess Sarasvati carries the Vedas in one of her four hands and the vina (ancient Indian stringed instrument) in another. Thus she is the holder of speech and sound. In tantric speculations Vak becomes the female power known as Shakti. Yogic practices consist in arousing her from her dormant state of Kundalini (the snakelike energy curled at the basic plexus of our spine) or Vak Devi (goddess of speech) and tapping into her powers by raising her up from the lowest centers of the body to the highest.[7]

In the Sikh tradition, "the navel of immortality" is called *bani,* denoting word, speech, or sound. She is not deified or limited in any fashion, and flows dynamically through the interpenetrating realms of Sikh metaphysics, history, and aesthetics. Kristeva's "semiotic" enables us to recollect the primordial Body of *bani* in the five hymns recited during the Khalsa rite of initiation, and daily by the Sikhs. Since the five hymns issue from the sacred text, they lead us back metaphysically, historically, and aesthetically to the Guru Granth, and we too shall follow their reciprocal movements. In Sikh parlance, each individual hymn and the collective corpus, are both called *bani*. In our semiotic mnemonics we remember

1. *bani* as the physical and dynamic body of the immutable Transcendent
2. *bani* as the body of plenitude and *jouissance* savored by the Sikhs.

Our memories are not mere meditations, but, as Judith Newton would say, "gestures towards history and gestures with political effect."[8] For us it is not simply a matter of interpreting, but a modality for changing the consciousness of those who read and recite *bani*, and for changing their relationship with what they read and recite. By seeing beyond the male symbolic, women can rid themselves of the male mind imposed on them and become free to partake of their heritage, which genuinely belongs to them. Remembering how their experience was articulated and legitimized, Sikh women can begin to live afresh with confidence. Men too can add a whole new dimension to their divided and dualized selves, and together, they can reproduce the whole and healthy Khalsa. Then will we fulfill Guru Gobind Singh's Baisakhi.

Body of the Transcendent One

Amid religious divisions, political conflicts, and social stratifications, the Sikh gurus from Nanak through Gobind Singh experienced the Ultimate as the One Reality. The Guru Granth begins with Nanak's preamble to the Jap "Ikk Oan Kar" [One Being Is]," and the 1,430 portfolio pages of the holy book are a poetic embracing of this quintessential Sikh principle. That infinite and formless One is also the focal point of Guru Gobind Singh's vision, and remains the subject of all his utterances, including Jaap, Swayyai, and Chaupai, which are recited during *amrit* initiation, and daily by devout Sikhs.

The Sikh gurus continuously perceive and conceive That One in both male and female configurations. They express their intimate and passionate experience of the Divine as father, mother, brother, sister, friend, lover, beloved, water, earth, skies, bumblebee, ocean, drop of rain. Their expression, the revelation of that One, is the feminine *bani*. In her we have a total fusion of content and form, for the very utterances of the gurus manifest the One. Thus, the subject is not apart from the language. However, the collective memory forged by the powerful male academy has invariably registered the vast infinity expressed by the Sikh gurus in male terms. This constricted symbolic disrupts the emotional, linguistic, and philosophical charge of *bani*. Through *bani*, in *bani*, the Ultimate enters our diverse and vibrant world, and in turn becomes the Body that produces and sustains timeless generations of various species. As the navel of Being and Truth, *bani* parallels the mother who bodies forth out of her own flesh and blood.

Semiotic *bani* reveals an organic process in which the Transcendent is rooted in our world. That One does not enter into our world from outside or above but rather exists as the basic ingredient of the cosmos: "[I]nside and outside, it is your *bani*" (GG, 99); "[W]ithin every heart resides true *bani*" (769); "[T]he Guru's *bani* permeates every being" (1075). In different ways, the Guru Granth pronounces *bani* as the "primal source [*dhuri ki bani*]." (628). She is the first principle, the original force, the sole reality. As such there can be nothing beside her and nothing outside of her. No segment of the universe could be separate from her. Cracking patriarchal edifices, she points to the primordial womb from which everything and everyone originates, and in which everything and everyone lives.

Bani is mentioned often in Guru Nanak's Jap. Initially recited by Nanak during his encounter with the Divine (as we discussed in chapter 3), this inaugural hymn of the Khalsa (and that of the Guru Granth as well) flows with the placental waters of River Bein: "Salutations! You are the World, the Word (*bani*), the Creator Truth, Beauty and Joy Eternal!" (Jap, stanza 21). With a strong rhythmic momentum, Nanak exalts the One as the World, Word, Creation, Truth, Beauty, and Joy. *Bani* is identified with the manifest world, with the flourishing creation, with the immutable truth, the beauty, and the eternal joy that are experienced by our senses. All of these modalities are identical and simultaneous: immutable truth is no different from the experience of it within time and space, and so *bani* is not an alternative aspect of the formless One. In fact, she is joyously equated with That One: "[W]onderful! wonderful! *Bani* is the formless One" (GG, 515). She is the Formless One, and she is the revelation and manifestation of That One. The unknown, unloved, immeasurable Transcendent becomes measured and defined and loved and known through her. As the beautiful and joyous body of the Transcendent One, she is the source of all our experience, sensuous and spiritual.

Sikh scripture celebrates *bani* as the modality of Truth. But she is not an abstract or rational conception. *Bani* is Truth that is lived out fully here and now, and it is through her that we become aware of Truth and are united with Truth. She is the one who inspires us to live truthfully in our variegated cosmos. The gurus repeatedly extol her as the body of truth—"Wonderful, wonderful is the truthful *bani*" (GG, 514, 1276). "True *bani* is truth, and true with truth unites" (954). Subverting conventional Indian and Greek philosophies that speculate upon the cosmos as a mere appearance of reality, and aspire to disentangle the transient physical forms from the immutable spiritual essence, Sikh ontology seeks the union of the temporal with the eternal, and truth with true living. *Bani* is the Body of Truth (*sat sarup*)—the corporeal self, the thing in itself. It is through her vital presence that we get to hear, see, touch, and experience the true nature of all phenomena. Individual life or the cosmos around us is no mere shadow of Kant's phenomenal self (*Ding an sich*); it is not the maya or illusion of Samkhya philosophy. It is Truth herself. The organic expression of the Absolute One, *bani* exalts human existence as truth and reality, and not as a condition of imperfection or falsity.

Since truth is not static but life and movement, the Body of Truth could not be an eternally immobile receptacle; she is forever diverse, moving, changing, and transforming. Our cosmos is a spontaneous and colorful unfolding and blooming of truth. Since both are truth, nature and *bani* become identified with each other: "[T]rue is nature; true is *bani*" (GG, 1074). Another reference to *bani* in Guru Nanak's Jap establishes a link between (countless) species and (countless) languages: "how many species! how many languages!" (Jap, stanza 35). The dynamic creatures of the world and their languages are intrinsically bonded together in the vision of the Sikh Gurus. As they echo one another in numerous instances, the Sikh Gurus offer an antidote to the alienation suffered in our technological culture. The first guru says: "[S]pecies and languages are yours" (GG, 580); the third: "[Y]ou yourself are the species, you yourself are the languages, you yourself create the continents and constellations" (552); the Fifth: "[Y]ours are the species, yours are the languages" (116), and so on. Derived from the same root, all species and languages belong to a single family. The divine, nature, and humanity are bound together rather than tiered into hierarchical levels with humans at the summit dominating and distorting the chorus of the planetary system.

With a quick rhythm, Guru Gobind Singh's Jaap exalts the animating and life-generating One who flows through and interconnects the myriad creatures: "[S]alutations to You in every country, in every garb" (Jaap, verse 66); again, "You in every country, in every form" (verse 117). Like Nanak's Jap, Guru Gobind Singh's Jaap rejoices in the presence of the Transcendent within the glorious diversity of the cosmos: "You are in water, You are on land" (verse 62); "You are the sustainer of the earth" (verse 173); and (with a slight variation), "[S]ustainer of the earth you are" (verse 178). The Sikh guru wins back the sacred that is snatched from the world of matter by the Father and exclaims, "You are the language of all languages" (verse 155). The temporal becoming of all of us is lodged in Truth—the universal vocal and kinetic rhythm of us all.

Infinite species and infinite languages originate from the same source and in turn become the source of all communication, of life itself. The diverse and plural cosmos depends upon communication and union, which are brought about by language. In his Jap, Nanak says, "[B]y words we speak and by words we write, by words we communicate and unite" (stanza 19). In his Akal Ustat, Guru Gobind Singh reminds us of our common language, which bonds us across all borders: "same one language [*ekai ban*]" (verse 86). The infinite species of our cosmos are begotten through language, which precedes the paternal symbolic. Kristeva's claim that "genetic programmings are necessarily semiotic" underlies the Sikh hymns, for they poetically posit language as physical and elemental. Language clearly is not in the Father's grammar, nor is it cultivated by man alone. For the Sikh gurus, from Nanak to Gobind, it is that primal language which is common to the vegetal, human, and animal spheres. The "genetic programming" belongs to the myriad forms of life; her syllables are life and life's continuity; her sounds are breath, blood, water, sex, and food.

In fact, semiotic *bani* is integral to the development of consciousness. Guru Nanak's Jap concludes by launching readers and reciters into a deeper and deeper intensity through the realms of *dharam, gyan, saram, karam* and *sach*—Earth, Knowledge, Beauty, Action, and Truth.[9] With maps and charts drafted totally on the longitudes and latitudes of our planet earth (*dharat*), Guru Nanak enunciates the development of moral, intellectual, aesthetic, and spiritual capacities. The third stage in this fivefold spiritual odyssey, *saram khand*, opens with a striking note: "Form is the language of *saram khand*; here are created the most beautiful of forms" (Jap, stanza 36).

How can "form" be a language? Guru Nanak's innovative phrase contains Kristeva's feminist perception of language, but it has been undermined in Sikh exegesis. In his erudite commentary on the hymn, G. S. Talib emphatically writes, "In the original is *bani*, which here stands not for 'speech' or 'expression' but 'making,' 'forging.'"[10] My teachers also told me that the term *bani* in this verse could not possibly mean "language," and though it meant language everywhere else, in this instance it was derived from the verbal root *bana* ("to make," but this word has a short *a*, whereas the *a* in *bani* is long). The rejection of the word "language" rejects Guru Nanak's semiotic understanding of language: *bani* is not a symbolic mode that is spoken, read, heard, or thought about, but the very matter out of which shapes and patterns are formed and sustained. Language is the actual Form (*rup*); it is the physical body.

Interestingly, the Law of the Father cannot describe the processes of *saram khand*. Sikh theologians have always found it hard to analyze this realm enunciated by Guru Nanak. Some argue that it pertains to the Persian *sharam* or shame, while others trace it to Sanskrit *saram* or effort, and their polemics are effectively discussed by Hew McLeod.[11] Our exegetes, however, forget that Guru Nanak had cautioned: "[W]ords fail to describe it, and those who try only regret" (Jap, stanza 36). Creative activities cannot be pinned down by an intellectual narrative; their splendor cannot be categorized by a patriarchal language. Free from the imposition of univocal categorizations and rational logic, maternal language heightens our sensitivities and energies. She makes the "blunt sharp" (GG, 941). The refinement and honing that takes place in *saram khand* does not lead to the Father's Ideas but, as Nanak says, to the mystical and divine experience: "[T]here the consciousness is sharpened to that of the gods and mystics" (Jap, stanza 36). As we make our entry into the depths of the unconscious—hidden away from the superficial level of logical knowledge—the dominance of the male symbolic is uprooted. The supreme analogue of the male mind is replaced by the maternal womb, where growth is both physical and mental, and the experience of union ineffable and unfettered.

Breaking the childlike/sophisticated and primeval/civilized binaries, the force of *bani,* like a mother's hold, ushers us closer and closer to the Transcendent. The fourth and final mention of *bani* in Guru Nanak's Jap characterizes the realm of Action: "[F]orce is the language of *karam khand*" (stanza 27). The junction where the individual seeking the Divine meets with the benevolence of That One is indeed powerful, and so Guru Nanak's own language brims with might and strength. The guru depicts this stage as full of valorous heroes and heroines. But the only one mentioned by name is the ancient Indian heroine Sita. Literally, *sita* means "furrow," and prior to Valmiki's *Ramayana,* Vedic literature petitioned her as "the mother of gods, mortals, and creatures."[12] In our re-memory, Sita's primordial female energy is remembered by the Sikh guru, and *her* creative abundance permeates the spiritual realm of *karam khand.*

The ancient Indian paradigm of female power is presented in the plural by Guru Nanak—*sito sita.* His usage of *sitas* not only increases the figures numerically, but also takes away the distant "goddess" stature of Lord Rama's wife, and makes women like Sita accessible and realistic members of society. Again, Guru Nanak admits that language fails to describe their beauty: "[T]heir form is beyond words" (Jap, stanza 37). Whereas the Sikh guru clearly reproduces and magnifies the traditional Indian figure, the patriarchal exegetes of his text try to dismiss and disfigure her. G. S. Talib shrugs her aside: "It would be superfluous to dilate on the symbolic character of Sita as representative of all that is noblest and purest in human nature."[13] Other exegetes reduce the full-blooded woman to the process of "stitching." In his popular text published by the Shromani Gurdwara Prabandhak Committee, Professor Kartar Singh explains Nanak's usage of *sito-sita* as "perfectly stitched [*puran taur te seeta hoia*]."[14] Sita, and women like Sita, are misappropriated into a man "stitched" in devotion. And still other interpreters of the Jap congeal the lively Sita and her companions into solid ice (deriving the term *sita* from *sheeta,* meaning "cold")![15]

Such representations are not reflections but rather active processes that Jackie Byer defines as processes of "selecting and presenting, of structuring and shaping, of making things *mean.*"[16] The misrepresentations and excisions of the female person in Sikh scholarship are carried out by the male symbolic, which refuses to imagine the female sexuality of the Transcendent One. Generations of patriarchy have been programmed to fear her body, and this threat of her sexuality has kept readers and hearers from recognizing the semiotic significance of Sikh sacred verse. *Bani* permeates with female force and fecundity, but the fear and disdain of *her* presence has kept Sikhs from acknowledging female images in the poetic world of the gurus. It is encouraging for a feminist to come across a distinguished Sikh scholar who recognizes that Guru Gobind Singh "introduced a new maternal dimension to Sikh understandings of Ultimate Reality."[17] Nevertheless, it is sad that neither he nor the Sikh community in general have paid due attention to the fact that all of the Sikh gurus, going back to Guru Nanak himself, have had a deep awareness of the life-giving female source. Guru Nanak's Jap, recited daily by Sikhs, amply acknowledges the Mother who gave birth to the three manifestations: creation, preservation, and destruction (Jap, stanza 30). The epilogue of his Jap reminds us of the great Mother Earth (*mata dharati mahat*) on whose lap we play. The fivefold journey begins with our grounding in Mother Earth. While Nanak and his successors clearly remind us of a vital maternal dimension, the community hides *her* away from public consciousness. Symptomatically, the wide horizon full of possibilities offered by Nanak and his successors remains shut, and what dominates in Sikhism is a patriarchal structure, with a distorted configuration of the Transcendent, and of our cosmos and society.

The tenth guru does not introduce "a new maternal dimension"; he remembers and carries forth the maternal resources envisioned by the first one. His Jaap (the opening hymn of the Dasam Granth), which is based on Nanak's Jap (the opening hymn of the Guru Granth), recognizes the Divine as Mother. Guru Gobind Singh intensely experiences and freely utilizes the forceful language (*bani jor*) of *karam khand.* A poetic offering to the One, his Jaap in 199 verses is a marvelous profusion that flashed on his artistic consciousness. Powerful language set in a fiery rhythm addresses the One in a wide range of images and metaphors. The One is "crusher of the enemy, supporter of the poor, destroyer of foes, dispeller of fears" (Jaap, verse 153). The breath in which Guru Gobind Singh extols the Infinite culminates in "the Mother of the cosmos"—"[S]alutations to the wielder of weapons, to the hurler of missiles, to the knower of all, to the Mother of the cosmos" (Jaap, verse 52). Nanak's female creatrix is re-envisioned by Gobind, and the language, diction, and temper of Nanak's *karam khand* with both its mighty heroes and heroines is reproduced in the verse of the tenth guru.

But just as the female power is excised from Nanak's Jap, so is it from Guru Gobind Singh's Jaap. Her energy is withdrawn, and the multitude of vigorous actions and functions of the Transcendent are attributed only to a male subject by Sikhs. The Jaap profusely acknowledges the formless One as the creator of the entire universe: "produced the whole expanse" (Jaap, verse 83); "creator of the world" (verse 106); "creator" (verse 24). Guru Gobind Singh honors the One as the "life of lives" (verse 72). His hymn profusely acknowledges the formless One as the sustaining force of the cosmos: "protects all" (verse 78), "protecting all" (verse 79), " protector of all" (verse 85), "protects all" (verse 28). The infinite Subject is envisioned through a myriad functions and powers, and in the velocity of Guru Gobind Singh's imagination, the gender of the Subject is not specified. However, all of these powers—even those which are typically maternal—are defined, interpreted, remembered, and translated exclusively in male terminology. Never, never, do we come across their female version. So the verses may be recited daily without their powerful female configuration ever surfacing in the memories of the Sikhs.

Sita is abducted from the semiotic poetry of Guru Nanak, and Durga-Kali from the poetry of Guru Gobind Singh; deliberately or accidentally, the maternal image and female activities are erased from the *bani* of the Khalsa. The female victors of Indian mythology become victims of Sikh male symbolic analysis with the result that the rich Sikh mnemonic resources are deplorably reduced. Guru Gobind Singh's sumptuous re-creation of the ancient heroine in his *Candi* poems wonderfully substantiates his capacity for and interest in seeing *her* as an active agent. Consequently, when he envisions the Infinite performing powerful actions in the Jaap, the female was sure to have been a major figure on his mental canvas. The wide range of humanity envisioned by the Sikh gurus has the potential to activate our conscious and unconscious selves. Their comprehensive imagery broadens our mental landscapes and affects our attitudes and actions toward one another. Inversely, by excising the female mythological figures from their compositions, by excising the female configurations from the hymns we recite, we fail to utilize their broad-mindedness. We only perpetuate insularity, exclusivity, and sexism.

Guru Gobind Singh's Jaap contains an endless list of vital terms that significantly are gender unspecific: "hurler," "creator," "protector," "sustainer," "food of foods," "song of songs," "light of lights." These open-ended expressions have been reduced to male personifications, and many Sikhs would consider it practically sacrilegious to recognize them as female agents. To insert a "she" in place of the "he" in commentaries and translations would be sheer anathema. Sikh theologians fear idols, and yet, by refraining from including the female imaginary in the vision of the formless One of their gurus, they succumb to an idol of masculinity. They only end up making their "monotheistic" religion into an "androtheistic" one, which itself is a form of idolatry. Only in paternal codes have Sikhs received and conveyed the infinite One. The Father's symbolic dilutes the powerful language *(bani jor)* of the world of action, and in spite of Guru Gobind Singh's efforts, the heroines (and even true heroes) of Guru Nanak's *karam khand* are not reproduced in the family of the Khalsa.

We must be very clear that though *bani* rejoices in the maternal body of the transcendent One, the maternal imaginary in the Sikh *Weltanschauung* is not a matter of religious deification whereby women are idolized as distant goddesses and made objects of worship. As Simone de Beauvoir perceptively warned us in her classic *The Second Sex*, the goddess can be a dehumanization of women rather than their genuine exaltation. De Beauvoir felt that idolizing goddesses was largely a male urge to have women "smooth, hard, and changeless as a pebble."[18] Contemporary scholars are now seriously looking into the impact that the powerful Hindu and Buddhist goddesses have on the social status and psyche of their worshippers. The recent volume *Is the Goddess a Feminist?* explores the male desire to embody female deities in the South Asian context. In her introduction, Kathleen Erndl cites the view of an erudite Hindu professor who approves of their power so long as it remains distant: "We like them as goddesses but not as people."[19] His casual remark sums it all up: the power of the Hindu goddess exists, but it must not touch us in our social and political reality.

It is very important that we distinguish the Sikh gurus from such perceptions. They do not worship the goddess. They loudly prohibit Sikhs from worshipping any deity in chants, images, or idols. Guru Gobind Singh's Swayyais, which form a part of the daily repertoire of Sikh hymns, categorically denounce any form of idolatry. That would be a way of divorcing the external from the internal, the ideal from the real. In the Sikh world, Durga, Sita, and women like them are the continuum of the Body from whom we are created, the Body that is reproduced in our sisters, our daughters, our wives, our friends. Without being deified, the female figures in the semiotic *bani* of the Khalsa are cherished as strong, compassionate, intelligent, and creative personalities. We cannot erase Sita or Durga-Kali from the expansive vision of the gurus, because that would disrupt the infinity of the One. They are there not to be worshipped from afar but to be remembered as role models whom we must pull into the nitty-gritty aspects of life. *We want them as people.*

Nor must we understand the Sikh maternal imaginary as a romantic exaltation of women as mothers. In no way must we construe the maternal power of the Transcendent as an automatic and mandatory process whereby women are tied down to be reproductory machines who must beget sons. It is not a command that she be "the mother of a hundred sons"—a blessing commonly heard in the patriarchal society of India. Nor should she be misinterpreted as fertile nature, manipulated and exploited by her sons. As I stated in my introduction, I do not intend to equate the maternal with physical conception or limit the maternal to the domestic world; for me it is the germinative ocean, the formless potential, that every female carries within her body. The Sikh maternal imaginary reveals to us the Subject who carries in her womb the power to produce—or refuse. The power of creation is her body, her womb, in which the conventional opposition between maternal love and sexual desire is washed away. It is not necessary that women give birth to children; they can give birth, as Luce Irigaray says, to many other things, such as "love, desire, language, art, social things, political things, religious things." However, society forces biological reproduction on women, and stifles all other forms of creativity in women, and so we must, as Irigaray exhorts, "take back this maternal creative dimension that is our birthright as women."[20] We remember Sikh hymns conferring a sense of reality on women's creativity, and enabling each one of us to cultivate meaningful relationships with our past and future, with East and West, with our biological and geographical community, or in Guru Gobind Singh's vocabulary, "with all four directions [*catr cakre*]" (Jaap, verse 199).

Semiotic *bani* truly validates the importance of the maternal continuum; she retrieves the primacy of birth over death, and reaffirms the union of body and mind. She offers new openings to feminist perspectives that are underscored by scholars in their own different ways. Indeed, the Body of the Infinite connects each one of us with the two sequences of infinity: the past and future of every male or female. In her provocative book *In Spite of Plato*, Adriana Cavarero notes that "Both infinities, past and future, origin and perpetuation, always exist through the feminine."[21] At the outset of her study on Freud, Madelon Sprengnether writes, "Whatever our other differences, as human beings we have one thing in common: we are all born of woman." Sprengnether finds a vivid testimonial to the power of the mother's body in Freud's observation that "after a protracted labor it [the baby's skull] takes the form of a cast of the narrow part of the mother's pelvis".[22] Semiotic *bani* illuminates for us the views of contemporary feminist scholars that we are rooted in female genealogy, and returns meaning to the basic fact that we are all born of woman. Rather than an abstract mode of language, Primordial Bani (*dhur ki bani*), True Bani (*saci bani*), is a palpable portion of infinity in which each of us from every species becomes embodied and exists authentically.

The Body of the Transcendent disrupts patriarchal dichotomies and draws our attention to this world. Instead of fleeing the world and body, hearers and reciters are impelled to have positive perceptions of themselves, and to develop constructive relationships with the world around them. "Amid mother, father, brother, son, and wife has the Divine yoked us," states the Guru Granth (p. 77). In these divinely bound relationships, mother and wife are both significant, and women's maternal and sexual proclivities are equally celebrated. Guru Gobind Singh's Jaap teems with the presence of the One in all four directions, and retrieves the tight yoke between our universe and our ultimate Reality (Jaap, verse 74). The image of the One "tied to all" (verse 77) evokes the umbilical cord to which we are primally attached. The verses of the gurus open up our sensibilities and imagination, and increase our respect for our female progenitor.

By her sexual and maternal powers, the mother protects the horizon of the physical, which has been downgraded and severed by the patriarchal metaphysical order carrying death as the fundamental paradigm. Feminist scholars criticize metaphysics as a form of matricide, and in Luce Irigaray's words, "Its soil has become culture, history, which successfully forget[s] that anything that conceives has its origins in the flesh."[23] For Cavarero, "Man, with a masculine—universal—natural valence, is a term from a language that has turned its gaze away from the place of birth, measuring existence on an end point that bears no memory of its beginning."[24] In our first chapter we incorporated Grace Jantzen's view that the obsession with death is connected with "the obsession with female bodies, and the denial of death and efforts to master it are connected with a deep-seated misogyny."[25] For Jantzen the various forms of dominance—racism, capitalism, colonialism, homophobia, ecological destruction—are imbrications of the need to conquer death.

In contrast with the necrophilic imaginary of the male symbolic, we find the semiotic poetry of the gurus affirming life and living in diverse forms. The Granth states, "You yourself are born of the egg, from the womb, from sweat, from earth: you yourself are all the continents and all the worlds" (GG, 604). These words resonate in Guru Gobind Singh's *Bicitra Natak*: "You have produced the sweat-born, fetus-born, earth-born / You have created the egg-born and the continents and the cosmos . . . "(*BN*, 1:24). The hymns of the Khalsa invoke the Transcendent as an essential experience of everyday life. The Jaap abounds with descriptions of That One as living and breathing all around us in infinite colors and shapes: "[H]omage to you in every form" (Jaap, verse 19); "homage to you in every color" (verse 71). While reminding us of Kristeva's principle that "The reproductive system is the essential link between the living individual and the species,"[26] Guru Gobind Singh's images are vital reminders that we come into the world along with the Divine, and that we come into the world by a woman who could not be a man. As we hear him exalt the Transcendent in his Jaap, we hear reverberations of the Granthian exaltation "Blessed are the mothers!" (GG, 513). The maternal power with her paradigm of natality overturns the male ideal with death as its fundamental paradigm. Indeed, "the womb of Mother Earth yokes us together" (GG, 1021). Birth becomes the absolute possibility of orienting us in the physical world so that we experience fully—body and spirit together—the Absolute within the natural and social fibers of our being.

The semiotic poetry of the Khalsa constantly turns our gaze to our origin in the mother's body. She beckons us back to the womb—the *garbha* or *udar*—reminding us poignantly that it is the place where we become the self, both body and spirit. Even Guru Gobind Singh's usage of *rahime* (compassionate)—for example, *namastam rahime* (salutations to the compassionate One)! (Jaap, verse 25), or *rahime rihakai* (compassionate liberator) (Jaap 108)—draws us to her maternal space. In the speculations of the Muslim philosopher Ibn Arabi, the root of the word *rahimat* is "womb," and the meaning of compassion or mercy is derived from it.[27] Similarly, feminist scholars relate the Hebrew word *rachum*, the word for compassion, with *racham*, the word for womb.[28] Sikh scripture resonates with many positive memories of our lodging in the mother's creative organ: "[I]n the mother's womb are we taken care of" (GG, 1086) and "in the mother's womb you nurture us" (132). In order to retrieve the meaning of *bani*, in order to live our lives in accordance with the verses of the gurus, in order to experience the harmonious patterns between *bani* and *bana*, we need to refresh our memories and absorb them. In a melody of phonetic sounds and a collage of visual images, the following passage by Guru Nanak takes us to our primal lodging. Since the maternal womb perfectly illuminates the Body of the Transcendent One, it forms a relevant conclusion to this section.

> Semen and blood came together to create the body;
> Air, water, fire came together to create life;
> And the One performs wonders in the colorful body;
> all else is the expanse of illusion and attachment.
> In the rounded womb is the upside down thinker,
> And the knower knows every one's hearts;
> Each breath remembers the true name,
> for inside the womb flourishes the One.
>
> (GG, 1026)

Her creative site of pregnancy is here brilliantly photographed by Guru Nanak. But this is no scopophilic or fetishistic construction. Focusing on the maternal organ, his semiotic lens takes us back to that magical location where womb, ovum, and sperm come together, making us mindful of the locus where life is produced—life that is the body, life that is the spirit. The founding Sikh guru's recollection of our first home forms a strong contrast to the male conceptions noted by Luce Irigaray: "The womb is never thought of as the primal place in which we become body. Therefore for many men it is variously phantasized as a devouring mouth, as a sewer in which anal and urethral waste is poured, as a threat to the phallus or, at best, as a reproductive organ."[29] Her womb is no "devouring mouth," no "sewer," no merely "reproductive organ." The Sikh guru makes us cognizant of our ontological, epistemological, and aesthetic rootedness in women's physiology. "Woman is the stuff out of which all people are made."[30]

Feminist scholars have noted how Aristotelian doctrine attributes the father with the agency to create, and so the maternal womb is only a container of inert and cold matter to which the warm sperm gives life. Such patriarchal notions are also overturned. The guru posits the equality and unity of *bindu* (semen) and *raktu* (blood) as the source of life. Elsewhere, too, Sikh scripture maintains, that "mother and father unite, and with blood and semen they make the body" (GG, 1,013). "The union of mother and father earns us the body" (989), and it includes Kabir's statement, "Without mother or father there can be no children" (872). We can even hear the Guru Granth honoring the maternal space as a social utopia in which the fetus is free from all patriarchal labels: "[I]n the dwelling of the womb, there is neither name nor caste" (324). The scriptural verses transparently reveal that the waters of the River Bein and that of the Khalsa's *amrit* are no different from the placental waters of the mother—primal and nourishing, these waters are free of all distinctions and hierarchies.

In Nanak's feminist photography we discover a maternal space pregnant with the Transcendent One. Hers is a vibrant and active site where the One is fully rooted: as our passage reads, "The One performs wonders in the colorful body" (GG, 1,026). That One has not made the entry from the outside or above but constitutes an essential part of her physiology: "Inside the womb flourishes the One" (GG, 1,026). With the Infinite delighting inside her body, the fetus grows, drawing upon the nutrients of the basic elements that the mother herself shares with the rest of the cosmos. The male Sikh guru seems to have used the lens of modern feminists for whom natural elements "constitute the origin of our bodies, of our life, of our environment, the flesh of our passions."[31] Guru Gobind Singh in his Akal Ustat likewise reminds us that we are created from the four elements, "a combination of earth, air, fire and water" (verse 86). The Sikh gurus go further than our contemporary French feminist writer, Irigaray, for they even show us the Divine present visibly—performing wonders, as Nanak says—within the walls of her uterus! That the Transcendent is not an extraneous addition but the very core of our physical self is a salient theme in Sikh sacred verses. Being in the womb is therefore a most healthy and positive human condition, and the Guru Granth overall is full of palpable reminders that we are tenderly cared for by the Divine: "[I]n the mother's womb you protect us with your hand" (GG, 805). Fetuses do not fall into the womb. They are lodged in the maternal space where the Transcendent exists simultaneously with the physical elements. In her semiotic foundations, we are somatically alive to the touch of the Transcendent Hand.

And "in the womb is the thinker"! The embryo lodged upside down is the guru's paradigm for one rapt in meditation and contemplation—its each and every heartbeat remembering the True Name. Semiotic *bani* respects the womb as the locus for both biological and spiritual growth. "Upside down in the chamber of the womb intense meditation is performed" (GG, 251); "you generated meditative heat in the womb" (337); and "without remembrance, we rot in the womb" (362). Her womb is the space where body and spirit are harmoniously integrated. The embryonic unit is not split into the female body doomed to die versus the male mind destined to live for eternity. Its upside-down posture graphically represents spiritual devotion, since "each breath is that of the True Name." Indeed, the womb is the matrix for all mental and spiritual processes. Mind and body together grow and feed on the elements shared by the mother. In *her* body, with *her* body, we begin our immediate connections with the cosmos and come into the world with the "four objectives" identified in ancient Indian philosophy as *dharma, moksha, artha*, and *kama*. Each person comes into the world with moral commitments *(dharma)*, works and earns money *(artha)*, enjoys sexual relations (*kama*), and experiences spiritual freedom (*moksha*). The four goals belong to ancient philosophy, but their incubation in the intrauterine phase where we all, men and women, begin to live intensely in all four dimensions belongs uniquely to Sikh ontological memories. Birth—not death—is the absolute possibility of us humans, and the authenticity of Heidegger's *Dasein* is strongly established in the mother's womb.

Her anatomy beckons us back to the third spiritual realm of Nanak's Jap: "Form is the language of this realm (Jap, stanza 36)." In Aristotelian embryology, the mother's "container" merely holds what the father produces. Against androcentric perceptions of a temporary "little oven in which the paternal gene was nurtured and cozily leavened,"[32] *garbh* or *udar*, is claimed as the source of life. In Sikh metaphysics, the whole person is created by and in the womb, and so *garbh* is no different from *saram khand*. Both share the creative surge, both fashion and design the most beautiful and intricate shapes, and "form is their language [*bani rup*]."

I find it truly amazing that, living within the parameters of patriarchal society of medieval India, Sikh male gurus possessed a "feminist" sensibility. Their verses uphold the concerns and solutions articulated by contemporary feminists. They take female genealogy seriously, and affirm the category of birth that feminist thealogians, philosophers, and psychologists of our own times find so critical. Their poetic utterances form splendid overtures to modern feminist reflections: "Mother-*mater*-matter-matrix. 'Woman' is the stuff out of which all people are made. In the beginning was her flesh, and, after the beginning, she continues to suggest human historicity, to suggest human connection to and dependence upon the outside world. It is this deep memory of birth union, I think, which turns any serious reflection on women into a reflection on the interconnection of human beings with each other and with all the things which make up the body of the world."[33] The deep memory of birth union, celebrated in this powerful passage by Naomi Goldenberg, is vital to the Sikh gurus. Our spirituality is anchored in our bodies, and our physical and spiritual birth is from the mother's creativity. Her womb, the metonymic marker of woman, is not a passive receptacle but an active and powerful locus where our unified subjectivity is conceived and developed. A powerful reminder of our uterine relationship by which we are all siblings born of the same mother, semiotic *bani* inspires us to reflect on our complex contingency.

But as usual, the mother's body so boldly expressed and affirmed in the verses of the gurus is repressed or deleted in male hermeneutic. Whereas the Guru Granth explicitly affirms that the Divine permeates both the heart and the womb—"It pervades every heart and flourishes in the womb" (GG, 1,026)—the translators and commentators of Sikh scripture simply deem it unnecessary to remember *her* body or our origins, and so the unique emphasis of the Sikh gurus on the divine constitution of female physiology and of our integrated subjectivity is lost. In their English translations, both G. S. Talib and Gopal Singh register the heart (*ghat*) but utterly ignore the womb (*udar*) in Guru Nanak's feminist sensibility.[34] The particular female organ even gets altered into a generic "stomach" or "belly." The authoritative and most popular exegetical text, the *Sabdarath*, refers to *udar* as *pet* (the Punjabi word for "stomach"),[35] and an otherwise excellent Internet resource translates it as "belly."[36] The radical vision of the gurus and their invigorating overtures remain unseen, unheard. Their womb-respecting, birth-oriented glimpses and melodies need to be remembered so that their lingering can make each of us more wholesome, and our world a better place.

Free of male symbolic, the sacred utterances reveal the organic process in which the embryo is consubstantial with the mother and the Transcendent One. We see the wonderful delights performed by That One in the maternal womb, and feel the touch and warmth of the divine "hand" by which we are primally held. Guru Nanak's reminder that we are brought into the world by our first principle, our original source brimming with dynamic physical and spiritual nutrients, flows vibrantly into the poetry of his successor gurus. The first guru's vivid cartography of the female body is reconfigured in Guru Gobind Singh's "salutations to the Mother of the cosmos!" (Jaap, verse 52). A female creatrix is central to Guru Gobind Singh's imagination and vision. Connecting men and women with each other, the "mother of the cosmos," connects us with all the other species that make up the body of our cosmos. When the daily hymns of the Sikhs are not simply recited but duly remembered, they send ripples of joy and strength in each of our own bodies, male and female. Surely, we are not thrown into the world but bring with every new birth—male and female—exciting beginnings and perspectives to develop intimate relationships with our mothers, our families, our friends, our pluralistic society, our variegated cosmos, and our Singular Divine.

The Body of Plenitude and Jouissance

The body of the Transcendent is the body of plenitude and *jouissance*. It is drunk by the Khalsa: the sapiential ingredients of the verses are sipped by the initiates, they are tasted, and they are savored. Altogether it is a very oral activity, something akin to Hélène Cixous's venture, "I was eating the texts, I was sucking, licking, kissing them, I am the innumerable child of their multitudes. . . ."[37] By drinking *amrit* prepared in and with the sight and sound and touch of semiotic poetry, the Khalsa is born, and is thereafter daily nurtured and sustained by *her*. So not only are the verses the first sheaths and the first membranes that create the Khalsa, but they are also the nutrients that are physically taken inside the body and become a part of the bloodstream of the newborn members, and continue to feed them throughout their lives and that of their future generations. The hymns of the Khalsa are none other than Cixous's omnipotent mother figure, who is powerful and generous, a dispenser of life, love, and plenitude.

Semiotic *bani* is the vital link in Sikh genealogy. Her dynamic womb reproduces the drinking of *amrit* by Guru Nanak in the River Bein, and pushes the primal Sikh experience into the future. When the fifth guru compiled the poetry of his predecessors, it was his way of giving a concrete form to their very sensuous experience that would nurture the Sikh community forever. Guru Arjan did not construct theological treatises or list ethical injunctions for his Sikhs: he gave them a body of literature that he wanted them to eat *(khavai)* and savor *(bhunchai)*. In his epilogue to the Granth, he says, "[T]hey who eat, they who savor, are liberated." Guru Arjan here uses the analogy of a platter. The Guru Granth is a *thal* (large metal dish) on which lie truth, contentment, and contemplation. The epistemological value of these dishes is not intellectually conceived or logically argued, it is swallowed and digested by the body. The *thal* is antithetical to male episteme, which rests on nonmaterial ideas and formless essence, and with the *thal* enjoyment of the text becomes paramount. Savoring the words is the quintessential practice for the Sikh community. For the compiler and editor, the textuality of the Guru Granth lies in its physical sensuality and not in some rigid symbolic order. Clearly, the fifth guru envisioned poetry as the body of plenitude and *jouissance*, a body that is both eaten and savored. The medieval Indian male Guru and contemporary European feminist secularists voice an intimate relationship with their texts, and in the sacred verses of the Khalsa we can recover the multiple and endless *jouissance* that Irigaray and Cixous unabashedly write about.

The identity of knowledge and food lodged in the epilogue of the Guru Granth is prefigured in Guru Nanak's Jap, the opening hymn of the Granth: "[K]nowledge is the banquet, compassion the hostess" (Jap, stanza 29). Knowledge is a delectable banquet. This sumptuous array of dishes indicated by Guru Nanak is specified by Guru Arjan as truth, contentment, and contemplation.

We find yet another intriguing resemblance, this time between Guru Nanak's *bhandarani* (hostess) and Guru Gobind Singh's *kirpan* (sword). The features, personality, and proclivities of the hostess who distributes the food of knowledge in the Jap hymn reemerge in the Khalsa symbol of the *kirpan*. The physiognomy in each case is rooted in the symbiosis of knowledge and compassion, for both resources offer knowledge *(gian)*, and both are full of compassion *(daia)*. Compassion *(daia)* is actually the name of Nanak's *bhandarani*, and this virtue is shared by Guru Gobind Singh's *kirpan* (since *kirpa* means "compassion"). The figure of Nanak's "hostess" is incorporated in Sikh practice by the "sword." She is recalled in the daily hymns to guide us through our lives. She is the one who possesses the mystical recipe and prepares *amrit*. She is the one who gives final touches to Karahprashad, the Sikh sacrament, before it is distributed in the congregation.

Sadly, however, malestream interpretations dismiss her image from the guru's verse, and the male hands that prepare *amrit* and distribute Karahprashad in public worship keep *her* concealed and controlled. The trend to crush, conceal, and control the female person continues in Sikh homes and in the wider community. Mothers, daughters, and sisters who prepare food day and night are relegated to a low status and usually circumscribed to the private sphere of the home; mothers, daughters, and sisters who selflessly serve meals to their families are severed from links with wisdom and knowledge. Sikh *bani* and *bana* lyrically exhort us to acknowledge the wise and compassionate female agent in the vision of the gurus, and have her join us in both our public and private lives. Food and knowledge, body and mind, are not binaries; we receive them both from *her*. We must relearn to hear her voice, see her viewpoint, and recognize her hands as they constantly feed us with knowledge served in a variety of dishes.

The image of the hostess from the Jap shifts our sense of *gian*, or knowledge, from an isolated activity in cubbyholes within the walls of academia to the elemental processes of eating and living in the "feminine" space of the home. Indeed, *bani* absorbs abstract thought into the folds of the body. But this individual process branches out, to use Kristeva's analogy, "like a bridge between singularity and ethics."[38] As personified by the *bhandarani*, the experience of something so inward as tasting and digesting is shared with others. Nanak's *bhandarani*, or hostess, in the Sikh imaginary is engaged in sharing and distributing knowledge and does not place herself above her students. She draws us into kinship with fellow beings, and informs us that the meaning of *sangat*, the Sikh congregation, is essentially a relationship with others so that we can partake together of the delectable platter containing the dishes of truth, knowledge, and contentment. Fed by her, we extend ourselves to our families and to our human community. Knowledge is not the Father's discourse; it is not an end in itself. Knowledge is reaching out actively to help the underprivileged, the deprived, and the violated. Guru Nanak distinctly pronounces, "[K]nowledge and reflection are philanthropic deeds performed for others" (GG, 356). Knowledge for the Sikh gurus consists in *her*ethics, a relational and dialogic *practice* that is not a philosophizing about *his* moral principles and mere abstractions.

The female conception of knowledge actually pervades the holy book. Guru Nanak identifies mother with wisdom: "[M]other is wisdom" (GG, 151); which is later repeated by his successors (172, 1397). She is even regarded as the sister-in-law who is "the most admirable member of her entire family," because "she guides her brothers-in-law, both younger and older" (371). Women in the Guru Granth are not just figures of speech. They are vital subjects who are accorded a high status in the daily course of life.

The female is quintessential to Sikh epistemology, and as I discussed in my earlier work, she is beauty, clarity, and revelation; she is the sister with eyes that see through the Formless.[39] What I missed out then were the scriptural reminders of our intellectual development in the mother's body. Kristeva's semiotic lens has helped me see through their beauty and import. To begin with, the Sikh gurus declare that the human body is precious. But it is in the mother's womb, as Guru Arjan says, "that we acquire all recognition of relationships with mother, father, brother, friend" (GG, 1387). Revealing the affinity between the male Sikh gurus and modern secular feminists, *bani* inspires us to retreat to those initial moments and relearn the primal relationships we experienced in her oceanic womb, and from which we are now split and dichotomized. Our return would not constitute an act of regression, as our phallocentric psychoanalysts may speculate, but a real progression toward new forms of subjectivity and new avenues for discovering our human potential.

Food is a biological necessity, keeping us all from shriveling up and dying. So is knowledge. By equating it with food, the Sikh gurus make knowledge essential for all of us—not just for Plato's philosopher-king or the Brahmins of Vedic India. The cognitive and digestive activities are not relegated to either male or female domains, nor set apart from other activities. Knowledge is eaten, and just like food, it is necessary for our growth and fulfillment, for our being and becoming. Eating is a most creative act: we take something from the external world and turn it into ourselves! A tiny morsel makes a circuit in us, and through the bloodstream becomes a cell, a muscle, a neuron, a thought, an emotion, an embrace. The poets of the Guru Granth repeatedly wish that the Divine be remembered in every "morsel of food" (GG, 961), making our alimentary canals elementary to our spiritual progress. Keeping with the Granthian tract, the tenth guru extols the Transcendent as "the food of foods," "the drink of drinks" (Jaap, verse 187). He meditates on the One as "the elixir of elixirs": *amritamrit hain* (verse 177); *amritesvar hain* (verse 179); *amritamrit hain* (verse 179); *amritamrit hain* (verse 180). The Transcendent is to be fully absorbed and assimilated into every part of our bodies. The hymns of the Khalsa incite us to free ourselves from the surveillance cameras of our culture, which coerce women to hate their bodies and the food they take in. If fully digested, semiotic *bani* could serve as an antidote to our modern epidemics of bulimia and anorexia nervosa. Remembering Guru Gobind Singh celebrate the Divine as food and drink, our daily meals become means of enjoying that One in each cell of our body. How could we then possibly abuse our bodies, our divine cells and selves, or abuse others in any form? Contemplation of truth does not pull us away from the ordinary functions of our life; as elemental and sumptuous as eating and drinking, it only makes us aware that every bite on our plate has a transcendent value.

Guru Nanak provides a cosmic setting for the platter image *(thal)* that Guru Arjan used in his epilogue to the Granth. In Hinduism the *thal* is used for *arati*, the daily ceremony performed at home and in temples. With lamps, incense, flowers and fruits placed on the *thal*, Hindus encircle their beloved deities. In Guru Nanak's semiotics, this beautiful ritual performed by Hindu worshippers is choreographed by our cosmos. In his hymn Arati, which is recited by Sikhs every evening, the spacious and ethereal skies become the metallic platter *(thal)* on which the sun, moon, and twinkling stars are set to perform *arati* around the Infinite One! Unconstrained by patriarchal either-or logic, the Sikh gurus connect a human mode of worship with that of nature, just as they connect the food on our tables with the Guru Granth, and the dishes from our kitchen with the distant skies that constantly illuminate our lives.

Since *bani* erupts through fixed and constricted categories, patriarchal discourse finds *her* problematic. Objective historians convert her dynamic womb into a concrete ground on which they try to erect their rational constructs. In the quick dynamic motion of the verses from which can burst forth a multitude of spiritually erotic emotions, they search in vain for structure and syntax. Cixous incisively refers to syntax as "that famous thread" "which acts for men as a surrogate umbilical cord," but which drains and divides the maternal fluidity and sustenance.[40] *Bani* delivers the profusion of meanings in the languages of the mother tongue that Kristeva conceives—"A woman's body, with its thousand and one thresholds of ardor—once, by smashing yokes and censors, she lets it articulate the profusion of meanings that run through it in every direction—will make the old single-grooved mother tongue reverberate with more than one language."[41]

But seeking control over the mother's continuum, the father's syntax breaks it into subject and object, past and future, verb and adjective. The scrutiny and control that patriarchs exert on the bodies of women is exerted on the generative powers of timeless *bani*. Instead of savoring her beauty and wisdom, Western scholars have criticized her for being "incoherent," "dark," and "perplexing."[42] Erudite discourses are unable to get in touch with the palpable and fluid female puissance that procreates the Khalsa. How can they impose the "father's famous thread" on the semiotic pulsations of *bani*? Nanak had rejected outright the infliction of any such censorship on his body. "Censor the body and you censor breath and speech at the same time," remarks Cixous.[43]

Actually, like our bodies getting rid of invasive substances, semiotic *bani* rejects symbolic constructs. Many passages in the Guru Granth denounce scholarly volumes, grammars, and astrological texts that presume knowledge of our past and future.[44] The very first stanza of Guru Nanak's Jap opens with "Thought cannot think, nor can a million thoughts.... Though a thousand mental feats become a million, not one can go with us" (stanza 1). The morning hymn repeatedly flushes out the mastery of patriarchal thought: "No paper, pen or scribe nor any philosophizing help to realize..." (stanza 12). In a lengthy passage, Guru Nanak acknowledges scholars and divinities from many religious traditions expounding on divine greatness. Nevertheless, symbolic language is incapable of articulating the greatness of That One, for "That babbler who presumes to say is marked as the fool of fools" (26). The Jap, Jaap, and Swayyais overlap one another in their dislike for scholarly discourses. Guru Nanak claims, "[W]hen it comes to discourse, many speak out, each outdoing the other" (Jap, stanza 21), and Guru Gobind Singh rejoins, "None of the Shastras can fathom It" (Jaap, verse 86). The tenth guru retains Guru Nanak's resistance to erudition and scholarship, and his Swayyais also contain a harsh criticism of paternal presumptions and pedagogies. Without the fluidity of love, "Study of Vedas, Puranas, Kateb and Quran, of all scriptures from all times and places...go to naught" (Swayyais, 4), says Guru Gobind Singh categorically.

Now, the semiotic *bani* of the Khalsa does not reject world scriptures; it simply cannot bear the Father's pontificating answers, proofs, and mastery. In fact, the Guru Granth is a wonderful Body palpably holding together the verses of the Sikh gurus, Hindu *bhaktas*, and Muslim Sufis. The 1,430 pages speak the same language of love, and enfold us in our human kinship. In the mother's womb, said Kabir, there is no name or caste, and so maternal *bani* makes no distinction either between Hindu, Muslim, and Sikh, or between weavers, tanners, and scholars. In this maternal space all differences are abolished. The infinite species coming from the same matrix speak in the same language: "[S]ome utter Ram, some Khuda" (GG, 885). Similarly, in chapter 1 we heard Guru Gobind Singh celebrate the singular Divine One for speaking "the four Vedas, the Qur'an, and the Puranas" (*BN*, 1:24). In his Akal Ustat as well, Guru Gobind Singh emphatically extols "the same One as the Puran and the Qur'an" (verse 86). Ultimately, the Hindu and Muslim scriptures, one in Sankrit and the other in Arabic, share the same Author, the same Voice. For the Sikh gurus, the One Source transcends all conceptual constructs. Guru Arjan, who compiled into the Granth the utterances of the Sikh gurus along with those of Hindu and Muslim saints, declares our common vocal expression: "Vedas, Puranas, Simritis, and saints, utter this *bani* in their tongue" (GG, 1227). Hindus, Muslims, and saints of other different religious traditions speak in countless dialects our universal mother language. Guru Nanak even praises the tiny sparrow who joyfully calls *khudai khudai* for her divine beloved (1286). What is deeply felt comes out spontaneously and naturally in the mother's musical tongue, and that refuses to submit to paternal control and scrutiny. The semiotic fluids of the Khalsa's poetry wash out symbolic infections of mental feats, intellectual divisions, and religious hegemony, but they tightly hold on to the desire for our infinite Matrix shared by the myriad species through all time.

Preoedipal language is not repressed by the Father's grammar. Because there is an oceanic surge to unite with That One, there are strong tides and equally strong ebbs in the language of the gurus. When Guru Nanak utters "Ikk Oan Kar" a whole flow of waves comes rushing forth: "Truth by name primal creator without fear without enmity timeless in form unborn self-existent the grace of the Guru. . . ."

This has come to be known as the *mul mantra* or quintessential formula of the Sikh religion. During the Khalsa initiation it is repeated five times. The tenth guru fully understood and felt what Nanak uttered, and with the same momentum utters: "You have no trait, no trace whatsoever, No color, caste, or family. / How to describe Your features or complexion, the lines on Your palms or Your garb? / You are called eternal, self-illumined, of infinite power, / Supreme among countless deities, Ruler among rulers, / Guardian of the three worlds—gods, humans, and demons, tiny blades of grass, and towering forests all proclaim your infinity!"

This is the beginning of his Jaap, a natural expansion of Guru Nanak's Jap. Since the realities and processes of his predecessor's verse shaped his feelings and his unconscious, the strong verbal ebbs and tides of the first guru's poetry pour into the tenth's receptacle. The Utterly Transcendent is ruler among rulers, guardian of the three worlds, and yet has no trait, no color, no caste, no family. The Other, totally infinite and formless, is the One the guru tries to imagine in the minutest details—even looking for the lines in the palms of the hands! From Nanak to Gobind, Sikh gurus acutely imagine and feel the One. In a rapid succession they arrest concrete images, and in an equally rapid succession, they let them go—the Divine is never reduced or immobilized in their verse. Simultaneously deeply intense and vastly expansive are their emotions.

In fact, no terms were used by Nanak: the numeral "1" designates the Divine. Fifteenth-century India abounded with eloquent terms and philosophically sophisticated concepts from Sanskrit, Arabic, Persian, and from the Dravidic languages. Nanak utters "Oan" after the numeral "1." *Oan* is the primal vocalic syllable of the Indian languages. The elemental modality of language becomes Guru Gobind Singh's expression as well, for he calls the One "song of songs" (Jaap, verse 47); "the sound of sounds" (verse 48). In a recent work, André Padoux explains *nada* as the manifestation of the universe: "that which expresses."[45] Guru Gobind Singh shares this view, and admits that the infinity spoken of *(kahe)* by him is not solo; rather, it is in chorus with the entire universe including "tiny blades of grass and towering jungles." The tenth guru's language, too, is not in the father's grammar; his is the maternal language shared by the terrestrial and celestial worlds, connecting each of us with our cosmos. Whereas the Sikh gurus hear the One as the totality of the sonic energy that cannot be accounted for grammatically, their interpreters, translators, and reciters reduce their language of plenitude to a male "he," stifling the dynamic processes of their expression.

The geometric arc flying off Nanak's "Oan" is a dynamic gesture of motion and movement. The circle is not closed; it cannot be closed. Following the same pattern, Guru Gobind Singh's Jaap is left without a closure in 199 verses. He ceaselessly addresses the Infinite in plentiful ways. Like the rapid flow of oxygen, carbon, hydrogen, and nitrogen in our bodies, the guru generates an ensemble of paradoxes: *andkare-tejteje* (deep darkness-brilliant light); *khape-thape* (destroys-creates); *balanbalan-rankanrankan* (highest of the high-poorest of the poor); *ajanmai-subanmai* (unborn-most beautiful). His contradictory movements awaken us from the patriarchal stupor of linear language, and stretch our imagination. The paradoxes are set in unique and repetitious movements, measures both long and short, and words that are Persian, Arabic, Sanskrit, Braj, and Punjabi. The Jaap mentioned above is in the language of the body, which is never complete, never static; it never stops growing. In turn, hearing, reading, and reciting the verses of the Khalsa makes our heart beat faster, and in the literal sense, "quicken" the pulse of our life. Produced from the Primal Womb, they affect our diverse bodies in diverse and profound ways.

The gurus' endless ways of relating with the Divine illuminate Irigaray's words that "woman's sex is not one" and open up a space where our own pleasures can unfold in a variety of ways. The sense of plenitude strips off patriarchal stratifications and blots out masculine identity as the norm for imaging the Transcendent. Over and over the gurus repeat that the Infinite cannot be fixed, immobilized, incarnated. In stanza 5 of the Jap, Guru Nanak says, "That One cannot be molded or made," and in the same tone Guru Gobind Singh says, "Cannot be contained in a chant. Cannot be reduced to an idol. Cannot be captured in an image. Ever the elixir of elixirs" (Jap, verse 177). Nothing verbal or solid or visual, neither male nor female, can encapsulate the One. Guru Gobind Singh's juxtaposition of the negative processes of "containing" "reducing" and "capturing" with the positive "Ever elixir of elixirs" pulls the Infinite into the realm of pleasure and expands it. Elixir is drunk, taken into our bodies, and as it rushes into our bloodstream it brings up the serotonin levels, opening up even more avenues of enjoyment. In the Sikh gurus' rejection of images and idols we recover their strong tendency to exorcise rigid symbols of male dominance. In his Swayyais Guru Gobind Singh specifically denounces the "wearing of phalluses around the neck" (Swayyai 10). In his Chaupai he says, "The fool has no clue of the Formless One: he calls Lord Shiva the Eternal One" (verse 16). Lord Shiva's generative organ, the *linga,* represents the eternal creator, and is worshipped by his devotees with milk, honey, and sandalpaste. The hymns of the Khalsa decenter such male symbols and uproot the monopoly of the phallus. Semiotic *bani* incites us to shed the weight and burden of solidified phallocratic chains around our necks—"the phallus dangling from the neck" (Swayyai 10)—so that our bodies are unleashed for multiple *jouissance* with the Infinite.

Absorbed by the body, the Elixir produces the emotions of love and heroism, which expand the self and stimulate intimacy with the Transcendent. Four times in his Jaap Guru Gobind Singh addresses the One lovingly, and boldly as *amritamrite* (Elixir of elixirs), evoking each time the primal image of Nanak sipping the bowl of *amrit* in the River Bein. So love and heroism are not antithetical approaches—the former is not chosen by the "peace-loving" Nanak or the latter by the "warrior guru." They are not contrary movements, for love is not a withdrawal and stepping back into one's own space, nor is heroism a charging and stepping ahead into another's space. And they are not bifurcated into either "feminine" or "masculine" characteristics. Both love and heroism are basic hormones essential to life. They flow out together from the primal Sikh experience in the River Bein, and they are both suffused in *bani.*

Semiotic *bani* is the voice of Love, and as we discerned, the very first scriptural reference identifies her as the language of "infinite love" (Jap, stanza 4). The Ultimate is love, and the way to unite with That is also love, and so the two forces coming from each side intersect. With spasmodic energy, Guru Gobind Singh's Jaap invokes the Transcendent as the "embodiment of love" (Jaap, verse 26), as "the incarnation of love" (verse 55) as "the love of love" (verse 68). As verse 80 of Jaap says,

> The embodiment of love
> Extends to all lands, to every nook and cranny.

Guru Nanak's "language of infinite love" is indeed Guru Gobind Singh's "Body of Love" (*raga rupe*) that fills all space. There are no cracks or fissures in this Body, which is the source of all our bodies. The entire universe is the semiotic voice of her endless love, and all species play and enjoy themselves in the maternal lap of day and night. Nanak's Jap and Gobind's Jaap mingle, echo, and coincide as they place love into the very womb of language. The infinite body of Love—*preet preete* (Jaap, verse 68)—opens our bodies so that we revel together. "Devotees who win your affection, revel in your love" says Nanak (Jap, stanza 27), and the ambrosia that flows out from the crucible of love in the last stanza of Guru Nanak's Jap is relished by Guru Gobind Singh's "reveler of all" (Jaap, verse 77), whom he lovingly salutes as "enjoyer of all!" (verse 15). The hymns of the Khalsa are grounded in the powerful passion and intimacy between us and our Divine.

Guru Gobind Singh's Swayyais rhythmically repeat that without love, all religious practices are ineffective. He goes off in all directions, using ceaseless similes to make the point that studies, ablutions, charities, rituals, and all ascetic activities like "subsisting on air, practicing celibacy," are utterly worthless.

> How futile to sit in contemplation, like a stork with both eyes closed.
> While trying to bathe in the seven seas,we lose this world and the next . . .
> I tell the truth, do listen to me, they alone who love, find the Beloved.
> (Swayyai 9)

The guru appropriates love as the highest form of action. This final line in the above quatrain—"they alone who love, find the Beloved" (*jin prem kio tin hi prabh paio)*—resonates through the entire hymn. Whereas love expands us, rigorous physical and mental techniques or ritual practices to purify the body only confine us. They wall us in and separate us from relating with the beauty and diversity around us. Our bodies are not polluted; they do not need any ritual cleansing. They are so lovely naturally that they are all savored by the One—the *sarbam bhugta* (reveler of all). The Khalsa's long hair grows from this basic premise, and so do all the other *Ks*. Love is passionate and takes lovers to those depths of richness and fullness where there is freedom from all sorts of limitations and barriers. Love is the powerful maternal hormone, which dissolves the individual ego and opens our pores so wide that we savor the Other with an intensity and immensity that no father's language can ever record.

Feminist writers distinguish *his* form of love from *hers*. Cixous and Clement comment, "[H]e needs to love himself. But she launches forth; she seeks to love."[46] Their explosive expressions define "the motto of all phallocentric speculation/specularization, the motto of every Teste" as "himself." This masculine narcissistic self-absorption that ends with the sight and glories of the individual ego is contrasted with the feminine takeoff that descends deeper to "where a voice that doesn't know itself is lost in the sea's churning."[47] The male gurus endorse the feminine modality of love in which *she seeks to love*. Indeed, hers is a courageous plunge into the vast and churning sea where all divisions and circumferences break apart: "[T]he Divine is completely saturated in us like the mother in her child" (GG, 672). Heroism for the gurus is the essential element of *her* love—it shatters the mirrors of narcissism, it breaks solid walls of fear, it stops all arteries from clogging with pride, prejudices, or threats. *Her* heroism launches love to flow freely within the self and from one body to the other to That One in all of us—male and female, brown, black, and white.

The Sikh gurus physiologically link heroism with love, making the emotion even more vigorous and forceful. The prelude to Sikh scripture features the Transcendent with no fear and no hatred: "*ikk oan kar sat nam karta purakh nir bhau nir vair*. . . . One Being is Truth by name primal creator without fear without enmity." In the same breath Guru Nanak links the creativity of the One with the virtue of fearlessness. We can even spot the birthing process in the verbal root *(kr,* "make"). But the male symbolic fails to see the Nanakian link between procreation and valor, and refuses to acknowledge the maternal substratum of the Transcendent One. Instead, Herculean muscle becomes the sole signifier. The One is never translated, never recognized as a She. With the word *nirbhau* (without fear) a strong male dictator standing far above *his* creation with nobody to answer to is fixed in the Sikh public memory. Life does not develop from the fear of Him standing out there, but from the love that She has for all of her creation. The cosmos is bodied forth in love and not in animosity *(nirvair)* toward any offspring. In the memorable scene from the epilogue to the Jap, the whole universe plays in the "lap of day and night, the male and female nurses." Once they come out of their mother's body, all the variegated and complex creatures freely and delightfully cradle themselves on the melodious body of night and day. Without rivalries and enmity, they are together nestled on *her* body. The first Sikh hymn constitutes a remarkably organic textual body in itself, for the latent and hidden womb of its prologue proliferates into the open and spacious lap of its epilogue.

Guru Gobind Singh retains the nexus between love and heroism, and reminds us of Guru Nanak's vision that they are birthed alike from the maternal body. His verses are a flashback to the mother.

> Wielder of weapons
> Hurler of missiles
> Knower of all
> Mother of the cosmos.
> (Jaap, verse 52)

The chivalrous actions of the Invincible One are rooted in the fecund mother. Destroyer and creator are both aspects of That One, and the countless divine activities envisioned by the guru all rest in the maternal locus. In his hymn called Chaupai, Guru Gobind Singh says that "the countless bodies are an expansion of you, O creator" (verse 13). In the Jaap, too, he says, "You permeate everybody." The Divine is the "life of all lives, the breath of all breath" (Jaap, verse 143). Guru Gobind Singh's hymn resounds with the Divine as the very life, the very "breath[,] of all creation" (verse 117). Several times he exalts That One as "linked" with us—as though the entire universe were tied to the Creator with an umbilical cord. In the Nanakian modality, the tenth guru brings out the female puissance of the Transcendent, and he even salutes the "wielder of weapons" as the "Mother of the cosmos" in the very same breath. For the Sikh gurus heroism is embodied in the female figure, who is love and creativity.

From the first to the tenth, the gurus regard heroism very highly, and the Jap, the hymn of "peace and serenity," recited daily by the Khalsa during "the ambrosial hour" (*amrit vela*), is saturated with the presence of mighty heroes and heroines. Even at its outset Nanak mandates valor. Courageous chords are required to extol the One who transcends all threatening barriers. Semiotic voice does not belong to the weak and fearful: "Filled with might, we sing praise of the Might" (Jap, stanza 3). It is the "invincible heroes" who sing divine praise in the *karam khand,* and they are empowered from within. They do not seek power over others. In this fourth spiritual realm, then, a vast array of heroes and heroines live peacefully—without a hierarchy, without a division, without a leader, and without any sort of religious or gender biases.

That sphere with its language of valor, that sphere of equality and freedom, that sphere where mighty heroes and heroines reside, that sphere so close to the home of the Divine that the two realms of Action (*karam)* and Truth (*sach)* are located in the same thirty-seventh stanza of the Jap—it is the sphere Guru Gobind Singh aspired to make into a social and political reality. The heroes and heroines conceived in Guru Nanak's *karam khand* were delivered on Baisakhi 1699. Masculine rhetorics of rupture between the first and the tenth gurus have only fractured the Sikh psyche, leading Sikhs astray from the forceful confluence of their gurus. We recover an amazing continuity between them: Guru Gobind Singh wanted his contemporaries—reduced to weakness and passivity under political hegemony—to become like the citizens of Guru Nanak's *karam khand* who are "drenched" with the Divine. Clearly their might is the force of love. The gurus are in total consonance, for Arjan also defines valorous heroes as all those "who are colored by the love of the Divine in this very world" (GG, 679). Both men and women are clearly regarded as members of this heroic community, which lies not elsewhere but within the daily rhythms of our life on the lap of Mother Earth. In fact, we specifically heard Guru Nanak mentioning Sita and her peers as denizens of the *karam khand*. Though commentators may try to congeal her, Sita is definitely not "ice." Nor is she a man "utterly sewn in devotion." Nor is she a goddess whose body is immobilized into stone. For the Sikh gurus, Sita and women like her are real flesh-and-blood heroines residing in Guru Nanak's *karam khand*. To end political and social oppression, Guru Gobind Singh's Khalsa has to be heroic like them. Both men and women have to be courageous. For the birth of the Khalsa and for the reproduction of the Khalsa, the language of *karam khand* was necessary. So the tenth guru, inspired by the semiotic *bani* of his predecessors, uttered his words with great speed and velocity. His meters, his images, and his emotions come with spasmodic force, and when properly felt and applied, they shatter all symbolic hegemonies. The verses of the Khalsa can dispel cowardice and infuse the reciter with love and heroism, and we must welcome and acclaim them as such.

Indeed, they can charge us to live confidently and courageously without being scared to hold back love and creativity. Heroism is not muscle and power over others, but the powerful and healthy flow of creative liquids, which promote a healthy body, and love for our family, friends, nature, and our Creator by whom we are all birthed. Heroism incites us to contest sexism, racism, casteism, and classism. Heroism incites us to courageously discard narcissism, phobias, fears, and hatred. It is necessary that we boldly shatter all impediments that repress physical conception, artistic and literary productions, fulfilling social relations, and a true enchantment with the Divine. Thus, we passionately love the Infinite and revel in countless pleasures. That is the energy derived by tasting, seeing, hearing, reciting, and remembering the semiotic voice of the gurus.

Love and heroism come directly from the mother. The way we develop our notion of selfhood and relate with the world is contingent on our primal relationship with our mother. In his Jaap, Guru Gobind Singh extols the One in numerous ways, but the various functions and associations nestle on "the

Mother of the cosmos" (*lok mata*). Even in the hymn of Chaupai when Guru Gobind Singh solicits the Transcendent to crush his enemies in order to save and protect his Sikhs, we see him reaching out to a mother figure. Although he does not follow the rules and laws of grammar that would specify gender, a female Subject seems to materialize and linger in his imagination. She is present in the opening itself: "Give me your hand and protect me (*hamari karo hath de racha)*" (Chaupai, verse 1), and continues to prevail as we hear him implore through the entire hymn: "protect me with your own hands" (Chaupai, verse 5), "we seek your lap" (verse 21), "I seek your lap" (verse 24) "give me your hand and support me" (verse 25). The valiant guru constantly desires the physical sustenance and contact that is primally given by the mother. Strong female impressions, unrecognized in the father's symbolic, permeate Guru Gobind Singh's aesthetic *Weltanschauung*. We must attune ourselves so that in the sound of Guru Gobind Singh's heroic meters we can hear *her* life-giving breath, in his battle scenes we can see *her* creative space, in the dramatic movements of his weapons we can feel *her* nurturing hand, and in our daily activities and occupations we can sense *her* strength and support. We cannot let phallocratic memories obliterate our maternal link with the Transcendent established by the gurus.

The mother is explicitly addressed in Guru Amar Das's hymn called Anand, which forms the finale of the Khalsa initiation. Actually, all Sikh rites and ceremonies conclude with the recitation of six stanzas from the Anand by the entire congregation in unison. The same six stanzas here have also been incorporated into the evening prayer Rahiras, so before going to sleep, Sikh men and women enter into this primal mother-child relationship. Anand, meaning "bliss," opens with the lines:

> My Mother! I am in bliss, for I have found my true guru;
> My true guru I found so easily, my mind rings with felicitations!

The guru is in bliss, for he has found the true enlightener within himself. In his ecstasy we see him trying to seize the mother, *meri mae* (my mother)!

This vocative for the mother flows vibrantly in the Guru Granth. Coming from the lips of male poets, it is a verbal embrace gushing from the point closest to their unconscious. They ask of her passionate questions: "How can I live without the Name, O my mother?" (GG, 226); "How could I forget That, O my mother?" (349) "How do I unite with Truth O my mother?" (661); "What virtues will unite me with my life, O my mother?" (204). While they seek her knowledge, they also share passionate moments with her: "I am in love O my mother!" Each time the mother carries their language forward, making their experience come out alive. This is not a dualistic opposition between *the male gurus vs. her*, but, to use Mikhail Bakhtin's term, a "dialogic" relation that is rooted in openness and leads to a deeper self-awareness, to a deeper communion.

Clearly, it is not in opposition to but pulling toward the mother that Sikh gurus establish their identity. Since It is all space and time, that One of course has no gender, but when That One is felt, it is experienced as *both* father and mother. 'You are my father and you are my mother!" exclaims Guru Arjan (GG, 103). Attaining divine bliss is like "the heart blossoming when it beholds the mother" (164). In the Sikh communal memory, however, the paternal relationship is retained and underscored, while the idyllic mother-child dyad is cast away.

To our ears the semiotic verses of the male gurus resonate with the views of feminist thealogians and object-relations psychoanalysts who posit the maternal-infant relationship at the heart of a person's psychological and social development. Instead of the Freudian oedipal conflict, castration complex, and individuality, feminist thealogians like Naomi Goldenberg and object-relations psychoanalysts like Melanie Klein and D. W. Winnicott shift the focus to the maternal-infant relationship. Both thealogy and object-relations theory "derive their insights into the matrices that support human life from an image of a woman-in-the-past."[48] The semiotic language of the gurus displaces the father from his dominating symbolic and cherishes the love of the mother, the care of the mother, the caresses of the mother, the transverbal communion with the mother. The male gurus seriously remember her prebirth and postbirth creativity, and our re-memories in turn can help us improve the individual and social fabric of our lives. "Just as the mother takes care of her children, so the One sustains us" (GG, 680). The abundant joy of envisioning the Ultimate is "like the look between a child and its mother" (452). When we feel the divine arms around us—"like a mother tightly hugs her child" (629)—we cannot but recharge the innermost batteries of our own selves, and renew our relationships with our families, friends, and community.

So it is *with* the mother that Sikhs wind up each day, each ceremony, and every rite of passage. The fifth and final liturgical hymn of the Khalsa culminating all Sikh rites, Anand, starts out by addressing the mother as the source of wondrous experience. Guru Amar Das says "mind-and-heart ring with felicitations (*manu vajia vadhaian*)!" (Anand, stanza 1). This joyous space sparkles and glitters with the precious jewels of wisdom that flashed out in the first hymn—"wisdom comprises jewels, gems, and pearls" (Jap, stanza 6). He attains his enlightenment "very easily" without having to go through any rigorous techniques or disciplines. As the stanza proceeds, "jewel-like melodies with their families and fairies from afar have come to sing the Word within me" (Anand, stanza 1). Fairies who belong to the world of the unconscious add to the horizon of his female imaginary. This is not a male *logos* that is grammatically structured. Here is excitement and joy, and there are no defense mechanisms on his part. The guru is free, he is ecstatic. He hears beautiful music, and his body is sonorous with five instruments playing the Word. In a libidinal drive, his entire self reverberates with melodious rhythms. The guru merges oceanically with the world that we learn from her while we are still in her body.

> That True Name is my sole support, satisfying all my hungers.
> With peace and joy, it enters my mind, fulfilling all my desires.
> (Anand, stanza 4)

The poet's sole support, that true name (*sach nam*), feeds him, satiates him, gives him peace and comfort, and fills him with joy.

Because the mother's milk is nurturing, "all hungers are satisfied." Sikh semiotic poetry flows with mother's milk. In our re-memory we see the food of the hostess (*bhadarani*) overflowing with the food of the mother, just as we hear the language of the guru joining in with the words of Cixous, "Voice: milk that could go on forever. Found again. The lost mother/bitter-lost. Eternity: is voice mixed with milk."[49] Sikh hymns remind us that every individual is formed from the physical and psychological sustenance provided by the mother. Her milk is inexhaustible. Not only does she feed her fetus with her nutrients, but also suckles the newborn with her life-giving milk. "The child's original attraction is to the mother's breast milk," acknowledges Guru Nanak (GG, 972). The fifth guru recalls the experience of "her milk poured into the baby's mouth" (987), and claims that satisfaction and fulfillment come from the mother pouring milk into her child's mouth (1266). The gurus compare the intensity of saintly devotion to that of an infant's love for the mother's milk (613). In an unforgettable juxtaposition of analogies, the Divine is like a "cane for the blind" and "like mother's milk for the child" (679). In another tender passage we read: "Says Nanak, the child, you are my father and my mother, and your name is like milk in my mouth" (713). Throughout the Guru Granth, the Sikh gurus unabashedly express their attachment to the Divine through an infant's attachment to the mother's breast: "[M]y mind loves the Divine, O my life, like a child loves suckling milk" (538).

These scriptural images of the delicious and invigorating milk pouring into the mouth flow into the musical melodies and rhythms that Guru Amar Das sensuously registers in his Anand. Paradoxically, however, his music is played to *anahad*—the "soundless sound" "the unstruck melody"! This subtle, self-producing sound, or what is called "unstruck sound," vibrates constantly in our universe. Though within each and every body, it cannot be heard through the father's rational methods, but only through the mother's elemental consciousness. There is no linear discourse here by the guru to prove his supreme enlightenment. He experiences total unicity in which he lyrically and polymorphously delights. The semiotic verses of the Khalsa reverberate with "the primal source *(dhuri ki bani)*," the mother, who in Cixous's words "nourishes, and who stands up against separation; a force that will not be cut off but will knock the wind out of the codes."[50] The oral is the aural, and the milk that is drunk is no different from the *bani* that is heard: "[A]s milk quenches the child, ambrosial *bani* quenches all heat" (GG, 978). *Amrit* sipped in the River Bein, *amrit* prepared by Guru Gobind Singh in Anandpur, and *amrit* recited by the Sikhs daily in Punjab or New York overflow from the maternal surplus. In a plurality of sounds and rhythms, in a collage of artistic images, semiotic *bani* replays Guru Nanak's effervescent mnemonic, "[T]hat One is the calf, She is the cow, and She is the milk" (1190). The hymns of the Khalsa are intrinsically written in "white ink," and we need to absorb the maternal element in order to derive total nutrition and full benefit.

And so the True Name *(Ikk Oan Kar Sat Nam)* uttered by Guru Nanak in his Jap, the Mother of the cosmos extolled by Guru Gobind Singh in his Jaap, the Beloved envisioned by Guru Gobind Singh in his Swayyais, the hands and lap desired by him in his Chaupai, are poetically carried over into the Anand and merge into the body of the mother. The five hymns of the Khalsa are a flashback to the mother whose body is imprinted on the deepest memory. They serve as a reentry into the innermost core of ourselves—returning the reciter and hearer to the original source of wisdom and joy underlying all our conscious powers. There is an ultimate depth to our life below the plane of fatherly thinking and reasoning. Semiotic *bani* takes us away from a logical world where we are divided into subject and object, male and female; it brings us back to the semiconscious self where dualisms begin to dissolve, to the unconscious where we do not feel or imagine anything, to the ultimate experience of total Oneness (*Ikk Oan Kar*). We return to our primordial mother who is all, not divided into male or female. This is the abundant unity that the Sikh gurus were deeply aware of and thoroughly savored.

In turn our re-memories of the oceanic experience in her body and of her strength, wisdom, and snuggles melt away our splintered and patriarchal individuality. They replenish us with a new identity, which Guru Gobind Singh birthed on that historic Baisakhi celebration day by the banks of the Sutlej. Social, political, and religious divisions could only be eliminated by a new subjectivity suckled from the maternal *amrit* semiotically produced. Since they integrate the interior and exterior of Sikhs with the mother's patterns of love and plenitude, the five *banis* that Guru Gobind Singh gave his newly born Khalsa match perfectly with the five *Ks* in which he dressed them up. The once-in-a-lifetime rite of passage of the Sikhs and their daily routine tellingly endorse Naomi Goldenberg's feminist thesis that "Plato has it backwards; the search for the wholly transcendent is, historically and psychologically, the search for the remembered state of union with the wholly immanent."[51] The body of the Transcendent, circulating in the body of the gurus, is the body of *jouissance*. Sikh ontology, history, and aesthetics come together in the maternal experience of infinity—within the *body* of every Sikh, male and female alike.

Conclusion

> Different vestures from different countries may make us different
> But we have the same eyes, the same ears, the same body,
> the same voice.
>
> Akal Ustat, 86

> [W]e are in need of our *subject*, our *substantive*, our word, our *predicates*: our elementary sentence, our basic rhythm, our morphological identity, our generic incarnation, our genealogy.
>
> —Luce Irigaray, *Sexes and Genealogies*

I started out this project for personal reasons, and it has ended up being most fulfilling. The loss of my "motherly" father was unbearable for me. But launching the theme of birth at that tragic moment gave me much hope and sustenance. My father's unbounded love, his care for the minute details of my food, clothes, books, and lectures, his smiles and his tears, were really the reservoir I drew upon in my personal analysis of an event so deeply etched in the collective memory of us Sikhs. The tenderness of my father made me sensitive to the tenderness of the Sikh guru, whom I primarily upheld as a lordly patriarch. Researching and writing about Guru Gobind Singh's maternal role over the past few years has not only made me appreciate the complexities, thoughtfulness, and creative personality of the tenth guru, it has also given me a stronger sense of my history and of being a more wholesome citizen in the twenty-first century. My study has proved to be a "form of self-discovery, no less spiritual than political."[1] I conclude with two wishes, which are aimed at two different audiences. One, I want our Western contemporary society to become more familiar with the Sikhs. As Guru Gobind Singh said, despite the differences in our complexions, religions, and cultures, we are one family, and we have to get to know one another. My other wish is for my Sikh community to be self-reflective, and remember the feminist nucleus of its genealogy.

Our world is getting to be a smaller and smaller place. There are over 500,000 Sikhs in North America, and more than 150 *gurdwaras* (Sikh places of worship) on American soil. Numerous Sikhs maintain their five symbols, they celebrate their festivals and rites of passage, and there are even huge Baisakhi parades each spring commemorating the birth of the Khalsa in the metropolitan centers of Washington, D.C., Los Angles, New York, and Toronto. Punjabi, the language of the Sikhs, is the fourth most spoken language in Toronto, and in fact Sardar Sher Singh, an eminent Sikh-Canadian lawyer, informed me recently that Punjabi is vying with Chinese to occupy the third position in the Toronto area after English and French! Yet, many people in North America do not know much about the Sikhs, and whatever little is known is solely as stereotypically male.

The reason well may be that the first Sikhs that the West saw were men. It was with the British annexation of the Punjab in 1849 that Sikhs became a part of the imperial workforce and began to migrate to distant lands. After losing their enormous and splendid kingdom to the British—including the Kohinoor, the largest diamond in the world—Sikhs quickly became their most loyal subjects. Having surrendered his sovereignty, all his possessions, and even his religion (for he was converted to Christianity), the young maharaja Dalip Singh was exiled to England. He became a well-known symbol of Sikh identity, whereas his remarkable mother, Maharani Jind Kaur (1817–63), who had earlier proclaimed herself as his regent and cast off her veil and held court and transacted state business in public, was asked to go into purdah by the British! She was even kept captive till she managed to escape to Nepal under the guise of a maid. In spite of their strict surveillance, she "masterfully" criticized colonial rule, and wrote inspiring letters to her son reminding him of the message of the Sikh gurus (and Dalip did reconvert to Sikhism later in life). Lord Dalhousie, the governor general, described her as "the only woman in the Punjab with manly understanding."[2] When the young maharaja arrived in England, one of the first things Queen Victoria did was to get his portrait painted with his oriental sword and his "manly" turban—in spite of the fact that the young fellow had neither *kesha* (his long hair had been shorn) nor the *kangha* underneath. As Dalip was modeling for the German painter Franz Winterhalter (July 10–17, 1854), the queen sat with Prince Albert gazing across at her fifteen-year-old "subject" to compose her own sketches of his "Sikh costume" and his "extremely handsome" appearance.[3] Even the queen herself was carried away by this image of Sikh masculinity, and her subjects naturally adopted this "manly" impression of Sikh identity in their own minds. Such stereotypes have, of course, nothing to do with reality. The helpless confined prince had to be viewed as a male warrior, and the powerful free-ranging maharani had to be removed from view to preserve the colonial stereotype of what Sikhs should be.

The British also had political reasons for focusing on Sikh masculinity. They greatly admired the "martial" character and the strong physique of the Sikh men and recruited them in disproportionately large numbers to serve in the British army. The caste names that Sikhs had learned to cast aside were reintroduced when many of them were registered under the old system of family name, and the occupational boundaries they had discarded also came into play when the colonialists created "traditional agriculturists," "martial races," and "trading castes."[4] Likewise, the gurus' ideal of the "human family" was also ignored, for the Sikh regiments were clearly separated from the other "martial races" of the Pathans, Gorkhas, and Rajputs, not to mention their separation from the more peaceful Bengalis, who were denounced as "effeminate" by the British. A vigorous new patriarchal discourse with its patriotism and paternalism got attached to the "brotherhood of the Khalsa." Fiery speeches were made by influential Sikhs on behalf of the British army, stressing, as did the maharaja of Patiala, "loyalty to the King-Emperor, and Sikh readiness to fight and die as good warriors."[5] Sikhs formed about one-fifth of the army in World War I, with numbers reaching 100,000 by the end of the war. They valorously fought for the empire in Europe, Africa, West Asia, Burma, Malaya, and China. The Sikhs won fourteen of the twenty-two military crosses awarded to Indians for conspicuous gallantry. From Shanghai to Mesopotamia, Sikhs heroically guarded the outposts of the empire. In return, they received grand honors and handsome grants of land in the new canal colonies in the Punjab (which the muscular lads whom the British admired so much had helped to build) and became the richest agriculturists in Asia.[6]

Alas, the exciting ventures to new places and the gallant victories belonged to the Sikh men alone. Their sisters, wives, mothers, and aunts stayed home in the Punjab, where they became enshrouded with the heavy impositions of patriarchal Punjabi culture. Victorian morality and the masculinist economic and political policies of imperial Britain were added to the already burdensome indigenous cultural sexism. The revenue policies implemented by the colonial regime denied Punjabi women the right to inherit agricultural land and created an even greater demand for sons on a soil that had for millennia prayed for "heroic sons" (in the very first hymn to Agni from the Vedic corpus). In her compelling chapter "Local Customs and the Economy Grow Mustaches," Veena Talwar Oldenburg traces the current violence against women in northern India to the "massive economic and social pressures brought on by the colonial rule."[7] Indeed, with the admiration, martial tributes, land grants, and monetary rewards that they received from their imperial masters, the proud self-perceptions of masculinity among Sikhs only got more pronounced, the interpretation of their five *Ks* as symbols of warfare more reinforced, and the sexist attitudes and practices in their homes and community more horrifying.

For the British, the turban and beard had a macho military import. But ever since September 11, the same symbols have acquired a very negative and dangerous meaning. They have come to represent Islamic fundamentalism. Daily TV images flash a bearded Bin Laden wearing a turban and caressing his machine gun. The media projections have instilled such fear and hate for anybody with turban and beard that more than two hundred Sikhs have been victims of hate crimes in America since 9/11. In the mind of the attackers Punjabi Sikhs are the same as Afghani Muslims and Afghani Muslims are the same as Al Qaeda terrorists. In Phoenix, a Sikh gas station owner was murdered in that blinding rage. This is disastrous. We cannot hate or murder people because of what they wear. We need to respect the plurality of genders and cultures, and we need to read symbols properly instead of imposing our own political meanings on them.

The symbols worn by the Khalsa are not weapons of war to spark violence in the public or domestic spheres. Nor are they tools that cut and divide us from the human family. Nor are they hand-me-downs from fathers and brothers. Our female understanding of the hair, the comb, the bracelet, the underwear, and the sword animates and activates each wearer's consciousness of the Infinite and knowledge of our common humanity. Similarly, the verses of the Khalsa come from the lips of male poets, but we must not dismiss them as patriarchal because they come, as Cixous would say, from "the other country without boundaries," and they carry great force to connect us across cultures, complexions, and religions.[8] The five *Ks* are made up of the transcendent verse. They may be specific markers of Sikh identity, but the ideals that inspired them endorse the "singular caste of humanity" (said Guru Gobind) and the "singular sect of humanity" (said Guru Nanak). Their re-memory challenges us citizens of the world to question separatist assumptions long held by all of us about our "unique" ways of dressing up: it forces us to look beneath our different and colorful patterns into the common MATERial. I feel there is tremendous potential lying behind the *bana* and *bani* of the Khalsa that would braid together our Eastern and Western cultures. As Guru Gobind Singh himself claimed, differences are external that happen to be an outcome of our different geographical regions and cultural locales: "Different vestures from different countries may make us different./But we have the same eyes, the same ears, the same body, the same voice" (Akal Ustat, 86). Our differences should not stand in the way of getting to know one another, and it is not enough for the guru that we tolerate people of different religious backgrounds. We must actively recognize (*pahicanbo*) and know (*janbo*) our universal physical and metaphysical being. The Sikh guru thus urges us to move beyond diversity and embrace "pluralism." His Baisakhi 1699 compels us all, Easterners and Westerners alike, to reflect critically on our own identity.

We live in a remarkably diverse world, but our ideals and outlooks are still very Anglocentric. It is urgent that our global society gets to know and respect all its members, and we must all actively try to build bridges of understanding among ourselves. The "divide-and-rule" policies of the masters, both in the West in itself and in its empires, have kept us splintered far too long, and I know for sure that in the Punjab as well as in diasporic communites across the world, Sikh women remain insulated and isolated, which makes them timid and insecure. Even Sikh, Hindu, and Muslim women who may have grown up historically and geographically together stay alienated from one another. Ideological constructs of our fathers have kept us from bonding with one another; they have kept us from sharing our anxieties and problems, just as they have kept us from finding solutions and strength from one another. Their dualized structures—monotheism vs. polytheism, East vs. West, modern vs. traditional, Sikh vs. Hindu—have blocked our access to the Creator. How can we make use of the windows of opportunity offered by Sikh gurus, the Prophet Muhammad, or Vedic seers if we do not even communicate with one another? The dialogical relation is much needed.

Personally, growing up in a postcolonial Punjab, I attended Victorian schools, which introduced me and my peers to distant Western authors, but kept us away from our own Indian writers. The works of Rokeya Sakhawat Hossain (Muslim) and Mahadevi Varma (Hindu) which I discovered later, had great resonance for me, but they were not a part of my convent school curriculum. These feminist authors hold great validity for us even today. For instance, Rokeya, writing a century ago in prepartitioned Bengal, reports many cruel practices that still fester in our global community. Her account about a Muslim woman burned to death for the sake of purdah a century ago eerily resembles the one published by the *New York Times* in the spring of 2002: Fleeing without their scarves, fifteen Saudi girls in Mecca are forced by the religious police to return to their burning school building—back into the flames![9] Rokeya's Bengali Muslim lady walks back into her burning building to be licked by flames rather than be seen by strange men who were fighting fire in the courtyard outside![10] Such poignant narratives by Indian women—Muslim, Hindu, or Sikh—would have shed light on the radical vision of the gurus, who spoke against purdah and other forms of female victimization. But in postcolonial Sikh society it was safe and secure to go to convent schools and even attend Catholic services, because it was all very "distant." For, the Hindu and Muslim traditions—so close geographically, historically, anthropologically, and psychologically—were all too dangerous and threatening! Patriarchal rules and boundaries have prohibited us from visiting each other's homes and shrines; they have kept us from sharing and learning and empowering one another.

At the academic level, too, there is very little engagement. With our colonial false consciousness, many of us are so busy trying to prove our modernity and superiority to Indians of other religious traditions that we barely communicate with one other. Sikh women seldom enter the worldview of non-Sikhs, and with a few exceptions, scholars from other traditions have not seriously entered the world of Sikh women, either. The works of contemporary Western scholars like Doris Jakobsh, Cynthia Mahmood, Catherine Fair, Robin Rinehart, Eleanor Nesbitt, Constance Elsberg, and Stacy Brady are heartening contributions. For the most part, however, the multivalent and complex feminine imagery of the Sikh sacred text remains closed to feminist scholars in religion. We need to rectify the current imbalance and Anglocentrism of feminist perspectives on religion. In turn, Sikh women need to tap into the resources offered by their feminist sisters from other religious traditions. We must not be afraid of our differences, and we must, as Mary Daly urges, "befriend" one another. Together we can develop methods and techniques to break androcentric codes, and together we can figure out ways for uniting and supporting one another so that we will loudly hear the mother's language, and feel the divine splendor radiating in and through our bodies.

My other wish is for each member of my Sikh community to really remember the Baisakhi of 1699, and rediscover the feminist genes in Guru Gobind Singh's construction of Sikh identity. My "feminist re-memory" is not a cataloguing of facts. It is a threefold process, which *begins* with seating ourselves among men and women who had gathered together in Anandpur. It is activating our senses, imagination, and spirituality, and reexperiencing the sounds and the colors and the smells and the feelings all around us. Feminist scholarship has cautioned us about the ways in which the powerful erase those out of power from public consciousness and forge the collective memory that they select: "[H]egemony means the ability to control the formal machinery of representation; to design the past that a specific culture will then naturalize and teach," writes Catherine Stimpson.[11] Concentrating on the maleness of the protagonists, and the masculinity of the Khalsa institution, Sikh collective memory has ignored the female presence at Anandpur, just as it has ignored the feminine dimensions of Guru Gobind Singh's creative act, and the liberating implications for women generated by his memorable Baisakhi. Sikh historians and theologians have told us over and over that Brahmins, Kshatriyas, Vaishyas, and Shudras were present. But women? Even though Sainapat, one of the earliest poets, records their presence in his narrative of the Guru's Baisakhi, women are scarcely mentioned. The emphasis on the males of the different castes coming together has completely overshadowed the coming together of men and women. In our re-memory we see sisters, mothers, wives, and daughters arriving in Anandpur to celebrate Baisakhi. In outfits emulating the brilliant flora and fauna of the natural spring scenes, we hear them reciting scriptural verses, and we sense their joy as their bracelets clink when they walk or stand or prepare *langar*. We can even feel their tension when the guru asks for a life. We can see their necks straining to stand up to their guru's call and the rest of their bodies being pulled down by heavy societal norms. We can recognize in their eyes the gamut of sentiments rushing through them. We can hear their hearts beating loudly within the stunned gathering. Women were palpably present during Baisakhi 1699. With the men, women witnessed the creative act of the guru. With the men, women heard the guru's call. His term *koi* (anyone) included them too. Though the collective consciousness forged by those in power may continue to cast them aside, Guru Gobind Singh did not.

And so, sitting in the congregation, we witness the radiant guru deliver his Khalsa conceived in tenderness and love—a crucial act that he performed for the betterment of all his Sikhs, both men and women alike. Why should this dramatic performance of our spiritual guru embarrass us? The Jewish *aqedah* is such a vital part of that tradition's history, and in that case it is God himself who tests Abraham, but this does not, of course, imply that God is practicing any kind of deception. A similar fear that testing might somehow imply deception leads some Sikhs to reject this dramatic event in Sikh history, as I myself have witnessed. As I was unfolding the dramatic elements of Baisakhi 1699 at the *gurdwara* in Palatine, Illinois, a passionate young man from the congregation got very upset with me, tackled me after my talk, and sent me numerous e-mail messages in the following weeks. He could not imagine that the guru would stage the birth of the Khalsa, and he adamantly rejected the whole event. The "lordly" image prevents us Sikhs from seeing Guru Gobind Singh's multidimensional personality, and it prevents us from acknowledging the intense anxiety, pain, and joy through which he birthed the Khalsa. No wonder we do not recognize the human response and motivations that the guru expected from men and women in his society. Surely what the guru did was not drama for drama's sake, it was not a show of power over a huge gathering, and it was not the work of a distant commander giving out his orders. Guru Gobind Singh's sensitivity for people suffering from injustice had impregnated him with the desire to give birth to a new consciousness for his entire community, of both males and females. The autobiographical *Bicitra Natak*, written prior to Baisakhi 1699, attests to the critical phenomenon that the birth of the Khalsa was not some playful act, but a complex and natural process that gestated in the guru for a long time. Guru Gobind Singh was well aware that the conventional paternal methods of legislating rules and regulations would be futile. Only a new identity delivered through the process of giving birth would embody the transformation envisioned by his predecessor gurus.

Sitting in the Anandpur congregation, we see the guru labor in sweat and blood. His sword cuts off age-old oppressive hierarchies and reveals the purity and power of maternal blood. As he shatters inequities between Brahmin and Shudra, high and low, he shatters the inequities between *men and women* as well. Manu equates the touch of an Untouchable with that of a menstruating woman and a woman in childbirth (5.85). If Baisakhi 1699 is cherished as the moment that our guru eliminated the pollution of caste by passing the bowl of *amrit* to the hands and lips of people of different social backgrounds, how could he possibly have maintained the tradition that there was pollution attached with the female body and her blood? Casteism and sexism went hand in hand in conventional society. How could the guru have uprooted one and held on to the other? Sikhs have yet to acknowledge that both casteism and sexism were visibly eradicated on the maternity theater of Anandpur. Sikh society could not be equal without gender equality. Baisakhi 1699 was a dramatic rejection of all hereditary names, caste, and professional ties. In the patrilineal structure of North Indian society, the family name, caste, and profession come down from the father *and his father*. When we so well remember Guru Gobind Singh for his annihilation of all family and caste ties *(kul nasa)* and for his annihilation of all occupations that determined one's place in society *(krit nasa)*, how can we remain oblivious to his elimination of the father's hegemony? By rejecting the supremacy of the father, the guru affirmed the parity of the mother. He made the father and the mother equal; he made the son and daughter equal. Starting with Nanak, Sikh gurus had openly addressed the low status of women, just as they had the low status of the Shudra. They were against sexism, and they spoke against prevalent views such as that women were impure at times of menstruation and childbirth. They also spoke against the customs of sati (widow immolation) and purdah (veiling and seclusion of women) that were current in their society. What Guru Nanak and his successor gurus had proclaimed—but went unheard by Sikh society—was displayed by the tenth guru in front of the Baisakhi gathering. The scene with his sword dripping with blood was drastic. It had to be. People had to be awoken from their passive acceptance of stifling codes.

The guru does not exhibit the "lightness of dictators, generals, judges, bureaucrats, codes of law and abstract principles";[12] rather, he is weighed down by the heaviness of a mother in labor. From the womblike tent, invisible to the Baisakhi congregation, he proudly brings out the Five Beloved. Holding his Five Beloved tenderly, he shows them off to his community. He glows with the pride and joy of a new mother. He dresses up his offspring beautifully, and offers them the nutritious drink, reciting to them sensuous rhymes. He is the perfect picture of a mother rejoicing; he is the perfect picture of a mother devoted to her progeny.

By remembering him in this vital female role we do not make our male guru "effeminate." Quite the opposite: his "feminine" characteristics give us a fuller vision of his personality—which in turn could be very inspiring for the reconstruction of our own torn and fragmented selves. Why do we have to be stuck in our polarized male-female roles? We are human, each with anima and animus. But gender essentialism, with its mutually exclusive scripts, defines people and their behavior in terms of either female or male norms—which is harmful and dangerous. Starting with Guru Nanak, the Sikh gurus transcended gender divisions, and frequently wrote in the female voice. So it is in keeping with the Sikh tradition that we recover the female side of Guru Gobind Singh. His "tough guise" that is imprinted in the Sikh public memory does not work for everybody, and surely not all the time. It only makes us push aside our real fears, and act in ways that distract us from a holistic and balanced self, making things problematic for ourselves, for our families, for our community, and for the world at large. By releasing him from "male" images of mastery and control, we recover Guru Gobind Singh's responsiveness, his attentiveness, and his emotional investment in his people. We begin to appreciate his amazing tenderness. We are touched and transformed by his poetic muse, his maternal emotions, his female imagination, his womanly activities, and his motherly empathy and love for society. Memories of his maternal role fill us with love and confidence in ourselves.

A *second* aspect of our re-memory is a true understanding of the event. Male memories have led generations of Sikhs to boast about the equality and justice championed by the guru, but they did not actually understand his maternal intentions. In my mind, such memories only serve as a coverup for the androcentrism and sexism prevalent in Sikh society. For the three-hundredth anniversary of the Khalsa there were conferences and celebrations throughout the world with lectures on the liberating achievements of Baisakhi 1699. Scholars continue to comment on the high status of women in Sikhism without really thinking about what is going on in their families and in their community. We will look at two such examples, which paradoxically illustrate how close and yet how distant we are from concretizing the vision of our gurus.

In a fine book entitled *The Khalsa*, the authors, who are from Punjab, the Sikh heartland, claim: "The position of woman is also much better and more respectable among the Sikhs. Incidentally, a woman now heads the Shromani Gurdwara Parbhandhak committee, the democratically elected body responsible for the governance of all major Sikh shrines."[13] Now, the Sikh community has every reason to be proud because Sikh women were the first Indian women granted the right to vote by the Gurdwara Act of 1925. Precisely because of the democratic principles of the Gurus, Sikh women got the right to vote relatively early. Guru Amar Das (1552–74) had delegated women to lead Sikh communities, and we hear about Sikh women leaders appointed to faraway places like Kashmir and Afghanistan. Yet, in spite of the gurus' initiatives, which date back to the formative period of Sikh religion, and the right to vote, which Sikh women received relatively early, extremely few Sikh women have been politically active.[14] Bibi Jagir Kaur's victory in 1999 as president of the SGPC is surely a landmark in women's history. But her tenure was brief, and she had to resign under a lot of male pressure.[15] Why aren't more Sikh women holding positions of power in Sikhism? As a community we need to think about both our negative and positive characteristics. There has to be introspection on our part. We possess immense potential to become the most egalitarian society, but we need to be self-reflective as to why we have not actualized the egalitarian vision of our gurus.

Another respected Sikh academic, from California, the heartland of the Sikh diaspora in America, remarks: "The translation of Sikh doctrine into practice can be seen in the active role women play in family worship as well as in devotional practices in the gurdwara. In sacred activity both at home and in the gurdwara, gender distinctions do not play a significant role."[16] That "men only see women from the corners of their eyes," a generality expressed by the Sikh author Shauna Singh Baldwin,[17] is unfortunately true even of male academics. For, what is peripheral to them is indeed very central for us. Women surely play a very active role in devotional practices at home, but when it comes to leading worship in *gurdwaras*—whether they are located in the homeland or in the New World—it is invariably the men. We almost never find a female *granthi* ("the reader of the Granth," who is normally in charge of a *gurdwara*), and we rarely hear a woman recite Ardas or read the Vak in public (which are both recited in solo). Unwritten laws are the ones that govern Sikh life, for public worship is a privilege granted to men. Daily ceremonies like *prakash* (opening of the Guru Granth) and *sukhasan* (putting to rest in the evening) in *gurdwaras*, the annual celebrations of Baisakhi and *gurpurabs* (birthday or death anniversaries of the gurus), and all rites of passage for Sikh men and women are conducted and administered almost exclusively by men. Gender distinctions *do play* a very significant role because the superior role and privilege of men in public is unconsciously taken into the home, with the result that male domination is reproduced in the family, home, and Sikh society at large. In the praxis of the words, women are marginal and tangential, which is distorting for their self-image and the way they are seen by others. The sexism and subjugation they directly experience in public places resonates deeply in the inner psyches of Sikh men and women, legitimizing women's deference and subordination to their fathers, brothers, and husbands. No! Sikh doctrine has not been translated into practice. It is urgent we be self-critical, and not self-lauding.

If anything, by reciting the equality promoted by the gurus, the oppressive societal structures get neatly covered up. Patriarchal memories over the generations have so elaborated upon gender equality that they have anaesthetized Sikhs from seeing the rampant sexism festering in their community. We cannot hide our atrocious social reality behind the egalitarian message of our gurus or behind the legal equality typed on paper. "Equality" in theory ends up being even more frightful. Blatant patriarchy would obviously hurt more, but at least the cause of the pain could be diagnosed. Under the guise of equality, the symptoms are retained rather than cured. This parity on paper gives Sikh men an extra excuse to show off, contributing to their becoming even more patriarchal than the cultures surrounding them. They jump on the feminist bandwagon, which they are actually destroying. Paradoxically, then, theologians and exegetes have reminded Sikhs of their past in such a way that they have actually succeeded in making them forget their present. Indeed, they have promoted a false consciousness in which men and women have become oblivious to the discrepancy between the ideals of their guru and the reality of their situation. And so Sikhs continue to commemorate Baisakhi 1699 without truly comprehending the transformative praxis of their guru's deed.

Our re-memory makes us squarely face the fact that even after centuries, Guru Gobind Singh's radical egalitarian vision is far from being realized, and instead of concealing them, our flashback of his dramatic Baisakhi glaringly shows the gross maladies and handicaps in our daily conduct. We are disturbed and shocked by sexist attitudes, which emerge from the very conception of a child. The obsession with having sons is so great that modern technology is abused by Sikh families to promote the abortion of female fetuses. Ultrasound and other modern technologies are misused to preserve the legacy, business, property, and status of fathers and their sons. With all the technological and economic advancement, Punjab, the home of the Sikhs, remains the worst location of all. Celia Dugger's article "Abortions in India Spurred by Sex Test Skew the Ratio Against Girls" in the *New York Times* focuses on the tragedy of female feticide in the affluent, agrarian Punjab.[18] A "diabolic link" exists between sex-selection technologies and the abortion of female fetuses, with the result that there is an increasing imbalance in the ratio of males to females in the population of the Punjab. Since immigrant Sikhs maintain transnational ties with their families and friends in the Punjab, the customs and values from home are quickly exported to diasporic communities across the globe.[19]

In a culture resounding with the blessing, "May you be the mother of a hundred sons," the birth of baby daughter is a source of immense sorrow. No sweets are distributed at *her* birth. This early sexism is articulated touchingly by Roop, the eight-year-old protagonist in Baldwin's *What the Body Remembers*. Very early in life the little girl accepts that chicken is for her brother Jeevan; dal, the cheap lentils, for her. They may be born into the same Sikh family, but the son and daughter are fed different foods and assigned different roles and given a whole different set of obligations. Come to think of it, how can Sikh society claim that a woman is reborn equally into the Khalsa family when she is even denied the position her male counterpart is entitled to from the moment of his birth? The liberty granted by the Rahit Maryada that "Any man or woman of whatever nationality, race, or social standing, who is prepared to accept the rules governing the Sikh community, has the right to receive *amrit* initiation" serves as a license more than as the true fulfillment anticipated by Guru Gobind Singh.

During my research, I asked several prominent Sikh men if women are allowed to serve as the *panj pyare* (the Five Beloved chosen by the community to officiate Sikh rites). The answer was always in the positive. But when I asked whether they actually do so, the answer was no, and the absence was blamed on the women themselves: "They don't want to." Yet, in 1989 when a group of women asked to be the *panj pyare* to lead the Baisakhi procession in New York, they were rejected. For the most part, women are tacitly barred from taking up the special role of the Five Beloved. Even on Sikh Web sites, five handsome boys represent Sikh identity. The boys reclaim Sikh heritage, pronouncing, "We are proud to be Sikhs." Guru Gobind Singh's call on that historic Baisakhi Day in 1699 was to the entire gathering—to Brahmins and Shudras, to men and women. Guru Gobind Singh did not choose anyone and he did not exclude anyone. His Sikhs volunteered. The first five volunteers during Baisakhi 1699 happened to be men—but this was not Guru Gobind Singh's request. *Koi* represents anyone, male or female. In the late seventeenth century, women did not stand up. But instead of understanding and empathizing with the particular situation of women at that moment of Indian history, the incident of the five male volunteers has been cast in stone by Sikhs. The guru's model of five *volunteers* has been changed into a *selection* of the five, and his model of inclusivity has been distorted and reduced to an exclusive male club. Whereas Guru Gobind Singh destroyed the difference between the initiator and the initiates, Sikh society has only valorized it. All Sikh visual and aural narratives feature handsome men as the *panj pyare*.

Like the *amrit* initiation, all Sikh rites of passage are the same for both men and women in some ideal sense, but in fact they end up being absolutely different in Sikh practice. For example, both male and female children are named in consultation with the holy book. Sikhs do not even have different names for boys and girls! The addition of the name "Kaur" (meaning "princess") for girls and "Singh" (meaning "lion") for boys indicates the gender of the child. This is another great feature traced to Guru Gobind Singh: he freed women from the lineage of fathers and husbands. A woman is a "Kaur" and retains her own identity for her whole life. She does not adopt the name of her father at birth nor that of her husband at marriage. Sons and daughters, husbands and wives, were to retain their selfhood equally throughout their lives. This transformation in patrilineal structure has radical implications for the identity and autonomy of women, but this revolutionary change is forgotten by the Sikh community; it remains buried in discriminations imposed on girls and women by the Sikh community. So the name-giving ceremony might be the same for sons and daughters, and they may even receive the same article to wear—their first *kara*—but depending on their "biology," it ends up being a totally different event, with the *kara* having a whole different symbolic significance. In the case of boys, for instance, the celebrations are amazingly more elaborate and joyous, with huge *langars* (community meals) for *his* name-giving but *not for hers.*

Such sexism continues in all aspects of Sikh life. The Punjabi winter ritual of Lohri is celebrated only in Sikh homes where a boy is born. Sadness and tears, blame and abuse, is the lot of mothers without sons, sisters without brothers. Affluent Sikh families have also begun to celebrate the *dastar bandhan* (turban-tying) with great pomp and show. This tying of the turban for the first time in a boy's life is becoming a popular rite of passage for the "first sex."

There have been devoted Sikh women over the generations who have worn turbans. I recall my father's maternal aunt wearing one. We find many artistic depictions of historical figures like Mai Bhago, as well as fictional protagonists like Bhai Vir Singh's Sundari, who wear turbans and valorously fight their enemies on horseback. In the 3HO (Healthy, Happy, Holy Organization) started by Harbhajan Singh Yogi in California, the women adherents have worn white turbans just like the men. Even mainstream Sikh women teachers, lawyers, and financial consultants in North America are taking up wearing the turban as a symbol of sexual equality. There is a renewed use of the turban among contemporary Sikh women born and brought up in the West. In the *Guru's Gift: An Ethnography Exploring Gender Equality with North American Sikh Women*, Cynthia Mahmood and Stacy Brady recollect the experiences of young female Sikhs who appropriate this traditional symbol to renegotiate their personal, cultural, and religious identity. "These women are using a traditional symbol to reflect changing ideas about gendered identities in Sikhism, which has opened up a dialogue about representation, power sharing, and the dynamics of the *siblinghood* (classically, "brotherhood") of Sikhism."[20]

Insofar as the turban provides a sense of the self and validates the wearer, it is a fine choice. Women who wear the turban should not be ostracized either by members of their community as some form of Western "feminism" or by outsiders as some form of "backward fundamentalism." Nor should the turban be obligatory for all women. The Sikh Rahit Maryada quite rightly leaves this typical male-gear optional for them. Actually, we do not hear about the turban as one of the five *Ks* specified by the guru. Worn by Hindu and Muslim men, the turban became a practical and convenient garment to hold the hair (*kesha*) tidy and neat. According to W.H. McLeod, the symbolic importance of the turban is essentially a twentieth-century product. In the early phase of the Khalsa, "The turban would, however, amount to nothing more than essential head-gear, a covering for the item which certainly was essential. It would not be regarded as *Symbol* of the newly-adopted faith"[21] Along similar lines, Bernard Cohn traces the Sikh turban to the colonial enterprise. He argues that the distinctive turban of the Sikhs, different from that of Punjabi Muslims and Hindu Dogras, was constructed out of the colonial context "in which British rulers sought to objectify qualities they thought appropriate to roles that various groups in India were to play. . . . A distinctive style of turban, worn only by Sikhs and serving in companies made up of Sikhs, was the crucial item of their uniform, which represented and helped constitute the obedience that the British expected of their loyal Indian followers."[22]

Whether we choose to agree or disagree with the arguments offered by McLeod and Cohn, the turban has become the critical symbol of Sikhism, which means that the half of the population that does not wear a turban is excluded. Its counterpart, the *dupatta* (long scarf), is an essential form of attire for women. Even when they wear the turban, the *dupatta* is still worn by women. Along with neat braids and coiffures designed in various styles, the *dupatta* is a very effective way of maintaining and respecting the gift of the *kesha*. With women wearing the turban, we are only moving in the male direction. And that is very troublesome. Why don't we see men taking on wearing *dupattas*? Why, why should my question sound so far-fetched?

Perhaps there would not even be a need for women to wear a turban if they were treated equally by their families and society. The women cited by Mahmood and Brady felt the turban gave them a sense of respect and confidence, which to my mind suggests that they themselves had been deprived of them simply because they were women. Respect and confidence were granted only to those whom they had witnessed wearing the turban, i.e., their fathers, their brothers, and the men in their community. Sikh women should not feel that they *have* to wear the turban to receive the equality that is their birthright. It is the deep-seated notions of male hegemony that have to disappear rather than women's hair beneath a turban. Why should women have to wear what men wear in order to feel confident and free? It was Malcolm X who said that African Americans did not need to make their hair straight in order to be treated like the whites. Uniformity is quite unnecessary.

Now there is the practice of a female custom called *chunni charana* (the scarf giving) among the Sikhs, which is like an engagement. However, in this case, *her* light scarf conceals heavy burdens of cash, sweets, fruit, and jewels that the "girl's" family is required to give as gifts to her husband-to-be and his family. Prior to the wedding, the groom's family comes to the bride's house to present her the *chunni* accompanied by jewelry and clothes. It is quite telling that the scarf in this Sikh ritual is the *chunni*, a skimpy version of the *dupatta*. A *chunni* is narrower and shorter in length. Little girls wear *chunnis*; the *dupatta*, literally, double (*du*) border (*patta*)—is worn by respectable women. Inherent in this female rite of passage we therefore detect a slighting of the bride-to-be. This initial contact by the groom's family through the *chunni* in her natal home is simply a prologue to the second-rate position that the bride and *her* family are relegated to for the rest of their lives. *Her chunni* thus forms a total contrast to *his dastar*, which imparts pride and respect.

The most deplorable sexism comes out in Sikh marriages. This crucial rite of passage is exasperatingly different for sons and daughters. The name of the wedding ceremony, *anand karaj* (*anand*=bliss, *karaj*=event), is derived from Guru Amar Das's rapturous hymn Anand (bliss), which, as we discussed, ironically begins with addressing the mother. The bliss and psychic contentment envisioned by the gurus ends up replaced by women's bondage and misery. The Sikh rite of marriage began as a very simple ceremony, but this unpretentious ritual has grown into an elaborate commercial racket. Staging fancy receptions with popular singers and *bhangra* dancers is taking precedence over the simple and profound religious ceremony. Families of Sikh sons now demand elaborate receptions and huge dowries. Weekly newspapers in India and abroad are full of advertisements, offering daughters who are "fair complexioned," "convent school educated," "young, easily molded in any way." They are products to be marketed to the "tall," "handsome," "landowning," "doctor," and "engineer" sons. Many young women in the Punjab are married off to men settled in distant lands as a means of sponsoring their entire families for immigration. The process has been interpreted by sociologists as the "sacrifice of the daughter for the sake of the son."[23] The *Tribune*, a popular English-language newspaper in the Punjab, poignantly captured this modern tragedy: "Young bright promising girls are literally bartered away by their parents looking for an opportunity to send other members of the family to the land of lucre."[24] The economic and social demands of contemporary Sikh culture are so strong and pervasive that Sikh teachings against elaborate rituals and "object"-ionable treatment of women by the gurus goes unheeded.

The obligations of the father and mother do not end at the marriage of their daughter but continue till the day she dies and extend even beyond. When there is a death in her in-laws' family, it is *her* family again who has to offer a turban (in the case of a male) or a *dupatta* (in the case of a female)—but, of course, both modes of accoutrement are accompanied by cash. I could not believe it when my aunt (mother of two physician sons) and her husband got upset with my ailing father for having failed to send a scarf at the death of my aunt's ninety-eight-year-old mother-in-law! Since he was suffering from a stroke, Dad could not attend the funeral of his sister's mother-in-law. But as the sole surviver from my aunt's side, he had to fulfill his obligations even though he was bedridden. So he sent cash but somehow missed out on sending a chiffon *dupatta*—and the poor man was duly chastised. Such rigidity in Sikh customs helps no one. It does not alleviate anyone's pain or sorrow nor does it add any real joy to any rite or custom. It only rips families asunder, tearing apart husbands and wives, brothers and sisters, and even aunts and nieces. When a daughter dies, no matter what age or stage of life she may have been at, it is *her* family's responsibility to supply the meal following the cremation. From her birth till her death, a daughter is a debit. Women do not freely conduct ceremonies like their male counterparts, and the ceremonies lack meaning and joy for them and their families. One wonders whether Durkheim's definition of rituals as "collective effervescence" works out in the case of Sikh women.

Matters get even worse in diasporic communities. How to preserve Sikh identity in our contemporary world is a vital concern for Sikhs across the globe. Threatened by modernity and affluence, patriarchal formulations become even more stringent. Since women are literally the reproducers of the community, the preservation of "Sikhness" falls primarily on them. As a result, Sikh women are subjected to manifold restrictions. Control over their reproductive rights leads to the reproduction of the family's identity and that of the Sikh community at large. "Honor" or *izzat,* which is identified with manliness and belongs to hierarchical and patriarchal systems, has come to be a central virtue of the Sikhs. Feminists point to it as a "harness" with which women are bridled. Threatened by the actions of women in our modern society, men safeguard their honor by controlling their sisters, wives, and nieces. In her telling study "Migration of Sikh Women to Canada: A Social Construction of Gender," Gurpreet Bal reports the alarming increase of wife-beating, abuse, and battering in the Sikh community in Canada.[25] In our contemporary scene with abortions, dowry deaths, physical and psychological abuse, and even "honor killings" escalating among Sikhs both at home and in diasporic communities, a re-memory of Guru Gobind Singh's emancipatory event becomes ever more urgent.

When the tenth guru created such a radically liberating paradigm some three hundred years ago, how, how could Sikhs today shackle themselves to these oppressive and dangerous structures? How could Sikhs put up with such horrible sexism and continue to perpetuate it at the personal and community level? So the *third* aspect of our re-memory charges us—men and women alike—with the obligation to get rid of all injustices and disparities that stifle our lives. We cannot remain passive anymore. Women cannot continue to collaborate with androcentric attitudes and practices. We have to take responsibility for our situation. As Mahadevi Varma wrote half a century ago, "By merely carting the load of age-old principles, she [women] has become a load for herself."[26] Guru Gobind Singh awakens us to the duties we owe ourselves. We have to retrieve our natural rights, our own interests that we have neglected for the sake of our brothers, husbands, and sons. Once we truly remember that the Shudra and Kshatriya drank from the same bowl, that the guru bowed before his disciples, we cannot allow a sweeper to be treated differently from an officer, nor any woman to be treated differently from a man. The spirit of freedom kindled by the guru has to be reignited. In fact, the more clearly we remember the egalitarian birth of the Khalsa in Anandpur, the more intensely we are disturbed by the tragic inequities prevailing in our homes and in our communities, and the more urgently we need to react to eradicate them.

Rather than boast, we should internalize the spirit of Baisakhi. "[T]he ideas that have the most powerful hold upon us are not those *we think about*.... The most powerful ideas are those *we think with*. They are the ideas that lie 'behind' our eyes, enabling us to see; what we do see is shaped by them."[27] I believe that if we keep the liberating praxis of Baisakhi 1699 "behind our eyes," we will instantly start doing something about the problems facing the Sikh community in a real way. Our re-memory is not a superficial celebration of Guru Gobind Singh's accomplishment three centuries ago—it is changing our thoughts, our emotions, and our actions *today*. It is recognizing that our daughters are no different from our sons, and treating them lovingly, impartially, throughout their lives. Flashbacks to the guru's Baisakhi mandate that we feed our sons and daughters the same foods, they mandate that we provide our sons and daughters with the same education, they mandate that we inspire them with the same goals and expectations, and they mandate that we leave them equal inheritance, be it cash, jewelry, home, land, firm, or factory. There should be no disparities in rites, obligations, and roles at home and in public for Shudra or Brahmin, *man or woman*. There should be no double standards for sons and daughters in any Sikh household anywhere in the world. The ancient rules of compartmentalization and subordination were broken by Guru Gobind Singh, and we must not allow any later exploitations—either from colonial rule or from our modern consumerism—to poison his liberating *amrit*. The Khalsa is the birth of a subject dominated by none—neither by a tyrannical ruler, nor by a father, husband, uncle, or brother. Inspired with the memory of Baisakhi 1699, Sikhs should throw away the repressive patriarchal blinders and earmuffs, and begin to live anew, conducting their daily life and their rites of passage with a renewed spirit inherited from their gurus.

The historic event of 1699 was Guru Gobind Singh's dramatic reminder that our humanity is defined by the Infinite, and our re-memory in turn becomes a reveling in the Infinite that was initially sipped by Nanak. An opening into our present and future, this joyous experience is not merely a negation of fetters of pride and possession; it is also a positive springing forth of countless resources of our common humanity that help us grow and excel in literary, artistic, political, economic, and scientific fields with the "sky as the limit." Something new came on the horizon on Baisakhi Day 1699. How do we commemorate it? Do we follow men like Chaupa Singh, who segregated Sikh society, who codified *dos* and *don'ts* for men and women, who prohibited women from conducting public worship, who stipulated that women worship their husbands, who all along have erected dams behind which the Sikh psyche has sunk into the stagnant water of suppressive practices and oppressive institutions? Do we abuse the five symbols as the weapons of those in power? Or do we follow the current of the transparent *amrit* flowing with divine love, with the guru's love, with mother's love, as it murmurs Guru Gobind Singh's verse *jin prem kio tin hi prabh paio* (they alone who love find the Beloved) down the waters of memory to the River Bein?

I cherish the Sikh legacy my parents left me, and miss them both terribly during all the intersections of my personal and literary activities. I fondly remember how as a kid I used to send waves of joy through a drawing room full of men arguing about Punjab politics. It used to happen on Sundays, the day that Dad would always wash his *kesha* and leave it open in public to dry (a popular Sikh Sunday morning custom before electric hair-dryers penetrated the Punjab). With the visit of his politically charged friends, our home would get caught up in fiery discussions, while I, comfortably seated on my Dad's lap, would keep busy playing with his long hair, which was otherwise always in a topknot or hidden under his turban. And suddenly everyone would discover that Dad's *kesha* was flowing in soft pretty braids! I guess I have been a "feminist" since the age of three, and my community's reception has not been hostile. For the most part, it has encouraged me to keep up with my feminist research, and I feel very grateful to its many members who have invited me to lecture and write on feminist issues in the Sikh religion, and honored me with numerous awards for my scholarship in this area. Memories belong to each of us, as do the *Ks* that are worn and the sacred verses that are recited, and when *bani* and *bana* merge together, new reservoirs of energy and enchantment begin to flow in every*body*. As we have said, the Bein in which Nanak was immersed literally means a braid (from the Sanskrit *veni*), and this braid made up of waters reflecting the Infinite in our deepest selves was formalized into a new identity for the Sikh community by his tenth successor. Rather than just center on beards, topknots, and turbans, when we begin to celebrate the confluence of our gurus with the braids belonging to our daughters, sisters, nieces, wives, aunts, and mothers, and recognize that each of their knots is braided with tactile and transcendent dimensions, we drink from the font of humanity and reveal our true Sikh identity birthed by Guru Gobind Singh on that momentous spring day in Anandpur.

Appendix

Brief Biography of Guru Gobind Singh

1. Patna (1666–73), where he was born to Mata Gujari and spent his first few years.

2. Anandpur (1673–82), where he had his early schooling. On Baisakhi Day, March 29, 1676, guruship was conferred upon him after the execution of his father, Guru Tegh Bahadur (1621–75). His nuptials with Mata Jitoji took place ten miles north of Anandpur (later called Guru Ka Lahore) in 1677. He was married to Mata Sundari in 1684. His nuptials with Mata Sahib Devan also took place in Anandpur in 1700.

3. Paunta (1682–88), where he continued with his martial exercises and engaged in literary pursuits. The famous battle of Bhangani was fought September 18, 1688. His eldest son, Ajit Singh, was born to Mata Sundari in 1687.

4. Anandpur (1689–1705), where he strategically constructed four forts: Anandgarh, Lohgarh, Keshgarh, and Fatehgarh. His next three sons were born to Mata Jitoji: Jujhar Singh in 1691, Zorowar Singh in 1696, and Fateh Singh in 1699. On Baisakhi Day, 1699, Guru Gobind Singh created the Khalsa. Mata Jitoji died in 1700. In May 1705, the hill rajahs with the support of the imperial forces besieged the guru for many months. He and his Sikhs firmly withstood their successive assaults. At last, Anandpur was evacuated during the night of December 5, 1705. But on December 7, the imperial army caught up with them at Chamkaur. Guru Gobind Singh's two sons Ajit Singh and Jujhar Singh, along with a few other Sikhs, died, fighting valiantly in the Battle of Chamkaur. The younger two sons, who had escaped with their grandmother, Mata Gujari, were betrayed by their old servant and executed on December 13, 1705.

5. Damdama (1706). After facing many hardships, the guru reached Damdama in January 1706, where he was rejoined by a number of Sikhs. His

two wives, Mata Sundari and Mata Sahib Kaur, also came from Delhi to be with him. Damdama soon became the center of literary activity.

6. Nander (1707–8). After Aurangzeb's death in 1707, the guru marched with the new emperor Bahadur Shah to the Deccan. Later, he broke off and encamped at Nander, a small town on the banks of the Godavari, for about fourteen months. During this time he converted Madho Das Bairagi to Sikhism and gave him the name of Banda Singh. The guru was stabbed at Nander by a Pathan sent by the Nawab of Sirhind, who was extremely jealous about the new emperor's friendship toward Guru Gobind Singh. When the news reached Bahadur Shah, he sent expert surgeons including an Englishman, but unfortunately, the stitched-up wounds reopened, and the guru died on October 7, 1708. A day before, he made the Granth Guru forever.

Notes

Introduction

1. In the Mughal period, *khalsa* was used as a revenue term. It stood for the area that was directly under the emperor's dominion as distinct from that under a local feudal lord, so its revenue would be directly deposited into the royal treasury.

2. For other sources on the formation of the Khalsa, see J. S. Grewal, *From Guru Nanak to Maharaja Ranjit Singh: Essays in Sikh History* (Amritsar: Guru Nanak University, 1972), pp. 56–58.

3. W. H. McLeod, *Who Is a Sikh?: The Problem of Sikh Identity* (Oxford: Clarendon, 1989), p. 29.

4. Michel Foucault, *Language, Counter-Memory, Practice: Selected Essays and Interviews*, ed. D. F. Bouchard (Ithaca, NY: Cornell University Press, 1977), p. 131.

5. The ten Sikh gurus are Nanak, Angad, Amar Das, Ram Das, Arjan, Hargobind, Har Rai, Har Krishan, Tegh Bahadur, and Gobind Singh.

6. Foucault, *Language, Counter-Memory, Practice*, p. 133.

7. Ibid., p. 134.

8. Frederick Nietzsche, *The Use and Abuse of History*, trans. Adrian Collins (Indianapolis: Liberal Arts Press, 1957), p. 39.

9. Kanwaljit Kaur, "Sikh Women," in *Fundamental Issues in Sikh Studies*, ed. Kharak Singh, G. S. Mansukhani, and J. S. Mann. (Chandigarh: Institute of Sikh Studies, 1992), p. 104.

10. Doris Jakobsh, *Relocating Gender in Sikh History* (New Delhi: Oxford University Press, 2003), p. 8.

11. See Hayden White, *Tropics of Discourse: Essays in Cultural Criticism* (Baltimore: Johns Hopkins University Press, 1978), p. 53.

12. Hans-Georg Gadamer, *Truth and Method* (New York: Crossroad, 1989), p. 301.

13. Rita Gross, *Feminism and Religion* (Boston: Beacon Press, 1996), p. 72.

14. Judith Plaskow, *Standing Again at Sinai: Judaism from a Feminist Perspective* (New York: Harper and Row, 1990).

15. A touching plea for equality between brothers and sisters is expressed by an anonymous Sikh teenager growing up in America in her essay, "Things That Make You Ask *Kion*?" in *Asian Religions in America: A Documentary History*, ed. Thomas A. Tweed and Stephen Prothero, (New York: Oxford University Press, 1999), pp. 312–14.

16. Uma Narayan, *Dislocating Cultures: Identities, Traditions, and Third-World Feminism* (New York: Routledge, 1997), p. 6.

17. W. H. McLeod, *Sikhism* (London: Penguin, 1997), pp. 48–49.

18. "Immanent Mother," ed. Mary Giles "*The Feminist Mystic" and Other Essays on Women and Spirituality*, (New York: Crossroad, 1982), p. 79.

19. See Grace M. Jantzen's excellent work *Becoming Divine: Towards a Feminist Philosophy of Religion* (Bloomington: Indiana University Press), 1999.

20. Harold Coward, *Sacred Word and Sacred Text: Scripture in World Religions* (Maryknoll, NY: Orbis Books, 1988), p. 182.

21. I have taken this term from the title of the video recording *Tough Guise: Violence, Media, and the Crisis in Masculinity*, executive director Sut Jhally, produced by Susan Ericsson and Sanjay Talr.

22. Rabindranath Tagore, *Gitanjali* (NY: Macmillan, 1971), poem #95.

Chapter 1. Pregnant Text and the Conception of the Khalsa

1. Besides the verses of the Sikh gurus, the Guru Granth contains verses of Hindu and Muslim saints. For a fuller discussion, see my essay, "The Body of the Gurus: Sikh Scripture from a Contemporary Feminist Perspective" for *Religious Studies and Theology*, Volume 23, no. 2 (2004), pp. 27–42.

2. Kashi is the old name for Benares.

3. Robin Rinehart introduces us to the controversial and impassioned arguments in her chapter "Strategies for Interpreting the *Dasam Granth*," in *Sikhism and History*, ed. Pashaura Singh and N. G. Barrier (New Delhi: Oxford University Press, 2004), pp.135–50. See also Piara Singh Padam, *Dasam Granth Darsan* (Patiala: Kala Mandir, 1990), pp. 39–53, 96–109, and Jeevan Deol, "The Eighteenth-Century Khalsa Identity: Discourse, Praxis and Narrative," in *Sikh Religion, Culture, and Ethnicity* (Surrey: Curzon, 2001), p. 30.

4. I am only focusing on those few compositions that are popular in the daily life of the Sikhs.

5. The *Bicitra Natak* is placed third in the Dasam Granth, following the Jap and Akal Ustat. It is thirty-eight pages long.

6. See Indubhusan Banerjee, "The Chronology of Guru Gobind Singh," in his *Evolution of the Khalsa,* vol. 2 (Calcutta: AMC, 1978), pp. 168–73.

7. In chapter 13 of the *Bicitra Natak* we learn that the enraged emperor sent his son (verse 1)—which tallies historically with Aurangzeb dispatching his son Muazzam to settle affairs in the Punjab on July 13, 1696. See Harbans Singh, *Guru Gobind Singh,* (New Delhi: Sterling Publishers, 1979), p. 41.

8. Harbans Singh, *Guru Gobind Singh*, p. 15.

9. M. L. Peace, introduction to *Guru Gobind Singh's "Bachittar Natak,"* trans. M. L. Pearce and Rattan Kaur, (Jullundur: Basti Guzan, 1966), p. 10.

10. See Janet Varner Gunn's fine discussion in *Autobiography: Towards a Poetics of Experience* (Philadelphia: University of Pennsylvania Press, 1982), pp. 17–18.

11. Clark Blaise, "Autobiography and the Post-Modernist Moment," in *The Seductions of Biography* ed. M. Rhiel and D. Suchoff. (New York: Routledge, 1996), pp. 203–4.

12. Peace and Kaur, *Guru Gobind Singh's "Bachittar Natak,"* p. 5.

13. Harbans Singh, *Guru Gobind Singh.* Chapter 5 is entitled "A New Literary Metaphor."

14. The influential exegete Professor Sahib Singh explains, "The Guru has further exalted the symbolic value of the Sword as the Supreme Power of God (Father Symbol). . . . " Sahib Singh, *Guru Gobind Singh* (Jullundur: Raj Publishers, 1967), p. 110.

15. Tracy Pintchman, "Is the Hindu Goddess a Good Resource?" in *Is the Goddess a Feminist: The Politics of South Asian Goddesses,* ed. Alf Hiltebeitel and Kathleen M. Erndl (Albany: State University of New York Press, 2000), p. 191.

16. I have discussed it in length in *The Feminine Principle of the Sikh Vision of the Transcendent* (Cambridge: Cambridge University Press, 1993), pp. 121–26.

17. See Thomas Cleary and Sartaz Aziz, "Goddess of Rebellion," in *Twilight Goddess: Spiritual Feminism and Feminine Spirituality* (Boston: Shambhala, 2000).

18. Wendy Doniger, *Other Peoples' Myths: The Cave of Echoes* (London: Macmillan, 1988), p. 165.

19. Ellen Umansky, "Creating a Jewish Feminist Theology: Possibilities and Problems," in *Weaving the Visions*, ed. Judith Plaskow and Carol Christ (New York: Harper & Row, 1989), pp. 187–98. Bella Debrida "Drawing from Mythology in Women's Quest for Selfhood," in *The Politics of Women's Spirituality* ed. Charlene Spretnak (Garden City, N.Y.: Anchor/Doubleday, 1982), p. 142.

20. "Things That Make You Ask *Kion*? in *Asian Religions in America: A Documentary History* ed. Thomas Tweed and Stephen Prothero (New York: Oxford University Press, 1999), pp. 312–14.

21. At a conference on Sikh theology, male participants vehemently disagreed with a female speaker for suggesting that the Sikh guru could refer to a Hindu goddess (New York City: Columbia University, March 31, 1990). The Bhasauria school has always rejected Guru Gobind Singh's authorship of poems with Hindu themes.

22. D. P. Ashta, *The Poetry of the "Dasam Granth"* (New Delhi: Arun Prakashan, 1959), p. 38. Trilochan Singh, in *Sikh Review* (Calcutta), May 1955, p. 34.

23. Peace and Kaur, *Guru Gobind Singh's "Bachittar Natak,"* esp. pp. 8–13.

24. Jodh Singh and Dharam Singh, *Sri Dasam Granth Sahib: Text and Translation*, vol. 1 (Patiala: Heritage Publications, 1999), p. 117.

25. I agree with Madanjit Kaur that the guru was not a worshipper of the goddess. See her chapter "Worship Story: A Critique" in *Fundamental Issues in Sikh Studies*, ed. Kharak Singh, G. S. Mansukhani, and Jasbir Singh Mann (Chandigarh: Institute of Sikh Studies, 1992), pp. 170–78.

26. See Harbans Singh, *The Encyclopaedia of Sikhism* (Patiala: Punjabi University Press, 1992) s.v. "Mai Bhago," pp. 323–24.

27. James Olney, *Metaphors of Self: The Meaning of Autobiography* (Princeton, N.J.: Princeton University Press, 1972), p. 44.

28. Diane Jonte-Pace cited by Grace Jantzen, in *Becoming Divine: Towards a Feminist Philosophy of Religion* (Bloomington: Indiana University Press, 1999), p. 132.

29. "Mohammed Atta's Last Will & Testament." See://www.pbs.org/wgbg/pages/frontline/shows/network/personal/attawill.html

30. Apparently Rabindranath Tagore was deeply impressed by the fact that Guru Gobind Singh "disclaimed any divinity and warned all his disciples against treating him as anything more than a servant of God." R. K. Dasgupta, "Bengal's Response to Sikhism," in *Guru Gobind Singh: The Saviour*, ed. S. S. Uppal (New Delhi: Sri Guru Tegh Bahadur Khalsa College, 1969), p. 59.

31. The Guru Granth utilizes the term *mansa* frequently to describe the female construction of our mental, spiritual, and imaginative self, as we shall see in our discussion of the Khalsa symbol of the sword in chapter 4.

32. C. H. Loehlin, *The Granth of Guru Gobind Singh and the Khalsa Brotherhood* (Lucknow: Lucknow Publishing House), p. 27.

33. Wendy Doniger, *The Rig Veda: An Anthology* (New York: Penguin, 1981), p. 38.

34. S. Radhakrishnan, *The Principal Upanishads* (London: George Allen and Unwin, 1953), p. 139.

35. *The Collected Works of Mahatma Gandhi* (Delhi: Publications Division, Ministry of Information and Broadcasting, 1967), 87: 201.

36. Ibid., 89: 274.

37. We heard the guru explicitly rejecting any notion of incarnation (*BN*, 6:32–33).

38. *Varan Bhai Gurdas* ed. Bhai Vir Singh (Amritsar: Khalsa Samachar, 1977), p. 39.

39. For an excellent study on the force of martyrdom for Sikhs, see Louis E. Fenech, *Martyrdom in the Sikh Tradition: Playing the "Game of Love"* (New Delhi: Oxford University Press, 2000).

40. Harbans Singh, *Guru Gobind Singh,* p. 19.

41. For example, D. S. Maini, ed, *Guru Gobind Singh: Reflections and Offerings by Puran Singh* (Chandigarh: Guru Gobind Singh Foundation, 1966), p. 23.

42. Frances Devlin-Glass and Lyn McCredden, *Feminist Poetics of the Sacred: Creative Suspicions* (Oxford: Oxford University Press, 2001), p. 4.

43. Diana Eck, *Encountering God* (Boston: Beacon, 1993), p. 195.

44. Virginia Woolf, "Women and Fiction," in *Granite and Rainbow: Essays* (London: Hogarth, 1958), p. 81.

45. Wolfgang Iser, "The Reading Process: A Phenomenological Approach," in *Modern Criticism and Theory: A Reader*, ed. David Lodge (London: Longman, 1988), p. 224.

46. G. S. Mansukhani and S. S. Kohli, *Guru Gobind Singh: His Personality and Achievement* (New Delhi: Hemkunt Press, 1976), p. 45.

47. Iser, "Reading Process," p. 224.

48. Madhu Kishwar, *Off the Beaten Track* (Delhi: Oxford University Press, 1999).

49. Harbans Singh, *Encyclopaedia of Sikhism*, p. 88.

50. Jodh Singh & Dharam Singh, *Sri Dasam Granth Sahib* p. 205.

51. In *Transcultural Poetics: Comparative Studies of Ezra Pound's "Cantos" and Guru Gobind Singh's "Bachittra Natak"* (Delhi: Ajanta Publications, 1988), Gurbhagat Singh uses the term "epistemic" for the process of inner transformation (p. 110).

Chapter 2. The Guru in Labor and the Birth of the Khalsa

1. Dalip Singh categorically rejects the story. See his comprehensive volume *Guru Gobind Singh and Khalsa Discipline* (Amritsar: Singh Brothers, 1992), p. 200.

2. Hans-Georg Gadamer, "The Ontology of the World of Art and Its Hermeneutic Significance," in *Truth and Method* (New York: Crossroad, 1989), pp. 101–34.

3. Gadamer, *Truth and Method*, p. 16

4. W. H. McLeod, ed. and trans. *The Chaupa Singh Rahit-Nama*, (Otago: University of Otago Press, 1987), introduction, p. 10.

5. In the scriptural context, Guru Ram Das (Nanak IV) is specifically addressing those men who are greedy, lazy, licentious, and follow similar women.

6. McLeod, *Chaupa Singh Rahit-Nama*, pp. 111–13

7. W. H. McLeod, *Sikhs of the Khalsa* (Delhi: Oxford University Press, 2003) p. 256.

8. Sallie McFague, *Models of God* (Philadelphia: Fortress Press, 1989), p. 69.

9. The term *baj* is used by Koer Singh, which itself indicates a Vedic allusion.

10. Joan Kelly, *Women, History, and Theory* (Chicago: University of Chicago Press, 1984), xii–xiii

11. In some passages, Koer Singh conjures up the Sikh Guru amid the supernatural world of Hindu gods and goddesses. The guru is even shown to appease and invoke the goddess Kali through severe austerities.

12. Even if other parts of Koer Singh's work show a strong Hindu influence, it is absent from this vital chapter, which represents the normative Sikh view of divinity.

13. Certainly in Guru Gobind Singh's milieu, and even in the period that Koer was writing, long hair was standard for women.

14. David Shulman, *The Hungry God: Hindu Tales of Filicity and Devotion* (Chicago: University of Chicago Press, 1993), p. 6.

15. "*Koi*" means "anybody" whatsoever—male or female.

16. In his opening chapter of *Mimesis*, Eric Auerbach compares the Homeric and biblical styles. See Eric Auerbach *Mimesis: The Representation of Reality in Western Literature*, trans. Willard R. Trask (Princeton: Princeton University Press, 1974), pp. 3–23.

17. Cited in ibid., p. 11.

18. See Bruce Lincoln's fascinating discussion of the identical patterns in Indic, Iranian, Old Russian, and Greek sociogonic myths in *Myth, Cosmos, and Society: Indo-European Themes of Creation and Destruction* (Cambridge, MA: Harvard University Press, 1986), pp. 140–71.

19. J. C. Hesterman, *The Broken World of Sacrifice* (Chicago: University of Chicago Press, 1993).

20. Schulman, *Hungry God,* p. 136.

21. Wendy Doniger, ed., *The Laws of Manu* (New York: Penguin, 1991), introduction, p. xvii.

22. Ibid., 4:208. Besides chapter 4, chapters 3 and 9 are quite derogatory toward women.

23. During my lectures, Sikh women have been pleasantly surprised to discover the radical message of their holy book.

24. Tom E. Driver, *The Magic of Ritual* (San Francisco: HarperSan Francisco, 1991), p. 81.

25. Indubhusan Banerjee, *Evolution of the Khalsa*, vol. 2 (Calcutta: A. Mukherjee and Co.), p. 103.

26. Caroline Walker Bynum. *Holy Feast and Holy Fast* (Berkeley and Los Angeles: University of California Press, 1987), p. 65.

27. Veena Talwar Oldenburg, *Dowry Murder* (Oxford: Oxford University Press, 2002), p. 165.

28. M. A. Macauliffe, *The Sikh Religion,* vol. 5 (Delhi: S. Chand & Co., 1963), p. 95.

29. Koer Singh's original term *cit* signifies both mind and consciousness.

30. Kapur Singh, *The Baisakhi of Guru Gobind Singh,* (Jullunder: Hind Publishers Ltd., 1959) p. 58.

31. Excellent entries on the Five Beloved are found in *The Encyclopaedia of Sikhism.*

32. Doris Jakobsh takes up this important topic in *Relocating Gender in Sikh History*, pp. 219–17.

33. The figure for India as a whole is 927 per 1,000 boys — a number that in itself is shockingly low, and once again, a result of aborted female fetuses. Reported by the *New York Times*, April 22, 2001, p. 10.

34. Gurmukh Nihal Singh, "Guru Gobind Singh: His Contribution to Nation Building," in *Guru Gobind Singh: The Saviour*, ed. S. S. Uppal (New Delhi: Sri Guru Tegh Bahadur Khalsa College, 1969), p. 38.

35. See Rita Gross, *Feminism and Religion* (Boston: Beacon Press, 1996), p. 25.

36. Jacques Lacan, *Ecrits: A Selection*, trans. Alan Sheridan (New York: Norton, 1977), p. 2.

37. *Varan Bhai Gurdas*, ed.: Bhai Vir Singh (Amritsar: Khalsa Samachar, 1977), p. 668. (The quotation is actually by another poet whose works are included among the writings of Bhai Gurdas.)

38. Brian Axel, "The Glorious Body of the Maharaja," in *The Nation's Tortured Body* (Durham NC: Duke University Press), 2001.

39. *kar masand sabhi duri khalsa kar lia*
(Sainapat, 5: 32)
The *masand* was removed, the Khalsa created.
(My translation).

40. For details see Macauliffe, *Sikh Religion*, pp. 22–23.

41. In Koer Singh's narrative, the guru explicitly rejects the *masands* for their egotism and their self-glorification: "[T]he Masands profess to be the Guru; they do not respect the Granth, they claim worship for themselves" (9:38).

42. J. D. Cunningham, *A History of the Sikhs* (Delhi: S. Chand and Co., 1966), p. 313.

43. McFague, *Models of God*, p. 69.

44. Catherine Keller, *From a Broken Web: Separation, Sexism, and Self* (Boston: Beacon Press, 1986), pp. 2–3.

45. Sheila Ruth, *Take Back the Light: A Feminist Reclamation of Spirituality and Religion* (Totowa, NJ: Rowman and Littlefield, 1994), p. xiv.

46. Some scholars, however, read into Khalsa Raj, the aspiration for political dominance of the Sikh community. For a recent discussion see Brian Keith Axel, *Nation's Tortured Body*, pp. 79–120.

47. Ruth, *Take Back the Light*, p. 173.

48. Adrienne Rich, *Of Woman Born* (New York: Norton, 1976), pp. 225–26.

Chapter 3. Mythic Inheritance and the Historic Drink of the Khalsa

An earlier version of this chapter was published in Pashaura Singh and N. G. Barrier, eds., *Sikhism and History* (New Delhi: Oxford University Press, 2004), pp. 51–76.

1. Pashaura Singh and Gerry Barrier, eds., *The Transmission of Sikh Heritage in the Diaspora* (Delhi: Manohar, 1996), p. 169.

2. Animal killed in one stroke, as opposed to the slow purification process of *halal.*

3. Sansrkit *v* survived in *Puratan Janamsakhi* Punjabi, but became *b* in modern spoken Punjabi.

4. Mircea Eliade, *Myth and Reality* (New York: Harper and Row, 1963), p. 6.

5. Ibid., p. 140.

6. B. Malinowski, "*Magic, Science and Religion*" *and Other Essays* (Garden City, NY: Anchor, 1948), p. 146.

7. Ibid., p. 96.

8. Prithipal Singh Kapur and Dharam Singh, *The Khalsa* (Patiala: Punjabi University Press, 1999), p. 51.

9. G. S. Talib mentions the heroic symbols and images through which the Sikh tradition exclusively remembers the tenth guru: "Lord of the Plume, the Lord of the Hawk, the Protector of Faith — all evocative of noble heroism and chivalry. His figure is conceived of as the Rider on the Bay Charger, shooting gold-tipped arrows and destroying in single combat tigers and other wild beasts." *The Impact of Guru Gobind Singh on Indian Society* (Chandigarh: Guru Gobind Singh Foundation, 1966), p. 12.

10. See my discussion of his hymns called "Baburvani" in "Text and Praxis," in *Research in Human Social Conflict*, ed. Joseph Gittler (Greenwich, CT: Jai Publishers, 1999), pp. 279–314.

11. Harold Bloom, *The Anxiety of Influence* (New York: Oxford University Press, 1973), p. 6.

12. I have used the third edition, edited by Bhai Vir Singh (Amritsar: Khalsa Samachar, 1948).

13. Painting by Phulan Rani, in *Life of Guru Nanak through Pictures* (Amritsar: Modern Sahit Academy, 1969), p. 17.

14. Anil Chandra Banerjee, *Guru Nanak to Guru Gobind Singh* (New Delhi: Rajesh Publications, 1978), p. 218.

15. Ibid., p. 218.

16. Ninian Smart, *Worldviews: Crosscultural Explorations of Human Beliefs* (New York: Charles Scribner's Sons, 1983), p. 95.

17. Martin Heidegger, *Poetry, Language, Thought*, trans. Albert Hofstadter (New York: Harper and Row, 1975), p. 76.

18. Talib, *Impact of Guru Gobind Singh on Indian Society*, p. 12.

19. Mircea Eliade, *Rites and Symbols of Initiation* (reprint, Dallas, TX: Spring Publications, 1994), pp. 2–3.

20. Brian Smith, "Ritual, Knowledge, and Being," *Numen* 33, no. 1, (1986): p. 73. See also Axel Michaels, *Hinduism: Past and Present* (Princeton: Princeton University Press, 2004), pp. 77–99.

21. Quoted in Kapur Singh, *The Baisakhi of Guru Gobind Singh* (Jullundur: Hind Publishers, 1959), pp. 4–5.

22. Malinowski, "*Magic, Science and Religion*," p. 47.

23. Bruce Lincoln, *Myth, Cosmos, and Society* (Cambridge, MA: Harvard University Press, 1986), p. 38.

24. H. Clay Trumbull, *The Blood Covenant* (New York: Charles Scribner, 1885), p. 100.

25. Grace M. Jantzen, *Becoming Divine* (Bloomington: Indiana University Press, 1999), p. 138.

26. Ibid., p. 132.

27. Rita Gross, *Feminism and Religion: An Introduction* (Boston: Beacon, 1996), p. 237.

28. Victor Turner, *The Forest of Symbols* (Ithaca, NY: Cornell University Press, 1967), p. 96.

29. *Puratan Janamsakhi Guru Nanak Devji* (Amritsar: Khalsa Samachar, 1946), "Vein Parvesh," pp. 16–19.

30. Sandra Steingraber, *Having Faith* (Cambridge, MA: Perseus, 2001), p. 66.

31. Elizabeth Moltmann-Wendel, *A Land Flowing with Milk and Honey: Perspectives on Feminist Theology* (New York: Crossroad, 1986), pp. 74–75.

32. Discussed in my earlier work, *The Feminine Principle in the Sikh Vision of the Transcendent* (Cambridge: Cambridge University Press, 1993), pp. 33–47.

33. Clifford Geertz, *The Interpretation of Cultures* (New York: HarperCollins, 1973), p. 93.

34. Bruce Lincoln, *Discourse and the Construction of Society* (New York: Oxford University Press, 1989), pp. 8–9.

35. Turner, *Forest of Symbols*, p. 103.

36. Ibid., p. 110.

37. Heidegger, *Poetry, Language, Thought*, p. 49.

38. Ibid., p. 77.

39. Mircea Eliade, *Myths, Rites, Symbols* (New York: Harper Colophon, 1976), pp. 192–93.

40. Lincoln, *Discourse and the Construction of Society*, p. 88.

41. Eliade, *Rites and Symbols of Initiation*, p. ix.

42. Nikky-Guninder Singh, "The Myth of the Founder: The Janamsakhis and Sikh Tradition," *in History of Religions* (Chicago: University of Chicago Press, 1992), vol 31, 4, May 1992, pp. 329–43.

43. Riffat Hassan, "Feminism in Islam," in *Feminism and World Religions*, ed. Arvind Sharma and Katherine Young, (Albany: State University of New York Press, 1999), p. 270.

44. Eliade, *Myth and Reality*, p. 141.

45. Victor Turner, *The Anthropology of Experience* (Urbana: University of Illinois Press, 1986), p. 33.

46. June O'Connor, "The Epistemological Significance of Feminist Research in Religion" in *Religion and Gender,* ed. Ursula King, (Oxford, UK: Blackwell, 1995).

47. Mary Midgley, "The Soul's Successors: Philosophy and the 'Body,'" in *Religion and the Body,* ed. Sarah Coakley (Cambridge: Cambridge University Press, 1997), p. 61.

Chapter 4. The Five Ks and the Accoutrement of the Khalsa

An earlier version of section 5 *(kacha)* was published as "Sacred Fabric and Sacred Stitches: The Underwear of the Khalsa" in *History of Religions.* 43, #4, 2004, pp. 284–302.

1. See his comprehensive and valuable work, *Sikhs of the Khalsa: A History of the Khalsa Rahit* (New Delhi: Oxford University Press, 2003), p. 3.

2. Ganda Singh, "Hair and Turban, Their Importance for the Sikhs," *Punjab Past and Present*, 15, no. 31 (April 1982), pp. 201–7.

3. Michel Foucault, *The Care of the Self:* trans. Robert Hurley, vol. 3 of *The History of Sexuality*, (New York: Vintage, 1988), p. 43.

4. Ibid., p. 51.

5. Patrick Olivelle, "Hair and Society: Social Significance of Hair in South Asian Traditions," in *Hair: Its Power and Meaning in Asian Cultures ed.* Alf Hiltebeitel and Barbara D. Miller, (Albany: State University of New York Press, 1998), pp. 40–41.

6. Bernard S. Cohn, *Colonialism and Its Forms of Knowledge: The British in India* (Princeton, NJ: Princeton University Press, 1996), pp. 106–11. See also Hew McLeod, "The Turban: Symbol of Sikh Identity," in *Sikh Identity: Continuity and Change,* ed. Pashaura Singh and N. G. Barrier, (New Delhi: Manohar Publishers, 1999), pp. 57–67.

7. Brian Keith Axel, *The Nation's Tortured Body* (Durham, NC: Duke University Press, 2001), p. 45.

8. Puran Singh, *Guru Gobind Singh: Reflections and Offerings* (Chandigarh: Guru Gobind Singh Foundation, 1966).

9. Ibid., p. 41.

10. Judging by its Sanskrit roots, as we discussed.

11. S. S. Johar, *Handbook on Sikhism* (Delhi: Vivek Publishers, 1977), pp. 91–95.

12. Ravi Batra, *Leadership in Its Finest Mould* (Amritsar: SGPC, 1979), pp. 23–24.

13. Khushwant Singh, *A History of the Sikhs* (Princeton, NJ: Princeton University Press, 1966), pp. 89–90.

14. Nesbitt in Sarah Coakley, *Religion and the Body* (Cambridge: Cambridge University Press, 1997), pp. 295–96.

15. Mircea Eliade, *The Two and the One* (New York: Harper Torchbooks, 1965), pp. 201–8.

16. Nancy J. Chodorow, *The Power of Feelings* (New Haven, CT: Yale University Press, 1999), p. 2.

17. Prithwish Neogy, ed. *Rabindranath Tagore on Art and Aesthetics* (Calcutta: Orient Longmans, 1966), p. 23.

18. Fatima Mernissi, *The Veil and the Male Elite* (Reading, Massachusetts: Perseus Books, 1991), p. 10.

19. Alf Hiltebeitel, "Hair Like Snakes and Mustached Brides: Crossed Gender in an Indian Folk Cult," in Hiltebeitel and Miller, *Hair*, p. 172.

20. Charles Berg, *The Unconscious Significance of Hair* (London: George Allen and Unwin, 1951), p. 92.

21. Dalip Singh, *Guru Gobind Singh and Khalsa Discipline* (Amritsar: Singh Brothers, 1992), p. 474.

22. Olivelle, "Hair and Society," pp. 40–41.

23. J. P. Singh Uberoi, "The Five Symbols of Sikhism" in *Perspectives on Guru Nanak: Seminar Papers*, ed. Harbans Singh (Patiala: Punjabi University, 1975).

24. Olivelle, "Hair and Society," p. 27.

25. Uberoi, "Five Symbols of Sikhism," p. 508.

26. Kapur Singh, *The Baisakhi of Guru Gobind Singh* (Jullundur: Hind Publishers, Ltd., 1959), p. 104.

27. Olivelle, "Hair and Society," p. 20.

28. The four hymns are collectively known as "Babarvani" (Babur's Decree).

29. For example, *Sabdarath Sri Guru Granth Sahib*, vol. 1, 4th ed. (Amritsar: Shromani Gurdwara Prabandhak Committee, 1964), explains the term *kesav* as "the beautiful-haired Vishnu" (p. 98). Similarly, G.S. Talib, *Sri Guru Granth Sahib: In*

English Translation, vol. 1 (Patiala: Punjabi University, 1987), footnotes "Vishnu" in brackets for *kesav* (p. 204).

30. For example, the case of Sita, which we shall discuss in our next chapter.

31. See K. Murthy, *Hair Styles in Ancient Indian Art* (Delhi: Sundeep Prakashan, 1982) p. 10.

32. Gary Ebersole, "'Long Black Hair Like a Seat Cushion': Hair Symbolism in Japanese Popular Religion," in Hiltebeitel and Miller, *Hair*, p. 98.

33. The overlapping beliefs at the popular level amongst Punjabis—Hindus, Muslims, and Sikhs—is discussed by Harjot Oberoi in his fascinating chapter, "An Enchanted Universe," in *The Construction of Religious Boundaries: Culture, Identity, and Diversity in the Sikh Tradition* (Chicago: University of Chicago Press, 1994), pp. 139–203.

34. Murthy, *Hair Styles in Ancient Indian Art*, p. 10.

35. Michael Ondaatje, *The English Patient* (New York: Vintage International, 1993), p. 217.

36. Toronto, April 1998.

37. Olivelle, "Hair and Society," p. 12.

38. According to Ganda Singh, *Hukamnama* (June 25, 1699) pronounces *kesha* as the guru's insignia. See Gunda Singh, "Hair and Turban," p. 202.

39. Uberoi, "Five Symbols of Sikhism," p. 508.

40. Olivelle, "Hair and Society," p. 39.

41. As we noted, Sanskrit *v* survived in *Puratan Janamsakhi* Punjabi, but became *b* in modern spoken Punjabi.

42. An interesting set of stories entitled "The Porcupine and the Woman Who Climbed to the Sky" can be found in George A. Dorsey and Alfred L. Kroeber, *Traditions of the Arapaho* (Lincoln: University of Nebraska Press, 1998), pp. 321–41.

43. Ebersole, "Long Black Hair," p. 92.

44. Ibid.

45. Ardas is a prayer, recited individually or as a congregation, at the end of Sikh morning and evening prayers, and at the beginning and conclusion of any significant undertaking. Ardas opens with the words "prathami bhagauti simarkai."

46. G. S. Mansukhani, "Sikh Rahat Maryada and Sikh Symbols," in *Advanced Studies in Sikhism*. ed. J. S. Mann and H. S. Saraon, (Irvine, CA: Sikh Community of North America, 1989), p. 184.

47. Hang-Georg Gademer, *Truth and Method* (New York: Crossroad, 1989) p. 73.

48. In his discussion of "picture" and "symbol." Ibid., p. 153.

49. This good explanation comes from Hew Mcleod, *Guru Nanak and the Sikh Religion* (Oxford: Clarendon, 1968), p. 180.

50. *Saram khand* is enunciated in Jap, the first hymn of GG, pp. 7–8.

51. David Kinsley, *The Goddesses' Mirror* (Albany: State University of New York Press, 1989) p. 237.

52. Gadamer, *Truth and Method*, pp. 153–54.

53. Kapur Singh, *Baisakhi of Guru Gobind Singh*, pp. 141–42.

54. Ibid., p. 142.

55. Uberoi, "Five Symbols of Sikhism," p. 508.

56. Olivelle, "Hair and Society," p. 27.

57. Batra, *Leadership*, p. 24.

58. "Hair and Turban," p. 207.

59. Sahib Singh, *Guru Gobind Singh* (Jullundur: Raj Publishers, 1967), p. 64.

60. Ibid., p. 109.

61. Gadamer, *Truth and Method*, p. 306.

62. Carol Christ, "Symbols of Goddess and God in Feminist Theology," in *The Book of the Goddess*, ed. *Carl Olson* (New York: Crossroad, 1985), p. 234.

63. Batra, *Leadership* p. 26.

64. Johar, *Handbook on Sikhism*, p. 96.

65. Olivelle, "Hair and Society," p. 27.

66. Sahib Singh, *Guru Gobind Singh*, p. 109.

67. Kapur Singh, *Baisakhi of Guru Gobind Singh*, p. 153.

68. Ibid., p. 146.

69. Ibid., p. 149.

70. G. S. Mansukhani and S. S. Kohli, *Guru Gobind Singh* (New Delhi: Hemkunt Press, 1976), p. 106.

71. Nita Kumar, ed. *Women as Subjects* (Charlottesville: University Press of Virginia, 1994), p. 21.

72. Ursula King, ed. *Religion and Gender* (Oxford, UK: Blackwell, 1995), p. 5.

73. Virginia Woolf, *Orlando: A Biography* (New York: Harcourt, 1928), pp. 170–71.

74. Kapur Singh, *Baisakhi of Guru Gobind Singh*, p. 148.

75. Geoffrey Parrinder, *Sexual Morality in the World's Religions* (Oxford: Oneworld, 1996), p. 45.

76. Audre Lorde, "Uses of the Erotic," in *Weaving the Visions: Patterns in Feminist Spirituality*, ed. J. Plaskow and C. Christ (New York: Harper and Row, 1989), p. 210.

77. Sandra Lee Bartky, "Suffering to be Beautiful," in *Gender Struggles: Practical Approaches to Contemporary Feminism*, ed. Constance L. Mui and Julien S. Murphy, (Totowa, NJ: Rowman and Littlefield, 2002), p. 248.

78. Ajeet Cour, *Kooda Kabada* (New Delhi: Kitabghar Prakash, 1999), p.1.

79. Luce Irigaray, *Sexes and Genealogies*, trans. Gillian C. Gill (New York: Columbia University Press, 1993), p. 16.

80. Ibid., p. 132.

81. Carter Heyward, "Sexuality, Love, and Justice," in Plaskow and Christ, *Weaving the Visions*, pp. 295–96.

82. Gadamer, *Truth and Method*, p. 78.

83. Sandra Lipsitz Bim, *The Lenses of Gender: Transforming the Debate on Sexual Inequality* (New Haven, CT: Yale University Press, 1993), pp. 194–96.

Chapter 5. Semiotic Poetry and the Reproduction of the Khalsa

1. For a detailed account see W. H. McLeod, *Sikhs of the Khalsa*, pp. 396–401 and Owen Cole, *Six World Faiths* (London: Cassell,1996), pp. 320–21.

2. *Sikh Rahit Maryada* (Amritsar: Shromani Gurdwara Prabandhak Committee, 1950). The code is accepted as an authoritative statement of Sikh conduct.

3. Ibid., p. 24.

4. Julia Kristeva, *In the Beginning was Love: Psychoanalysis and Faith*, trans. Arthur Goldhammer (New York: Columbia University Press, 1987), p. 5.

5. Taittiriya Brahmana, 2.8.8.4–5; for translation and further discussion, see André Padoux, *Vac: The Concept of the Word in Selected Hindu Tantras*, trans. Jacques Gontier (Albany: State University of New York Press, 1990), p. 11.

6. Guy Beck, *Sonic Theology: Hinduism and Sacred Sound* (Columbia, S.C.: University of South Carolina Press, 1993), p. 29.

7. S. Radhakrishnan, *The Principal Upanishads* (London: George Allen & Unwin, 1968), p. 76.

8. Judith Newton, "Making—and—Remaking History: Another Look at 'Patriarchy' in *Feminist Issues in Literary Scholarship*, ed. Shari Benstock (Bloomington: Indiana University Press, 1987), p. 124.

9. I have discussed these five stages in depth in my chapter "The Spiritual Experience in Sikhism," in *Hindu Spirituality: Postclassical and Modern World Spirituality*, ed. K .R. Sundararajan and Bithika Mukerji) (New York: Crossroad, 1997), pp. 530–61.

10. G. S. Talib, *Japuji* (Delhi: Munshiram Manoharlal, 1977), p. 63nn.

11. W. H. McLeod, *Guru Nanak and the Sikh Religion* (Oxford: Clarendon, 1968), pp. 222–23.

12. David Kinsley, *The Goddesses' Mirror* (Albany: State University of New York Press, 1989), p. 93.

13. Talib, *Japuji*, p. 135.

14. Kartar Singh, *Japuji Sahib te hor bania da steek* (Amritsar: Shromani Gurdwarara Prabandhak Committee, 1996), p. 72.

15. The term "Sita" is taken by some exegetes in the sense of *seetal* (cold). For example, Gyani Harbans Singh, *Japu-nirnaya*, preface by Gyani Lal Singh, (Chandigarh: 1963 n.p., p. 230. Even in his commentary, *Japuji: The Immortal Prayer-Chant*, G. S. Talib includes the possibility of its meaning "cold." He writes: "*Sito Sita* in the line may be either 'Sita by herself'—that is, few others like Sita attain to that realm. Or, *sito* may be an epithet, meaning cool (*Shital*) of great poise, one who has subdued all passion" (p. 135).

16. Jackie Byars, *All that Hollywood Allows: Re-reading Gender in 1950s Melodrama* (Chapel Hill: University of North Carolina Press, 1991), p. 69.

17. Harjot Oberoi, *The Construction of Religious Boundaries* (Chicago: University of Chicago Press, 1994), p. 97.

18. Simone de Beauvoir, *The Second Sex* (New York: Vintage, 1974), p. 179.

19. Alf Hiltebeitel and Kathleen M. Erndl, *Is the Goddess a Feminist?: The Politics of South Asian Goddesses* (Albany: State University of New York Press, 2000), p. 12.

20. Luce Irigaray, *Sexes and Genealogies*, trans. Gillian Gill (New York: Columbia University Press, 93), p. 18.

21. Adriana Cavarero, *In Spite of Plato* (New York: Routledge, 1995), p. 60.

22. Madelon Sprengnether, *The Spectral Mother: Freud, Feminism, and Psychoanalysis* (Ithaca, NY: Cornell University Press, 1990), p. 1, quoting *The Standard Edition of the Works of Sigmund Freud*, ed. James Strachey (London: Hogarth, 1974), 1:169.

23. Irigaray, *Sexes and Genealogies*, p. 109 (also cited in Cavarero, *In Spite of Plato*, p. 69).

24. Cavarero, *In Spite of Plato*, p. 69.

25. Grace Jantzen, *Becoming Divine* (Bloomington: Indiana University Press, 1999), p. 132.

26. *In the Beginning was Love*, p. 45.

27. Ibn al'Arabi, *The Bezels of Wisdom*, trans. R. W. J. Austin (NJ: Paulist Press, 1980), p. 29.

28. Phyllis Trible, *God and the Rhetoric of Sexuality* (Philadelphia: Fortress Press, 1978), pp. 31-59.

29. Irigaray, *Sexes and Genealogies*, p. 16.

30. Naomi Goldenberg, "The Return of the Goddess: Psychoanalytic Reflections on the Shift from Theology to Thealogy," in *Religion and Gender*, ed. Ursula King (Oxford: Blackwell, 1995), p. 154.

31. Irigaray, *Sexes and Genealogies*, p. 57.

32. Cavarero, *In Spite of Plato*, p. 74.

33. Goldenberg, "Return of the Goddess," p. 154.

34. G. S. Talib, *Sri Guru Granth Sahib: In English Translation* (Patiala: Punjabi University Press, 1987), 3:2098: "In each being's heart pervasive. . . . " See also Gopal Singh, *Sri Guru Granth Sahib: English Version* (Chandigarh: The World Sikh University Press, 1978), 4:979: "And he pervaded the hearts of all. . . . "

35. *Sabdarath Sri Guru Granth Sahib*, 4th ed. (Amritsar: Shromani Gurdwara Prabandhak Committee, 1964), 3:1026.

36. See srigranth.org A valuable source. For the most part very thorough and accessible. Nevertheless, uses belly for womb! on p. 1026.

37. Toril Moi, *Sexual/Textual Politics: Feminist Literary Theory* (London: Methuen, 1985), p. 118.

38. Julia Kristeva, "A New Type of Intellectual: The Dissident" in *The Kristeva Reader*, ed. Toril Moi (New York: Columbia University Press, 1986), p. 297.

39. Nikky-G.K. Singh, *The Feminine Principle in the Sikh Vision of the Transcendent*, (Cambridge: Cambridge University Press, 1993), pp. 69–77.

40. Hélène Cixous, "The Laugh of the Medusa," in *Feminisms: An Anthology of Literary Theory and Criticism*, p. 342.

41. Ibid., p. 342.

42. Ernest Trumpp in his preface to his 1877 translation, *The Adi Granth or the Holy Scriptures of the Sikhs*: "[T]he Sikh Granth is incoherent and shallow in the extreme, and couched at the same time in dark and perplexing language to cover these defects" (New Delhi: Munshiram Manoharlal, 1970), p. vii.

43. Cixous, "Laugh of the Medusa", p. 338.

44. GG, 476.

45. André Padoux, *Vac: The Concept of the Word in Selected Hindu Tantras*, trans. Jacques Gontier, p. 98.

46. Hélène Cixous and Catherine Clement, *The Newly Born Woman*, trans. Betsy Wing (Minneapolis: University of Minnesota Press, 1986), p. 94.

47. Ibid., p. 94.

48. Goldenberg, "Return of the Goddess," p. 155.

49. Cixous and Clement, *Newly Born Woman*, p. 93.

50. Cixous "Laugh of the Medusa," p. 339.

51. Goldenberg, "Return of the Goddess," p. 159.

Conclusion

1. Arvind-Pal Mandair, "Thinking Differently about Religion and History: Issues for Sikh Studies," in *Sikh Religion, Culture and Ethnicity*, ed. Christopher Shackle, Gurharpal Singh, and Arvind-Pal Mandair (Surrey: Curzon, 2001), pp. 68–69.

2. Harbans Singh, *The Heritage of the Sikhs* (New Delhi: Manohar Publishers, 1983), p. 206.

3. Brian Axel has a very interesting chapter, "The Maharaja's Glorious Body," in his book *The Nation's Tortured Body* (Durham, NC: Duke University Press, 2001), pp. 39-78.

4. Veena Talwar Oldenburg, *Dowry Murder* (Oxford: Oxford University Press, 2002), p. 154.

5. DeWitt C. Ellinwood, "An Historical Study of the Punjabi Soldier in World War I," in *Punjab Past and Present: Essays in Honor of Ganda Singh*, ed. Harbans Singh, (Patiala: Punjabi University, 1976), p. 344.

6. For many of the historical details, I have relied on Khushwant Singh's *History of the Sikhs*, vol. 2 (Princeton, NJ: Princeton University Press, 1966), see esp. p. 160.

7. Oldenburg, *Dowry Murder*, p. 173.

8. Hélène Cixous and Catherine Clement, *The Newly Born Woman*, trans. Betsy Wing (Minneapolis: University of Minnesota Press, 1986), p. 98.

9. The incident took place on March 11. See the report in the *New York Times*, March 19, 2002.

10. Rokeya Sakhawat Hossain, *Sultana's Dream: A Feminist Utopia* (New York: Feminist Press at CUNY, 1988), p. 26.

11. Catharine Stimpson, "The Future of Memory: A Summary," *Michigan Quarterly Review* vol. 26, no. 1 (Winter 1987), p. 260.

12. Simone de Beauvoir, *The Second Sex*, trans. H. M. Parshley (New York: Vintage, 1974), p. 680.

13. Prithipal Singh Kapur and Dharam Singh, *The Khalsa* (Patiala: Punjabi University Press, 1999), p. 127.

14. They were Jagdish Kaur, Jagir Kaur Faguwalia, and Nirlep Kaur. *Tribune* (Chandigarh, India), September 3, 1996.

15. Bibi Jagir Kaur was replaced by G. S. Tohra.

16. Gurinder Mann, in *The South Asian Religious Diaspora in Britain, Canada, and the United States*, ed. Harold Coward, John R. Hinnells, and Raymond Brady Williams (Albany: State University of New York Press, 2000), p. 272.

17. Shauna Singh Baldwin, *What the Body Remembers* (New York: Doubleday, 1999), p. 47.

18. *New York Times*, Sunday, April 22, 2001. See also Gurjeet K. Gill, "Female Feticide as a contemporary cultural practice in the Punjab" in *Dialectical Anthropology* 23 (Netherlands: Kluwer Academic Publishers, 1998), pp. 203–13.

19. See C. Christine Fair, "Female Foeticide among Vancouver Sikhs: Recontexualizing Sex Selection in the North American Diaspora," *International Journal of Punjab Studies* 3, no. 1, (1996), 1–44.

20. Cynthia Mahmood and Stacy Brady, *Guru's Gift: An Ethnography Exploring Gender Equality with North American Sikh Women* (Mountain View, California: Mayfield Publishing Company, 2000), p. 47.

21. W. H. McLeod, "The Turban: Symbol of Identity" in *Sikh Identity: Continuity and Change*, ed. Pashaura Singh and N. Gerald Barrier (Manohar Press, 1999), pp. 58–59

22. Bernard S. Cohn, *Colonialism and Its Forms of Knowledge: The British in India* (Princeton, NJ: Princeton University Press, 1996), p. 110.

23. Gurpreet Bal, "Migration of Sikh Women to Canada: A Social Construction of Gender," *Guru Nanak Journal of Sociology* (Amritsar), April 1997, 107.

24. *Tribune*, June 15, 1996.

25. Bal, "Migration of Sikh Women to Canada," p. 108.

26. Mahadevi Varma, "The Art of Living", in *The Penguin New Writing in India*, ed. Aditya Behl and David Nichols (Harmendsworth, UK: Penguin, 1995), p. 100.

27. June O'Connor, "The Epistemological Significance of Feminist Research in Religion in *Religion and Gender*, ed. Ursula King (Oxford: Blackwell, 1995), p. 47.

Index